SOFTWARE
TECHNOLOGY TRANSITIONS

WALTER J. UTZ, JR.

SOFTWARE TECHNOLOGY TRANSITIONS

Making the Transition to Software Engineering

PRENTICE HALL
Englewood Cliffs, New Jersey 07632

Library of Congress Cataloging-in-Publication Data

Utz, Walter Julius
    Software technology transitions : making the transition to
software engineering / Walter J. Utz, Jr.
        p.   cm.
    Includes bibliographical references and index.
    ISBN 0-13-824939-3
    1. Software engineering.   I. Title.
QA76.758.U79   1992
005.1--dc20   91-22173
                                                                    CIP

Acquisitions Editor: Paul Becker
Production Editor: Gretchen K. Chenenko
Copy Editor: Linda L. Thompson
Cover Designer: Wanda Lubelska Design
Prepress Buyer: Mary McCartney
Manufacturing Buyer: Susan Brunke

The publisher offers discounts on this book when ordered in
bulk quantities. For more information, write:
    Special Sales/College Marketing
    Prentice Hall
    College Technical and Reference Division
    Englewood Cliffs, New Jersey 07632

Printed in the United States of America

10 9 8 7 6 5 4 3 2 1

ISBN 0-13-824939-3

PRENTICE-HALL INTERNATIONAL (UK) LIMITED, *London*
PRENTICE-HALL OF AUSTRALIA PTY. LIMITED, *Sydney*
PRENTICE-HALL CANADA INC., *Toronto*
PRENTICE-HALL HISPANOAMERICANA, S.A., *Mexico*
PRENTICE-HALL OF INDIA PRIVATE LIMITED, *New Delhi*
PRENTICE-HALL OF JAPAN, INC., *Tokyo*
SIMON & SCHUSTER ASIA PTE. LTD., *Singapore*
EDITORA PRENTICE-HALL DO BRASIL, LTDA., *Rio de Janeiro*

To Martha

Contents

Preface

SOFTWARE TECHNOLOGY TRANSITIONS

Software is applying for full membership in the engineering community. Software has grown in application breadth and technical complexity to the point where it requires more than handcrafted practices. Software engineering will use new methodologies, tools, training, and measurements. Although it is still possible for three to five experienced software developers to put a working program together, today's applications and operating systems can require hundreds or even thousands of analysts and programmers. Large-scale computer systems require extensive programming and significant funding. In many large computer manufacturing companies, software developers often outnumber and sometimes outearn their hardware counterparts. As software quality and reliability become essential, the winds of engineering change are moving us into the next millennium.

Suddenly software engineering seems to be at hand. A few years ago the terms CASE (computer-aided software engineering) and IPSE (integrated project support environment) were being whispered in progressive circles. Today these terms have become buzzwords that are shouted from every "lab top." Although these concepts hold great promise, the actual deliverables for the most part do not live up to the expectations. CASE/IPSE experts are heralding the arrival of these new technologies, but many programming departments, EDP groups, and management information services (MIS) departments are being consumed by software defects. Are CASE and IPSE really software engineering? Is software engineering really at hand? What does one do to get ready for the transition to software engineering? How does one make the transition? When should one make the transition?

CONTENTS

This book explains software technology transitions, the elements of a transition, the proper time to make a transition, and offers guidelines for making a successful transition. The reader will understand what is happening to software, what to do about it, and the reasons to make technology transitions that lead to software engineering. The book enables readers to place themselves, their development groups, and their companies, along the software development continuum and understand the next transition steps. Managers will find a global framework for making technology transition decisions; software designers and developers will be able to understand the technology challenges of this decade.

READERSHIP

This book is intended for three types of readers:

1. Industry software developers, including technical line managers, who must understand and manage software technology transitions. Software developers are on the front line and in many cases are swept along in the flow of the technology rapids. They must understand that it will take a series of planned and well-executed transitions to complete the move to software engineering.
2. Students who will develop software as they move into their chosen work and the professors who teach them. The students will be software engineers, and at the same time they must be able to deal with today's handcrafted software. The students must understand the fundamental concepts of software engineering, and they must know how to make successful technology transitions as they enter the development world.
3. Hardware engineers who wonder what this software business is all about and when software will be able to be understood in an engineering framework. This book will give them an overview of this emerging discipline called software, and it will help them to understand the role of software in the fast approaching world of concurrent engineering.

There are other readers who may find this book helpful. I have attempted to minimize the jargon and explanations of the internal workings of the system in order that these readers may also gain a new perspective of the software environment.

SOFTWARE STAGES

The development of CASE/IPSE tools could be the keystone in the transition to software engineering. We are going to examine the major product development stages: needs, requirements, innovations; problem definition and product specification; development, integration, and test; and release and support. This book explains each of these stages and outlines the essential functions within the stages. Successful software engineering requires tight coupling of the stages and the integration of the communication, data storage, and other supporting elements.

Software engineering also requires a complete set of project management tools that feature both horizontal breadth and detailed depth. Major functions of project management are explained, and accurate project estimation and control roles are outlined.

Software engineering requires a completely new methodology, although a complete methodology has not yet emerged. The book explains the technology transitions leading to the new methodology, why it is absolutely essential to success, and how to recognize an emerging methodology.

The successful transition to a new technology requires a balanced program that includes the elements of methodology, tools, training, and measurement. There are ways to use these elements in successful test sites and to initiate full implementation of a new technology. The transition to software engineering should be a planned transition with a high probability of success. The transition should be timely and natural to the development environment.

This book puts software evolution, software quality, software productivity, and software engineering into perspective. All these factors play a role in software technology transitions, and they allow us to understand the future direction of software. This book looks beyond CASE/IPSE and sees some fundamental product process changes at work. These changes will profoundly affect the relationship of research and development, manufacturing, marketing, and support. These changes are further justification for understanding software technology transitions, and the importance of making the transition to software engineering.

There are some basic differences between hardware and software; this book will examine both the differences and the similarities. The fact that software does not have a formal manufacturing phase appears to be one difference, but standard systems and smaller applications are "manufactured" in programming departments, whereas large systems, networks, and applications are handcrafted by field engineers. This dichotomy has caused quality departments to change their traditional approach in dealing with software, and it is leading to some surprising changes in the way advanced quality departments are functioning today.

Understanding technology transitions is also necessary to understand and deal with software engineering. There are fundamental phases in all technology transitions, and engineering disciplines (including software) follow these phases. There are specific criteria for each phase of technology transition and established time lines for moving through each phase. Understanding technology transition allows us to estimate the coming changes more accurately and to plan for, rather than simply react to, these transitions.

MAJOR AREAS OF FOCUS

Technology

This book is divided into three areas of focus. The first area is the technology focus (Chapters 1 through 7), which includes a brief history of software technology, an overview of development lifecycles, and an overview of software engineering.

Technology Transition

The second area is the technology transition focus (Chapters 8 through 11), which includes transitions, quality, and transitions to software engineering.

Business and Management Practices

The third area is the business and management practices focus (Chapters 12 through 18), which includes information and skills needed for successful transitions and the emergence of software engineering as a profession. Understanding this area is necessary to successful planning and implementation of software technology transitions.

Software began as an art or a craft and is beginning to move into the mainstream of engineering. The development of existing tools and the emergence of CASE/IPSE are orderly and logical transitions. The evolution will not end with CASE/IPSE, but it will most certainly affect all medium-to-large software teams using crafted software development techniques. As the reader gains an understanding of technology transitions, time frames, and tools, these transitions offer hope in addressing the current dilemma of software complexity. Software engineering will allow engineers to focus on their work with dramatic improvements in productivity and creativity while improving the quality and reliability of their software.

SOFTWARE PROFESSIONALS WHO MAKE TECHNOLOGY
   TRANSITIONS HAPPEN

During the course of my career, I have been fortunate to serve in the very finest computer companies, work with outstanding members of the academic community, and meet with top computer consultants. This book is based on my observations, meetings, analysis, and experience in programming and managing programming activities. This book is not about any one company or activity; it is a generic look at the development of software. Many of these ideas have been used in my lectures at universities, companies, conferences, and research centers. During these lectures the audiences often smile in recognition of a problem (area of opportunity) or antiquated practice. If you recognize one of these while reading this book, do not hesitate to smile. I was not pointing to your group; we simply share common victories and defeats. This is a wonderful endeavor, and we are on an exciting journey.

When I began the serious study of computer programming in the days of paper tape and punched cards, the term *software* was gaining acceptability. Our software instructor informed our class that we would do well to consider the career path that we had chosen. There was an emerging technology called *firmware* that threatened to engulf software. In addition, the instructor advised us that software was not a profession; it was somewhere between a trade and a racket.

As I have always held trades in high regard and as rackets were usually very profitable, I concluded that I had made a wise choice indeed. What I did not understand was that I had chosen a craft that was going to become one of the dominant professions of this technological era. I did not understand that the software revolution would include all the elements of a western movie. There have been fortunes made and lost; shootouts over technology and architecture; and a constant parade of fast-talking, slow-thinking promoters.

The best news is that the adventure has only just begun. Software did indeed have handcrafted origins, and those days are rapidly coming to a close. The emerging discipline will bring about software engineering and allow professionals to emerge from their cottages. This technology transition is happening in a manner that is strikingly similar to transitions in other engineering disciplines.

Today there are some critics who argue that software will always be an art or a craft and as such must be crafted. As the software problems move into the domains of scientists and universities, a major technology transition is beginning. That transition is moving us rapidly into a new era of software engineering. This book places technology transitions into a chronological framework that will allow engineers, managers, professors, and students, to know what to do. The book is also intended to serve as my personal career-planning guide. I would very much like to retire just before software becomes a totally honest profession; fortunately, this final transition is not yet in sight.

I have always had the privilege and pleasure of working with computer professionals who are working to make software a profession. My colleagues have listened patiently to my understanding of software phenomena, and they have added immeasurable value with their critiques, encouragements, and wisdom. I would like to thank Marc Barman, Tom Bean, Lynne Brown, John Burnham, Fred Clegg, Dan Costa, David Crockett, Vince D'Angelo, Robert Dea, Sally Dudley, Robert Heldt, Jr., Donna Ho, Chuck House, Henry Kohoutek, Robin Maybury, Peter Nicklin, Jay O'Dell, Tim O'Konski, Ian Osborne (of the UK), Kathy Osborne (of Silicon Valley), Jim Peachey, Ray Price, David Pugmire, Steve Schloss, Anil Shenoy, Chuck Sieloff, Keith Stobie, Bruce Thomas, Armen Varteressian, Lois Watson, Phil Way, and Daniel Wu. If there is value in what I have written, they have guided me; if there is error, I have failed to listen.

Reviewers are critical to a book's success. I want to thank Ilene Birkwood, Brian Claes, Ted Park, Marvin Patterson, Patricia Pierce, Sandra Sheehan, and Rebecca Smith; special thanks to Robert Boothby for two reviews. These reviewers devoted their considerable expertise to helping me share software technology transitions with you. I wish them continued success in their work.

Finally, I want to thank my son, Kevin, for his work on the ideas and drafts of the graphics. It is difficult to illustrate something that has never been seen and exists mostly in the memory of the machine. The visual illustrations are most helpful in aiding our understanding of software engineering toolboxes, platforms, and linkages.

PART ONE
Software Technology Transitions:
Technology Focus

1

Software
Technology Transitions

The software development process evolves in two ways. First, there is continuous process improvement that takes an existing process and selectively changes one or more parameters. Second, there are discrete technology transitions that allow significant gains in the effectiveness of a software development process. Figure 1.1 shows both types of changes. Continuous process improvement is necessary to maintain a competitive position. There are limits to the productivity gains possible for a given technology, and there comes a time when it is necessary to move to a new technology. Discrete technology transitions are necessary (at the proper times) to retain a competitive position and to offer the possibility of gaining a leadership position.

There are many excellent sources of information about continuous process improvement, and this text will refer to this practice only in the context of technology transitions. There are far fewer sources of information about discrete software technology transitions, but every software development group and company must make successful transitions to stay in business. Companies that achieve only partial success in software technology transitions are surrendering opportunities for competitive gain.

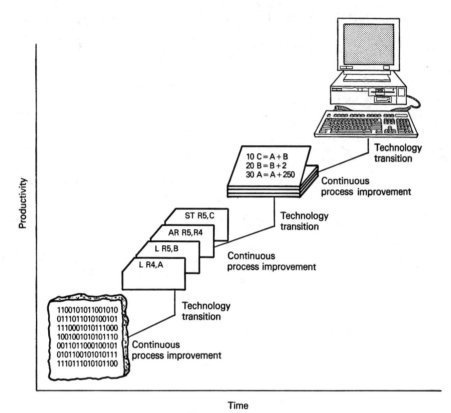

Productivity

Time

Figure 1.1 Software technology transitions.

TRANSITION

Transition means changing state, or moving from one position to another. Transition also means a passing, including the final transition to the end of the program. In an emerging technology, the transitions will happen, one way or the other. It is very important that technology transitions be understood and mastered, or they will pull us along, in a series of events that we do not control, to an uncertain end.

This book is concerned with major technology transition. These include changes of language, computer systems, data storage, life cycles, applications, and the like. These transitions are expensive and time consuming. They must be planned and managed.

Software transitions began as a series of technology pulls. Figure 1.2 shows that over time this is evolving to a series of customer pulls.

Today successful companies must plan and execute software technology transitions in such a way as to maximize customer satisfaction with the highest possible quality in software products at the lowest possible cost of ownership.

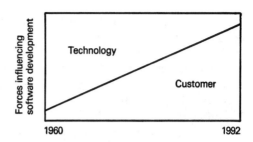

Figure 1.2 Evolution of customer need for software.

When technology was the driving force, the customer was expected to be pleased with all of the latest developments and to find a way to use software products. The early model is shown in Figure 1.3.

As customers began to understand the strengths and weaknesses of software, they began to call the shots. Figure 1.4 shows the present model.

In addition to the customers becoming the primary driving force, there are also emerging standards and global market conditions that must be addressed by successful software companies. This book explains software technology transition in a customer satisfaction framework.

Software technology transitions involve many elements. A major transition can include changes in methods, language, tools, measurement, facilities, technology, and management. Major transitions often include changing fundamental components of the software development process.

Management of software technology transitions is usually entrusted to managers who are skilled in the present technology and often have only limited understanding of the new technology or the transition process. These managers find it difficult to assess the risks and rewards and to plan for the

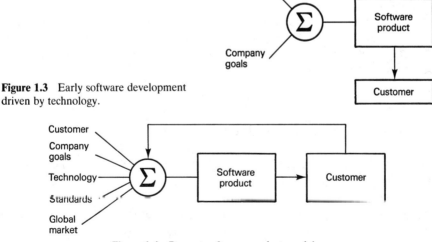

Figure 1.3 Early software development driven by technology.

Figure 1.4 Present software product model.

transition. Some tend to rush the start; others tend to give up when victory is almost at hand. Yet none of these managers can afford to stay with an obsolete technology; they must learn to manage transitions.

There are two fundamental mistakes made during technology transitions. Figure 1.2 shows a decision to make a transition because the existing process shows no further productivity gains. The mistake is in making a technology transition when none is needed at this time. What is needed is continuous process improvement; what is missing is process measurement and control needed to support continuous process improvement. The dotted line shows that process improvement would produce the same benefit as the introduction of new technology. Transition without prior process improvement usually results in no gains from the new technology, and low productivity continues.

The second fundamental mistake is shown in Figure 1.3. In this situation there had been continuous process improvement, but present productivity gains were slowing, and some competitors had switched to another technology. A software technology transition was made, but it was not well planned, understood, or executed, and the net gain was slightly worse than the old process. The opportunity to gain leadership in this transition has been lost, and extra work will be required to get the new technology working properly. The mistake can be compounded by concluding that the problem is having selected the wrong technology. In this situation, management may decide to try again by selecting another technology.

Technology focuses on the application of science to business; transition involves switching from one state to another. Although technology transitions are different than continuous process improvements, the goal should be the same. Both techniques should yield productivity and quality gains, both should be well managed, and both should be part of the management practices of every software organization.

Major software technology transitions have happened in the past; the most significant software technology transitions are in our future. Let's begin by looking at major software transitions to date, then examining the transition elements, and finally looking at the transition to software engineering.

TRANSITION TO PROGRAMMING

Who really put the "soft" in software? There have been various claims to this name. The origin of the term has to do with the apparent ease with which a programmer can create and modify computer programs. Hardwired connections can be inspected; they are permanent in nature. Software connections must be imagined; they appear to be easier to change.

Software: Temporary and Small

Software was often viewed as temporary because it was easy to change; it did not generally have a life expectancy beyond the current experiment. Scientists were delighted to be able to program computers by translating their formulas into computer programs (FORTRAN). Scientists were able to envision the mathematical process for finding a solution; they could write computer programs with little or no outside assistance. As their research was constantly moving forward, so their computer programs were supposed to be changing and constantly moving forward.

Programs were very small. Early computers with 8000 bytes of memory were shown to visitors who stood in awe. As loadable subroutines and overlays came into use, they allowed increased complexity. But programs that were considered large in the 1950s and 1960s could fill only a fraction of today's laptop computer.

The first daring programmers who worked in the clay of machine and assembly languages were able to design in their minds and program from their mental image of the problem. Many early programs were the product of one mind. First-generation programmers were creators, designers, builders, and users. Programming was an elite domain; it would take another generation to get down to basics and the BASIC language.

Software Development as an Art

Software began as an art form. The products were one of a kind. Software was free; it was part of the system purchase. The 1960s saw the transition to a new breed of self-taught experts who specialized in compiler design and construction. Individuals or small teams consulted with computer companies. The compiler expert was almost always language specific and moved from company to company as a compiler was completed. This was a mysterious and little-known craft; small fortunes were made by those who possessed the best secret formulas for high performance and compact code. Today it is not uncommon for traditional computer science programs to require undergraduates to design and code several compilers as part of their normal course of study. Today some universities have made the transition beyond traditional computer courses; undergraduates are no longer required to design and write compilers. Future compilers will be engineered by specialists.

Data communications specialists were next to attain prominence. Early data communications approximated two tin cans and a string, which often broke. If one or more lines went down during a computer run, it was often necessary to take the entire system down to reestablish the connection. The best lines were often the promises provided by those pretenders to data communications expertise who promoted well and programmed poorly.

Software almost always had defects. If you asked why this was so, you were told that this was a very complex and elusive art. All analysis was done by perspiration and was based on the ability to read "dumps"; later it was also based upon the ability to read job-control language. During one of my first runs on an early FORTRAN compiler, the compilation simply stopped in midstream. There was no cryptic error code; it just halted. The technical expert explained that I had discovered a compiler bug, and it could not be fixed until the next release. The solution was to modify the FORTRAN source until the program would compile.

Software Development

As the first software teams evolved, software was in the minds of three to five creators. This tradition has been preserved to the present day; crafted software is characterized by small teams or individuals who use informal methodologies and techniques. The tradition has been maintained because it works amazingly well for software projects of limited scope and minimum dependencies. Many popular computer games are crafted; today's artisans can create a million bytes of microcode for just one game. In Japan, the successful crafter who creates a superior game usually finds that it is not possible to duplicate the feat. Such a crafter then assists others to create future successes. Crafters will continue to have success in the one-of-a-kind computer game market. This book focuses on getting many small teams to be able to function as one large team on software projects that must be engineered.

Early small teams developing software systems often believed that software was the product of technically innovative minds. They prided themselves on knowing many programming "tricks" and used them with reckless abandon. Computer memory was a scarce resource, and swapping the contents of two memory locations generally required a third location (move A to C; move B to A; move C to B). Can you use the exclusive OR command to swap two locations without requiring a third location?

```
XC A TO B
XC B TO A
XC A TO B
```

This sequence swaps the contents of A and B. It also baffles anyone who does not know the logical basis for this swap. Even if there is a comment statement, a novice programmer might not understand.

Another example depends upon understanding the microcode that implements the move instruction to blank an entire field.

```
MOVE " " TO (A)
MOVE (A) TO (A+1) FOR 255 BYTES
```

This sequence will blank a 256-byte field. The microcode in this instance moved the field 1 byte at a time. Thus A was moved to A + 1, leaving A intact. Then A + 1 was moved to A + 2, and so on. This propagated the blank byte down the entire field. It would not work if you did not place a blank in the first byte or if you did not move A to A + 1. A programmer who used this type of crafted programming to the extreme might be guilty of making a "crafty move." But other crafters may find both the move and the pun hard to follow.

These examples will suffice to show the nature of the problem. There is no doubt that another book could be written containing thousands of these types of programming shortcuts. They are hard to understand, stylized, and personal. This type of programming began to be suppressed in the 1970s with the advent of higher-level languages and institutional pressure for programs that could be maintained easily.

Early Software Teaching Techniques

Early software techniques and practices were passed along by personal example and word of mouth. This was especially true for debug and analysis techniques. Assembler code, microcode, and machine level code were machine specific. FORTRAN, BASIC, COBOL, and dozens of other languages moved toward machine independence. At this point the first great schism occurred. The assembly level programmers had better control of the machine; they could optimize the code by tuning it to the machine. Assembly code was more efficient than early compiler-generated code. It would take a number of years for this to change, and in some cases assembly code is still more efficient. The ability to read dumps was essential to survival. The programmer had to second-guess the compiler, linker, loader, and so on. This was vital when the programmer was able to get only one or two batch runs a day. Batch systems created the need for the notorious job-control language (JCL) wizards. Every site had at least one such wizard, and the programmer gratefully accepted two decks of punched cards, always putting the first deck in front of the program to be run and the second deck at the rear. It was good practice to keep multiple copies of these decks. Other computer vendors required different wizard skills, but at every site the wizards were essential, revered, and sometimes feared.

Early Computer Resources

During the first 20 years of the computer age resources were limited. Computer time was very expensive; computer memory was bulky, slow, and small. Programmers quickly became skilled in saving memory. The machine or assembly language programmer often had a memory map posted on the wall, with segments blocked out in colors. This memory-saving skill later proved to be a handicap when memory blossomed and new emphasis was placed on solving the problem quickly. Early programmers enjoyed a memory-saving renaissance when early pocket calculators and personal computers required programming.

Peripherals were limited in capacity and speed. Printers were slow and listings were hard to read. Early storage devices used tape for large files. It was not uncommon to spend months planning the sorting strategy for a file that required 10 to 100 reels of tape. There were no integrated databases, and most file systems were sequential in nature.

On-line debugging was simply the dream of a few visionaries. Early programmers learned to be attentive to detail. It would be unthinkable to let the computer find syntax errors; the computer was supposed to find those that the programmer missed. Programmers who had a limited number of computer runs available quickly learned to pour over their listings and dumps. They learned to run code in their minds to understand exactly what their program was doing. To this day I have friends who are able to read object code to understand what a module is doing and how well it was written.

Another interesting characteristic of early programmers was their need for a computer "fix." In order to get computer time they stayed near universities or took jobs with large companies when, in fact, they really did not want industrial careers. What they did want and need was lots of computer time. In our present day, computer enthusiasts can have all the computer power and time that they require for a modest investment; the entire system can sit comfortably on a kitchen table. Early computing behaved as a logical cottage industry; today computers have evolved to a point where selected types of programming can actually be done as a cottage industry.

Computer access was limited. The cost of a computer was so much greater than the cost of a programmer that it made economic sense to have programmers waiting for the computer. The computer systems were so fragile that an inexperienced programmer could make a mistake that cost thousands of dollars and days of downtime. Special hands-on privilege was accorded only to those senior programmers who were trustworthy and very skilled. Many computer operations were run as closed shops where punched-card decks were submitted through a window and returned decks and listings were found in a bin. The computer was a huge engine, and multitasking allowed multiple jobs to be run concurrently on the engine. It was very important to stage the jobs and keep the mighty engine filled with programming fuel. Prior to program execution all the required tapes and discs had to be mounted; operators were constantly moving back and forth to keep the behemoth happy. Today the economic balance between computer time and programmer time is reversed.

The next transition was time-sharing, which allowed program development and application execution to be done by more than one programmer and user at a time. Most applications were developed by an in-house programming group. There were very few off-the-shelf, ready-to-run applications. There were some consultants and early "software houses" would develop custom applications.

Crafted Software for Minicomputers and Microcomputers

Crafted software followed the emerging development paths of minicomputers and personal computers. As minicomputers evolved, they needed compilers, file systems, databases, data communications, and the like. Personal computers (PCs) followed this same path. Many crafters followed this evolutionary development and were successful in using the same skills and applications three times over. Today there are many crafted PC programs that were developed by small teams. These programs are high in quality, low in cost, and very successful. As PC software increases in size and complexity, the need for software engineering will emerge. Crafters are being displaced in large-system and network development today; they will be displaced in PC development tomorrow.

While this walk down computer memory lane can be nostalgic for some, it is necessary here to give us the proper perspective for understanding software engineering. Figure 1.4 illustrates the domain of early crafted software. With hindsight we can see that it would be very difficult to develop large-scale systems using this model. It was difficult when it was first attempted; it is difficult today. This difficulty is one of the reasons for seeking a transition to software engineering.

EMERGENCE OF NEW CONCEPTS

Concepts such as functional module design, reuse of code, and controlled processes made a brief appearance in the early crafted software domain. These concepts received a broader interpretation as masses of programmers joined the early pioneers. This is not surprising as these concepts have suffered similar interpretations in every emerging engineering discipline. In the early days of the United States someone conceived the idea of having interchangeable replacement parts for rifles. Prior to this time each rifle was handcrafted, and replacement parts had to be built by hand. When this pioneer attempted to design and build some of these parts to specification, it was discovered that 12-inch rulers varied in length from town to town. Someone had to travel up and down the East Coast to calibrate the rulers. Manufacturers then learned about materials, tolerances, and the need for a controlled process. Software now has standards committees riding coast to coast in an attempt to get languages, databases, data communications, and the like standardized.

You must have specific standards before you can have interchangeable,

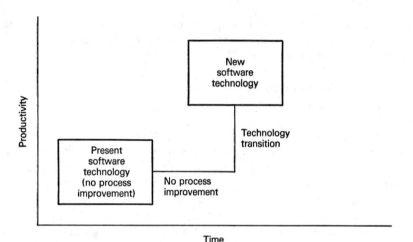

Figure 1.5   Technology transition with no prior process improvement.

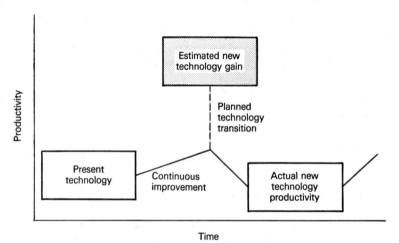

Figure 1.6   Ineffective technology transition.

reusable software parts in large-scale software projects. A measurable process is prerequisite for process improvement in development, manufacturing, support, and so on. Older and better-established engineering disciplines and manufacturing processes have enjoyed significant improvements in their technologies through the application of quality-control practices; the focus is on continuous improvement and refinement of the process. Continuous process improvement locates major process problems, fixes them, and then iterates this process. Process improvement fixes the process, not the product. Continuous process improvement has only limited success in a crafted environment where the development process varies widely from crafter to crafter.

The Need for Software Process Control

If software is being developed by crafted processes, it will prove remarkably resistant to a process-improvement analysis. A widely varying process, or lack of formal process, does not include process improvement opportunities. To make matters worse, the crafted process is best conducted as a collection of cottage activities. Each cottage team continues to adapt and modify their process. This creates widely varying and localized processes. Crafters do use tools, but they do not craft to a specified design. Crafters do strive for quality in their products, but they do not necessarily strive for continuous improvement of their software development processes. Early software tools focused on development and testing. If you ask a crafter what is needed to do a better job, you will most likely be told faster and better editors, compilers, debuggers, and so on. Although it is true that better tools are a valuable asset, large-scale projects using only these tools lead to a mentality of better tools to "make the mistakes faster so we can fix 'em faster." It is a case in which increased complexity leads to a defect rate that increases exponentially.

The crafted software process is well suited to small experienced teams working on small- to medium-scale projects, especially in market niches. This is the reason that small software companies prosper. Their software can achieve high quality, often with little or no modularity or reuse. The keys to high productivity and high quality include understanding the user's needs,

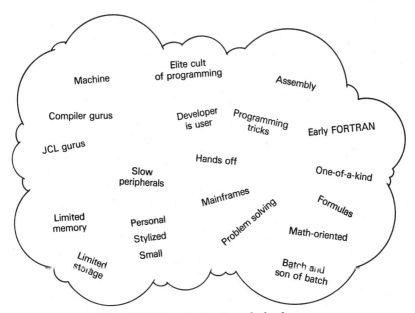

Figure 1.7 Domain of early crafted software.

analysis of the problem, design of the solution, integrated development, reuse, support tools, high levels of modularity, and a repeatable and predictable process. Crafted software did require some sort of development life cycle to explain the process and allow management to maintain some actual control and the illusion of greater control.

The earliest software technology transitions were almost totally driven by a very strong and rapid technology pull. As programmers began to work in larger teams, the need for a development life cycle became apparent. We shall now look at the transition to a development cycle and the evolution of that cycle.

2

Beginning of Software Development Life Cycle

In the beginning there were widely varying programming styles that supported the delightful idiosyncrasies of the early programmers. The one-of-a-kind nature of early crafted software did not allow for conformity. The earliest form of development cycle may have been: think, code, debug; some historians may record that it was code and debug; the harsher may simply say code and run; the harshest would say code and ship. The move toward a development cycle probably began when someone asked a programmer, "Can you write a program for me?" The answer was often based on the theme "Of course I can, I have done something like that before." In many cases the program requester was asked to modify the original request to meet the programmer's skill.

EARLY PROGRAMMING SCHEDULES

As the first programming teams evolved, there was a need to agree upon dates for programming completion. Later there were requests for dates for integration, testing, and release. The initiation of programming teams for operating systems, compilers, file systems, and the like formalized the need for a software development cycle with specified deliverables and dates. Managers love to manage; they want to know what they are going to get, when they will get it, and what it is going to cost. They also have great interest in the return on their investment. Technical project managers have less interest in schedules and costs and greater interest in technical accuracy, innovation, and technical contribution.

Early software managers often operated on the basis of being happy for almost any return on their investment. This caused them to seek out programmers with a proven track record; the validity of the track record depended on how many times the programmer had developed this type of code before. In early times entire teams of programmers and managers would move to a new company or contract. From the investors' point of view, buying a "package deal" increased the probability of success. Often it did not ensure success. Teams that could do it right prospered; teams that could do it right—and on schedule—were legendary. The importance of the team has not diminished. Today's software engineering managers have begun to think in terms of the correct programming process to support the right team; traditional programming managers search for the right team, with less regard for finding the right process.

Documentation was one of the ways in which management hoped to stay informed. The external specification was supposed to describe what was being developed; the internal specification would explain how it was built and how it worked. Other documents emerged with the increasing need to know what was happening and how to sell, configure, install, and support it. In many cases the documents were only partially completed prior to development; they were then reworked to more or less match the product somewhere around release time. This resembles a master's thesis where the introduction is written last, after the thesis is completed, so the author knows what was intended.

Managers needed a generic "process flow" to plan, execute, and control software development activities. They looked to the computer hardware community for examples of success and realized that some sort of cycle was needed to describe the software process. Early software development cycles were fashioned after the general engineering development cycle. The general cycle is a natural problem-solving process, and it has been used since the beginning of engineering practice.

CRAFTED CYCLE

A "waterfall" form of the crafted development cycle is shown in Figure 2.1. Software development "flows" from analysis to design to coding, and so on. The cycle contains all classic development activities and shows the completed product being released to customers and moving into the support phase.

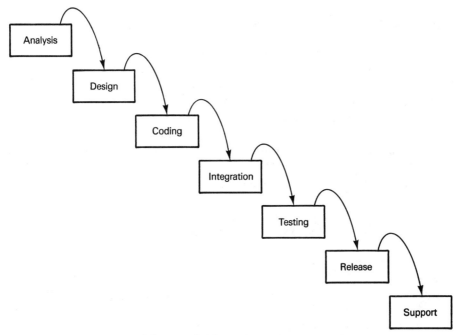

Figure 2.1 Waterfall form of crafted software cycle.

Support can still be part of the cycle because software development teams often remain involved in support, perhaps even for the life of the product.

The crafted cycle boldly stated major steps such as analysis and design, which in fact were often done on a very informal basis. Management felt comfortable with the left-to-right flow. The crafted cycle did support some communication between marketing and development regarding the software process. The problem is that the great majority of software projects never matched this development cycle. It was an illusion that served as a tranquilizer for managers. A monthly report might state that the project is "60% completed in the coding phase." It did not explain that the remaining 40% was still in the mind of a stressed-to-the-limit software developer. It did not explain that the 60% was not well designed, well documented, or well understood. Testing would find the defects and make everything better.

Despite the limitations of the early development cycles, they were absolutely necessary. If a larger programming organization did not follow any form of cycle, the results bordered on chaos. Large amounts of money were spent to get a consistent cycle, and it did help. When everyone understood the required cycle, there was a common understanding of the deliverables, dates, and importance of meeting those dates. There was a consistency of schedules and sometimes a consistency in the supporting documents.

SOFTWARE LIFE CYCLES TODAY

Development cycles have been treated in depth in other books, standards, and courses. The most comprehensive efforts in the United States are the Department of Defense (DOD) military specification (DOD-STD—2167), the IEEE Standard For Software Life Cycle Processes, and IEEE Standard Glossary of Software Engineering Terminology. Major phases in the DOD document include system/software requirements analysis, software requirements analysis, preliminary design, detailed design, coding and unit testing, computer software component integration and testing, computer software configuration item testing, and system integration and testing.

THE CONCEPT OF SOFTWARE ENHANCEMENTS

Earlier software development cycles were not well suited to the concept of enhancements. Early software was one of a kind; operating systems and major software applications can be enhanced for years. Ongoing compatibility has proven very effective in selling computer systems. There seem to be two truths that are self-evident:

- Software will always live longer than intended.
- Software that is used will be enhanced.

Enhancing crafted software is somewhat like adding a room to your home. In some cases it is easy to add one room; in other cases it proves to be a difficult task. The case of large computer systems where the original system software is 10 or 15 years old can be similar to attempting to build a 20-story addition on a single-level home that was never intended to become an apartment building.

EARLY QUALITY ASSURANCE BY TESTING

Original forms of the development cycle challenged early attempts at software quality assurance by quality assurance (QA) departments. The original idea was to verify software quality by testing at the end of the development cycle. Although testing is only a subset of quality as we know it today, it was a logical first step. Quality today includes not only testing for functionality but also human engineering, supportability, performance, and more. Software quality of yesteryear focused on defect detection and correction. Programming teams were supposed to be doing their own unit and integration testing, but the main thrust was at the end of the cycle just prior to release. This produced a warp in the cycle. Many software teams felt that it was the job of the testing team to check the software, and so they did not do full testing. In some cases, it got to the point where teams would release the software to the test team on schedule and have a party. The testing team would then work on the software for a week or two and pass it back to the software team. The cycle would continue until one side tired or management stopped the cycle and released the software. Management was responsible for allowing the cycle to occur. There should have been clear assignment of responsibility for quality and testing.

As we now know, you cannot test quality into software. Testing can prove that defects exist, but you cannot be certain that software is defect-free just because testing failed to uncover any defects. The quality process must permeate the entire development cycle. But testing had proven very effective in smaller software releases, and it still has a very important role in modern software development. We examine the quality dimension of software engineering in Chapter 9.

The Achilles' heel of testing can be shown by examining a hardware analogy. Figure 2.2 shows an iterative testing process that might be used on bits in a computer chip. At one point in the test a single bit is turned on and all the other bits are turned off to measure the leakage outward. Later in the test, the same bit is turned off, and all the nearby bits are turned on to measure the leakage inward. If we did the complete iteration of the bit pattern in a 1K chip, it would take a matter of minutes to completely test the chip. If we attempted to test a 4M chip with the same logic using the newest high-speed test equipment available, the test would exceed the number of seconds that the universe is estimated to have been in existence. Thus if someone is testing 4M chips in this way, that person has not yet completed the tests.

In a similar fashion it was possible to test a small software function by testing every permutation and combination of inputs. Today's large networked

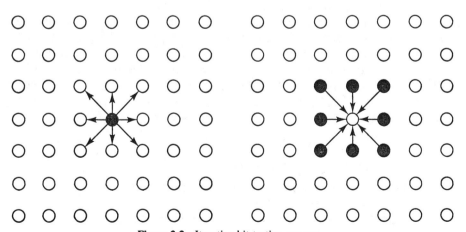

Figure 2.2 Iterative bit testing process.

systems approximate the 4M chips. Testing is very important; a good testing program does not attempt blind iteration; rather, it uses other principles and mathematical techniques to ensure that the tests meet their objectives.

Today's 4M chips are very reliable. The engineers discovered some wonderful techniques that include heating, cooling, and stressing the chips. Those that pass the tests will run for years. The problem is that we do not know how to heat and cool software; we are just learning how to apply stress in a controlled testing environment.

The old-style "QA software at the end of the cycle to see if it passes the tests" was a feeble attempt to put up a gate at the end of the cycle. In addition to being more like a leaky sieve, the original QA process was also unable to deal with the problem of incorrect specification or design of the solution. If you and I each invest $5 million to make a movie, we must submit the finished product to the rating board prior to distribution. Should our movie receive an X rating, we have a problem. Our $10 million is already spent, and we cannot get into the general film-distribution channel. The only thing to do is snip two seconds at a time until the rating board finally gives us an R rating. But now what do we have? The X scenes are for the most part gone, and the movie never had a good plot. So we have spent our $10 million and have almost nothing.

The problem is that software developed the same way is no laughing matter. If we must spend $10 million to develop a large software system and then find that it is almost nothing, the only thing that can be done is to cut and paste in an effort to salvage the project. Poorly designed software does not meet the customer's needs and expectations. The software does the wrong things and is generally awful to watch in operation. Thus the old style quality assurance department was at a loss to determine if software products really were quality products that met customer needs. At best they could make some estimation of how well the product met the external specification, without knowing how well the product met customer needs.

The problem centers on definition and specification. In many cases the users were not able to gain an understanding of how the product would function by reading technical specifications. In some proposed products users became enamored by the "sizzle" of new features and new technology. In other products users read more into the functionality plot than the software product could deliver. This led to the belief that testing would somehow ensure that the correct software product operated according to specification. The result was that

- functionality was difficult to test;
- usability, appropriate solution of the original problem, and performance were almost impossible to test;
- testing worked best on software development tools as test teams usually

understood the qualities of a good product. In some situations the testers were not familiar with user requirements and environments.

These obstacles posed sufficient challenges to the testing community but an even greater challenge is the increasing size and complexity of software, which grows faster than the ability to test.

Problems of validation and verification are similar throughout all engineered products. Early telephone switchboards, vacuum-tube devices, steam boilers, networks, telegraph systems, and the like could be tested completely. There were testing evolutions and revolutions as the development cycles evolved, and product complexity increased.

In all these developments there was almost always no effort made to conduct testing at earlier stages in the development cycle, to test designs, or to test needs. Instead, there were significant efforts to ensure full test coverage, development of standard test suites, and specification of performance goals. Again, these are all worthwhile activities, but they are not enough by themselves.

OTHER LIFE CYCLE MODELS

There have been numerous variations in software development cycles. In addition to the waterfall cycle, there are also pragmatic "expand it as you go" models, formal specification models, and spiral models, which recognize complexity and approach the solution by making multiple passes through the development stages, allowing high-risk issues to be identified and addressed at the lowest possible level.

The spiral model allows a logical "building" of the software product by a repetition of software development processes. Each cycle is subject to review, which includes all progress to date and planned progress for the future.

The spiral model has found favor in the largest aerospace projects as well as in smaller projects throughout all types of software applications and systems development. Whether one of the present forms of the spiral development cycle will meet the needs of software engineering is not clear. The important element in alternative models such as the spiral is recognition that actual software development does not proceed through all the steps one time only; it does not flow smoothly from left to right. There is a need for iteration, a need for change during development, a need to minimize risk.

Five main points relate to software transitions.

1. The evolution of crafted software development cycles continues.
2. There has been one major transition from free form to the sequential waterfall cycle.

3. Software engineering will require more than a modification of one of these cycles; another transition is needed.

4. The development of object-oriented programming is focusing on the encapsulation of data and procedures, and this will result in a new life cycle, perhaps even a new paradigm.

5. There are several major approaches to software life cycles today.

There is an amazing lack of focus and concern about software development cycles in the colleges and universities. Students either have not heard of the concept, do not find it relevant, or have forgotten it entirely. When these students take a position in industry, they often begin work without any introduction to the life cycle concept. This makes their knowledge fragmentary and dependent upon that passed on by senior crafters.

There are many excellent academic computer science programs, but some of the best do not have any team programming projects. Those that attempt such projects report that students who work together without the benefit of development cycles or schedules usually have major problems in less than 8 weeks. They cannot successfully complete their team projects on schedule without using a development cycle. A software development cycle is required for success in all team programming environments.

As we follow the transition of software from crafted to tooled phase, the software development cycle has been under constant pressure to evolve to support the use of software tools. This support requires the use of a repeatable, predictable process for software development. A stable process is one of the prerequisites for successful use of tools in software design and development.

The software development cycle is one way of attempting to overlay consistency, structure, and method onto a crafted process; it is a transition to a systematic approach. Such an approach should include all phases of software engineering development, and we have not yet covered all those phases in this book. The phases will be outlined and described as we build a complete software engineering process.

The waterfall cycle made a real contribution to software development and allowed teams to function. There has not been a major technology transition beyond variations on this original cycle, and one or more transitions will be required to support software engineering.

Before beginning our process journey, it is necessary to take a look at the fundamental differences between hardware and software. Earlier examples have focused on similarities, but differences will help us to understand the importance of required segments in the software engineering process.

3

Software Distinctions

DIFFERENCES BETWEEN HARDWARE
AND SOFTWARE

There are six major distinctions that contribute to the uniqueness of software when compared to hardware:

1. Hardware is manufactured; software is duplicated. Hardware manufactures multiple numbers of a product. Software has only one copy of the operating system, application, database, or utility, which is duplicated many times (the detection of duplication errors is a trivial process).

2. Software cannot break. Every defect that turns up in software use was present from the time of creation. All software defects are the result of human error.

3. Software systems are enhanced and grow in size over time. Computers are superseded by new models. Software systems and applications are similar to living plants. They tend to grow and expand over time as users upgrade to new versions, and they are used for many years.

4. Hardware is governed by the laws of physics; software is governed by human minds.

5. Software is a virus carrier.

6. Software is built or assembled on-site.

These are the major distinctions. The next few pages expand on those distinctions.

Hardware Is Manufactured; Software Is Duplicated

In hardware the "release to manufacturing" step is always a significant milestone. Figure 3.1 illustrates the step as part of the development cycle. Manufacturing takes the responsibility of producing 100,000 or 1,000,000 terminals, computers, automobiles, and so on, by machining, welding, soldering, assembling. Statistical quality control ensures that each of these units is as close as possible to the original. But the software product as released by development is the final product. There is only one set of programming instructions, and duplication is reliable and verifiable. Hardware is designed once, mass-produced, and usually replaced rather than upgraded; software is developed once and run many times; larger systems are upgraded many times. In one sense, every user of a given software product shares the same code.

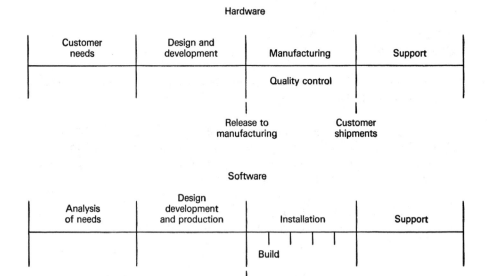

Figure 3.1 Hardware and software development cycles.

Software Cannot Break

Hardware can change states; printer mechanisms wear out and stop functioning; chips can stop functioning; CRT screens can go dark. Software does not change state without human intervention. If software is developed defect-free, it remains defect-free. In this sense, it is the ideal product and has no manufacturing cost (only a duplication cost).

Another nuance in software distinction comes after the release of the software product. Figure 3.2 shows the total number of defects remaining in a software product that has not been further enhanced or otherwise changed; each of the subsequent software ("patch") update tapes has reduced the number of remaining software defects. This could be a software product that has been placed on the obsolete list, which will be removed from the product line after several additional years of support. In this situation, there were three patch tapes that followed release 11.0 of the product. Each of the patch tapes corrected known defects in the product. Remembering that software cannot break, there will be no additional defects "creeping into" the product (other than those introduced by the update tape). In many such actual cases, the software support team will be hard-pressed to find the source code of release 11.0 in the fourth year of support. If Figure 3.2 is correct, why do we have so many problems with ongoing software?

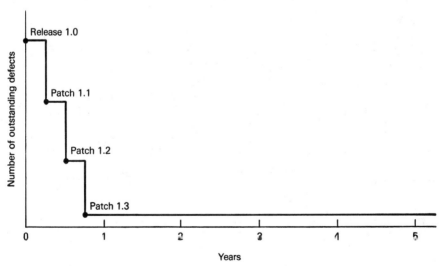

Figure 3.2 Software release with patch tape containing only defect corrections and no enhancements.

Software Systems Are Enhanced and Grow in Size over Time; Computers Are Superseded by New Models

The answer to the preceding question is shown in Figure 3.3; the problem is usually caused by enhancements to the software product. In many competitive situations, other vendors are upgrading their software products, and new products are constantly entering the market to challenge our software product. Figure 3.3 shows release 1.0 and the decrease of the total number of known defects as patches 1.1 and 1.2 are released. Then release 2.0 comes along, leading to a higher total number of defects due to significant enhancements in the functionality of the product. This raises the starting defect plateau. The problem continues to grow with releases 3.0 and 4.0. The most frustrating fact is that many customers who wanted the features in release 1.0 would have been happy to stay with release 1.0, which follows the path shown in Figure 3.2.

It must be noted that software releases can contain defects that make their first appearance years after the initial release. This is a separate problem.

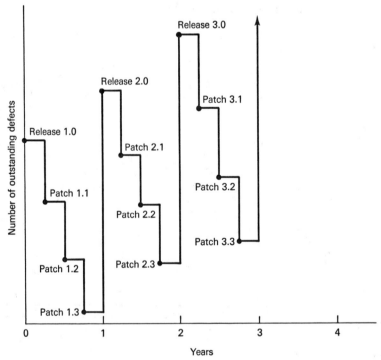

Figure 3.3 Software releases with patch tapes containing defect corrections and enhancements.

We are concerned here with those customers who would be happy if we did not add enhancements; they like the software just as it is.

Although some customers are fully satisfied with release 1.0, other customers have come to expect increased functionality with each subsequent release of the software. Hardware comes out with new models, and you trade in or replace the old models only if you want the new features. There are some software trade-ins today, but larger systems usually have the customer buying an initial product that later comes to be viewed as the "starter" version, and the customer expects it to be upgraded periodically.

A similar situation might occur if the customer took an expensive car into the garage for service and was told that several major modifications must be added to the car before having an oil change and normal service performed. The enhancements allow the car to be driven at a maximum speed of 150 miles per hour. However, the car now runs erratically at lower speeds. When the customer complains he is told that the car will run smoothly at speeds above 100 miles per hour, but he was satisfied with the original version, which allowed a top speed of 90 miles per hour.

The example of an upgrade to a state of unhappiness applies only to packaged software supplied for general sale and distribution. Custom-designed software users expect continuous changes and improvements. The need for changes is one of the reasons for creating an internal programming department. The user expects custom-built software to meet today's needs fully and to be expanded and upgraded to meet future needs. The capability for enhancement is a very strong software benefit. The economic realities of creating custom-built software versus packaged software drive all but the largest users to select packaged software. Standardization drives custom-built software producers to produce similar products. The combination of development costs and the need to build to standard makes prototyping very desirable.

In hardware development the prototype and the specifications are released to manufacturing. Hardware developers can afford to spend millions of dollars on a prototype prior to spending billions on the manufacture of millions of the item for sale. Software duplication is a small fraction of the total cost of the product. In a sense, the software prototype is the finished product.

The hardware release-to-manufacturing step is a major accomplishment. Manufacturing will not accept a new product without a proper prototype, full specifications, known tolerances, full testing reports, and more. Hardware has to measure up to be released to manufacturing; software is released to duplication and distribution.

Customers are now asking for a product that is beyond the limits and scope of the original crafted design. If vendors do not add functionality and performance, the software does not sell in today's market. If vendors release software to customers, they upset many who might never have been upset if vendors had a more flexible support policy. Customers who liked the original version of the product have been exposed to all the additional defects shown in Figure 3.4. If vendors change the support policy to support all previous software releases, they might threaten the financial security of their company. In a traditional software development environment, the added burden of having to keep more than two versions of the system in active support requires additional computers, staff, documentation, training, and the like.

This frustrating set of circumstances occurs not only because vendors are making enhancements to the product but also because vendors believe that each new version of the software is better. Perhaps vendors believe they were doing their customers a great service by forcing an upgrade to a "superior" version of the product. Instead vendors forced customers to endure additional defects.

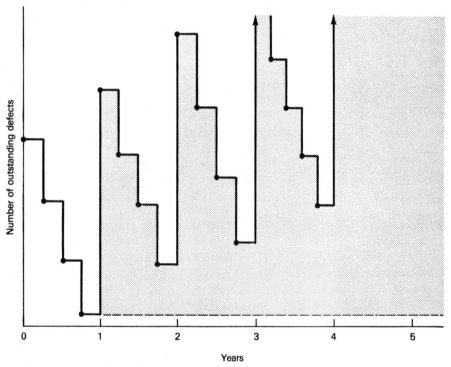

Figure 3.4   Delta software engineering evolution.

HARDWARE AND SOFTWARE PROCESS CONTROLS

In hardware manufacturing, the management, working with quality managers, would not hesitate to put a manufacturing "hold" on the production line if the production process went beyond the control parameters. In software there is no manufacturing control. This led to a role crisis. Marketers often sell things before they are ready for release. Senior engineers often move to newer and more exciting projects before they finish the current projects, leaving the final details to the newer engineers. Senior engineers do not want to stay around and maintain software. Who was to save customers from software that was not yet a completed prototype but was still in various stages of development? Who was to save customers from a new engineer who possessed great courage and entry-level skill but had little familiarity with the several hundred thousand lines of code assigned for maintenance?

The responsibility fell on the quality assurance department. It was supposed to verify that software met all the specifications and was free of defects. As we have discussed earlier, the near infinity of permutations and combinations swamped the quality assurance effort. In some cases quality assurance dependence led software teams to abrogate their responsibility. The attitude that quality assurance should find the defects prevailed. Teams started to make software releases to quality assurance on schedule, regardless of the fact that the release would be back to the software team a week later. The inescapable conclusion that software teams are responsible for software quality is enjoying a renaissance. The first software developers were responsible for their work; responsibility then became diffused as projects grew in size; today we understand that everyone has responsibility for quality.

Teams should do testing, but they also have to fix the process, and quality should permeate the entire development cycle. It should become part of the development culture. In this sense quality assurance departments could be of great assistance in consulting and auditing quality aspects of the development process. Quality "police" catch few quality offenders; quality plans and programs promote proper quality practices by all departments.

Hardware Is Governed by the Laws of Physics; Software Is Governed by Human Minds

Hardware products are governed by the laws of nature. Physics has described these laws, and the mathematics is quite well known. Chip designers learn to work within these laws. If we were to argue about these laws, it would prove to be futile. Software is another story; software laws are more or less governed by human minds. There are some empirical rules emerging, but in general we must wonder, How big is a program? What is the best way to design a module?

In the evolution of computer science curricula, undergraduates were required to learn compiler design and development; now compiler design and development are becoming options. Today database design and construction are enjoying a similar "reductio ad undergraduum." As the empirical rules emerge and databases become standard, undergraduates will no longer be required to design them; they will then be free to use them. Human minds are hard at work on the guidelines for software development. The evolution of curricula are not transitions; they are a lagging indicator of technology transitions that have already happened.

Software Is a Virus Carrier

Viruses are deliberate sequences of instructions that cause a computer system to malfunction. Viruses propagate by "infecting" media and systems as software is distributed. Viruses have caused millions of dollars in damages and added untold stress to computer users who have work to do.

This is an increasing concern as the skill of the virus creators increases. It seems ironic that although software cannot break, it can infect an entire computer system. Although it is possible to plant virus-type defects in hardware circuitry, software has the unique distinction of being able to transmit viruses with apparent ease.

Software Is Built or Assembled On-Site

In general, software products are installed on a computer or a system. In the personal computer world this is a pretty straightforward process, and users generally install their own software. As systems grow larger, installation, configuration, and "tuning" of the system requires specialists. The difference between good performance and mediocre performance rests in the hands of these individuals. They also add special software and in some situations write special code to get the system up and running. In very large computer installations up to 25% of the total code in a system can be created, selected, or mandated by these specialists. While this complexity is worth noting, it should be noted that very large installations of hardware, including manufacturing hardware, are often installed and tuned by experts. Additional complexity is cited here because in one sense very large software systems are one of a kind "manufactured" in a crafted assembly process. The on-site assembly phase is largely neglected by the software engineering community.

Actual stories of network viral damage in dollars lost and gigabytes of corrupted data are sobering indeed. The nature and ease of network connectivity will probably allow viruses to wreak even greater havoc in the future. Ultimate control of viruses involves disciplines beyond the present scope of computer engineering. When hardware was the dominant technology pull in early computing, users believed they were free of viral threat; now users feel threatened and are not certain how to protect themselves.

The time has come to leave crafted software to crafted situations and move to engineered software. A firm foundation is needed to support the weight of necessary software transitions to an engineering discipline. The move to engineered software involves a technology transition. Our understanding of technology transitions is essential to knowing how and when to make the move to engineered software and the bigger moves to system engineering.

Changeable Nature of Software

Software is by its present nature very changeable, copyable, and vulnerable. The great advantage in being able to create programs to solve specific problems and select programs to run on a computer, workstation, or personal computer becomes something of a liability when security and copyright are issues. At this writing there is a trend to see software and hardware chip design as the same problems in logic; on the one hand we can write it in code; on the other hand we can put it on a chip. When we want to champion the cause of software engineering, it is handy to invoke these examples. However, software will not be replaced by chips, but it will be farther and farther removed from the end users.

Software Protection

As software writing and modification disappear from the user's view, it will be possible to provide better protection from outside viruses and better protection of copyrights. There are some similarities with the early days of radio when "pirate" transmitters were on the air. This was also complicated by unplanned interference from legitimate transmitters. The Federal Communications Commission entered the scene, established broadcast standards, allocated frequencies (including "clear" channels), and brought order to the airwaves. There were skeptics who believed that you could not "police" the airways or catch violators. Broadcasting seemed so free and vulnerable.

There is still a great deal of controversy today about digital audio tape being able to copy CD-ROMs. Software is naturally suited to storage and distribution on CD-ROMs, and so there is a much bigger problem to solve than software per se. In a situation similar to software, there is really only one original recording of the performing artist; this is then copied many times. There are plans in place to help recording artists; there will be help for software owners.

FUNDAMENTAL ACTIVITIES OF HARDWARE AND SOFTWARE

Although it is important to understand software distinctions, it is equally important to understand the fundamental activities that apply to both hardware and software. These activities include the following.

Logic.   Hardware and software contribute both individually and collectively to the logic used in the system.

System functions.   Software is part of the system; it cannot function alone.

System results.   Early hardware devices produced power changes; early software produced information changes. Computer systems produce process change and control.

Although software distinctions will remain, they will have less impact on the end user as software development and upgrades are further removed from the user. Distinctions will, however, remain very important to the software engineering community, which must learn to master distinctions without allowing them to trouble the end user in any way. Software engineering is still in its early stages; as software engineering evolves, distinctions will become strengths.

As software becomes an integrated part of system development, the transitions that take us to software engineering will also take us to an integrated development environment. This is discussed in a later chapter. The important point to be noted here is that the distinctions will dictate some of the software technology transitions.

4

Software Engineering Transition Phases: Crafted to Tooled to Engineered

The key to understanding what is happening in the transition of software engineering is to realize that software is similar to hardware in many ways, and historical precedents apply to the software evolution phases that are underway. The principal software phases are and will be the following.

Crafted. All emerging technologies begin in the crafted mode.

Tooled. Technologies progress to a tooled mode with stand-alone tools that later become loosely linked; the components are built to specification. (This is an advanced crafted stage. A crafter with loosely linked tools is still a crafter.)

Engineered. The engineering mode is marked by entire systems being built to specification.

Automated engineered. The automated engineering mode uses tightly linked tools and hierarchical methods for handling complex design.

Automated intelligent engineered. The automated intelligent engineering mode has complex interactions and connections handled within the system, freeing engineers to concentrate on solutions.

These phases, and the professional skills necessary for mastery have been evolving over the last 20 years. Some of the finest academic professionals are using software evolution data to conduct research on the potential of the software engineering concept. A sampling of their work is included in the bibliography. Academic research should lead the way; industry should use this work in making the transition to software engineering.

There may be some hesitation when professionals confront the idea that software engineering is still in its infancy, as shown on the software evolution phases chart. Figure 4.1 lists the key features of each phase and shows the progression toward software engineering.

Crafted	Tooled	Engineered	Automated Engineered	Automated Intelligent Engineered
Manual design; coding, testing, and release tools	Separate tools for analysis, design, code, test, etc.	Loosely linked tools used in all stages of software development	Linked and fully integrated toolsets	Artificial intelligence and other advanced techniques for software development
Cottage industry; built to order	Shop mode; built to component specification	Professional mode; built to system specification	Professional mode; built to industry specification	Professional mode; can be custom designed and optimized to industry specification
No two systems run exactly the same way	May be built differently but run the same way	Specialized reusable modules; little design reuse	Software "chips" with high levels of reuse	Software "boards" with high levels of reuse
Known and proven practices	Engineering practices and methodologies	Discrete practices and methodologies	Linked practices, processes, and methodologies	Integrated practices, processes, and methodologies
Almost no standards	Few product standards	Partial product; some component, some tool standards	Full product; full component, full interface standards	Full product, module, component; full platform and environment standards
Apprenticeship learning	Journeyperson learning	Specialist learning	Professional learning	Professional mastery
No division of labor	No division of labor	Some specialization	Recognized areas of specialization	Defined areas of specialization

Figure 4.1   Phases of software engineering evolution.

These phases have common threads throughout all engineering disciplines. The point is that software is following a similar evolutionary path, and our understanding of that path can help us to see what must be done and when it must be done. The *when* is also strongly influenced by technology transitions described in a later chapter. For the moment, let us assume that all technologies used in each software engineering phase are in the category of known and proven practices.

TECHNOLOGICAL PRESSURE FOR CHANGE

The rapid pace of technological advancement is pulling the computer industry into technology transitions. Figure 4.2 shows the industrywide gains as the technology pull causes companies to respond with transitions.

Technological pressure for change is shown in the figure. Quality and productivity are linked to the extent that a crafted technology involving hand-written reports can move up the curve only to the maximum gain shown by the crafted line. Those who use engineered technologies involving printing presses or laser printers can achieve far higher levels of quality and produc-

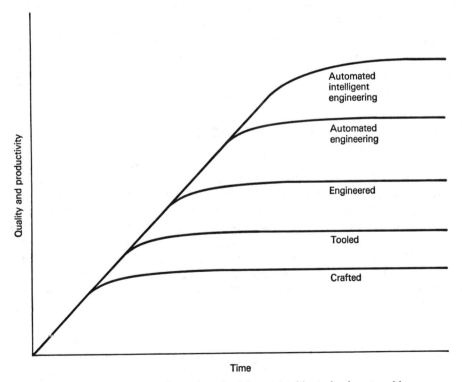

Figure 4.2   Gains in quality and productivity attained by technology transitions.

tivity than is possible with thousands of handwritten pages. Thus there comes a time when one must move to new technologies.

The same principle applies in the case of handcrafted ditches. The worker who digs with a shovel will be outdone by one who uses power tools; that worker in turn will be outdone by someone using a small bulldozer. Figure 4.2 allows us to draw some guidelines:

> If we delay too long in recognizing that it is time to change a phase, motivation will occur through pain.

> If we lead the curve and make a change before it is known to be a proven practice, the results will be unpredictable and involve higher risk but could have huge monetary or marketing rewards.

> The ideal situation would be to follow just behind the rise of the composite curve.

Figure 4.2 represents the industry as a whole. Individual companies will make discrete transitions as they respond to the technology pull and to changing customer needs. Successful companies will manage transitions; they will not be dragged through transitions.

The crafted environment is not well suited to an orderly progression of technologies. Crafters are primarily concerned with finding the right tool to get their jobs done. They are not concerned with developing new tools or planning technology transitions. An engineering environment should allow orderly progression through accurate measurement and planned technology transitions.

SOFTWARE SIZE AND SCOPE FACTORS

Remember, size and scope of the software effort are very important factors. Small specialty software shops will not have to spend as much time worrying about these phases and transitions. All software shops, software labs, and academic labs have one common warning indicator, which indicates it is time to change: Is the project technically manageable? Small shops can hold a project together by sheer force of will. Some of the smaller shops use the central designer model, in which one technical lead understands the entire project. The lead then directs others in coding activities. Other small shops use the multiple-designer model, in which everyone has an almost equal share in the project. Both models work up to a point, but almost all software projects increase in size and scope.

The problem begins when the project, with no formal design and no way to control design changes, grows. As mentioned in a previous chapter, software keeps expanding due to the increased functionality necessary to maintain a competitive position. At some point software becomes too complex for a few programmers to hold together. But it usually happens gradually. Meanwhile, programmers truly believe that they can still hold the software together; managers believe they can hold projects together.

They also believe that they can stretch the existing language, operating system, and files or databases to meet expanding functionality. At the same time another team begins again with an improved language, improved methodologies, and up-to-date training; this team makes the original product obsolete. When you combine this technology pressure with technological evolution, the combination passes the point of reasonable supportability. Finally you come to the point where it is necessary to get 30 programmers into a room to have a complete team that has read all the code. At this point the whole system begins to break down because it is not possible for 30 programmers to remember all connections and interdependencies, since each one has only read a portion of the code.

ENGINEERING TRANSITION

The software engineering evolution is happening. The move from machine and assembly languages to fourth-generation and to object-oriented languages is well underway. The move from cryptic job-control sequences to icon manipulation is well underway. The move from crafted to tooled to engineered has been underway for some time. It is very important to recognize this fact because the answer is not simply in finding the latest language, data structure, or software engineering tool. The answer lies in knowing the proper technology transition step, the components of that step, and the proper time to initiate the transition. Panic is the enemy; it becomes the energy that drives frantic transitions. There is sufficient time to understand what is happening and to plan for an orderly technology transition that matches the needs of the customers and the company.

Craft is associated with the ideas of trade or guild. Early programmers definitely fit this mold. *Tooled* is associated with the notion of cutting, shaping, or working within tolerances. Tooled also has the beginning glimmers of building to some sort of specification. *Engineering* is associated with the concept of the application of scientific knowledge that is useful to society. Computer-aided software engineering is quite simply a tool driven system that uses hardware and software components to support engineering solutions that offer potential benefit to society.

ENGINEERING SKILLS TRANSITION

If it were simply the case that we had only to purchase the toolset required for a craftsperson to tool software, this would be a much shorter book. Engineering goes far beyond purchased software toolsets; the problem is much more complicated. The software toolset is not complete as it stands, and the complete toolset would require a renaissance person to be able to use it. There is a similarity to one who works on automobiles. Such a person might be able to do a wide range of car repairs. An extremely clever person might be able to assemble an entire automobile from a pile of parts. But it would take a unique individual to be able to operate all the machines used in a modern automobile plant. Today some European automobile companies have small teams assemble an entire car. This change has become possible because equipment is automated and simple to operate. There are other benefits to this small-team experiment, such as a feeling of greater self-worth and importance of the job.

But this is only an experiment, prompted by the failure of the previous system. Even if using small teams to assemble automobiles is a positive, productive idea, it does not apply as well to design and construction of complex computer systems. For the near term (the next 5 to 10 years) there will be an increasing specialization in software engineering. In the longer term, anything is possible when we consider development of easily integrated and reusable software components. Perhaps the future will hold a return to the concept of small software teams assembling very large systems. Perhaps the answer lies somewhere between the crafter and the assembly line. For the near term, the software toolsets will remain sufficiently complicated to require larger teams to operate them successfully.

In a similar fashion the complete software engineering toolset will probably require a division of labor. This division has already begun with the advent of compiler experts, database experts, data communications experts, and so on. Several experts might be required to operate all the software development tools in the complete set of the software engineering toolboxes and platforms being outlined here.

While the complete software engineering toolset is still in the formative stages, there is no doubt that it will require a major technology transition, or perhaps a series of transitions, to complete the evolution to software engineering.

As we move to tooled mode, the approach will be to describe in some detail the complete functional toolset required for the five major phases of software development and support. All these tools do not exist in one package at this time, but the idea is to explain the full set and then move on to the linkages of the tools, which marks the beginning of the integrated toolset.

5

Transition to Software Development

Crafters require tools to attain a repeatable, predictable process, which is a pillar of continuous process improvement. The concepts of process control and process improvement are essential elements in successful software engineering. Continuous process improvement establishes a solid base upon which technology transitions are made. After completion of a successful technology transition, a new cycle of continuous process improvement supports the new technology.

This chapter addresses the toolboxes that are necessary to support the technology transition to software engineering. We discuss the major software engineering toolboxes and the functions performed by the tools within each toolbox. The intent of this chapter is to give an overview of the functions; there are other texts that explain the functions and specific tools in detail. We want to understand the functions and tools in terms of the magnitude of the effort required to make the transition to software engineering. The complete collection includes many tools, and we would do well to group the functions, tools, and their related attributes into logical toolboxes. There are eight software engineering toolboxes:

1. development and test
2. definition and specification

3. needs and requirements

4. installation and build

5. support

6. documentation

7. management planning and control

8. software engineering data repository

This chapter describes each toolbox and the functions provided by the tools within that toolbox. To be accepted and used successfully, these toolboxes need three characteristics:

1. simplicity

2. standards

3. linkages

Simplicity.   The toolboxes should support a natural problem-solving process. The toolbox functions should be simple to understand, and the flow from problem to solution should be easy to understand.

The Japanese have a beautiful philosophy regarding simplicity. They believe that there is beauty in simplicity. They often make a garden more beautiful by taking something away. Today's cameras have thousands of electrical circuits and multiple small motors and are definitely complex instruments. However, automated operation has taken away things that were formerly done by the user. Today's modern personal computers have followed the same concept; small children now delight in their computer creations. As we begin to describe the full functionality of a complete software engineering toolset, contained in eight toolboxes, there may be the temptation to look only at complexity. The following descriptions of eight logical toolboxes are intended to give an understanding of functions supported by each toolbox; tool linkages will be discussed in later chapters. Future software engineers should never have to wrestle with this complete toolset in some sort of stand-alone operation.

Standards.   When we plan telecommunications networks, we take communication standards for granted. This was not always the case. In the beginning there were many different types of connections and standards. Over time, national and international standards evolved. A similar situation happened in the evolution of plumbing. At first there were many standards, and the final standard has still not been approved. To this day there are still separate standards for pipe fittings in different sections of the country. Newer technologies also face the problem of arriving at a standard. When video-cassettes arrived on the scene, there were competing standards, although there now appears to be a winner. The concept of software engineering standards is still in its infancy, and it will take a number of years, a number of "tournaments of decisions," and a decision based on the will of the majority before mature standards arrive on the scene. Standards are necessary if we are to have a stable software engineering environment.

Linkages.   Linkage refers to a series of connections that allows the parts to function as a system. There are linkages in mechanical, electrical, and biological disciplines, among others.

In well-established areas of software development there is a tight linking of many functions associated with coding, debugging, and testing. The early days saw a separate invocation of editor, compiler, linker, and loader prior to run time. Today there are complete language management systems that track dependent files, linkages, and things to be done prior to run.

These advances have allowed the programmer to concentrate on the job at hand. Please note that the evolution to this ease of programming required the development of separate, stand-alone tools and slow and deliberate linking of those tools. This is somewhat analogous to the early days when photographers wrestled with filters, light meters, separate flashes, f-stops, focus, and so forth. By the time they were ready to shoot, the subjects had aged. Today's modern cameras take care of all these details, allowing the photographer to concentrate on taking pictures.

This is another one of those situations where it is easy for a technical person to become enamored of the technology. It is highly doubtful that Hemingway and Faulkner would have gotten together to show each other their typewriters. Tools are important, but why do we show each other our cameras; why not show the pictures we have taken? Why show word processors; why not show what we have written? Why show individual computers or workstations? Why not show the link to the solution? The same kind of transition is happening in software. The first step was to take pride in the mastery of the complicated craft. There was much bravado about the latest language, the best diagnostic routine, and the best terminal. Today we should be able to take pride in our software creations and show results that meet the objectives of the organization, rather than the latest software tools. Linkages will help to remove our concentration on individual tools. Linkages will make it possible to use the complete software engineering toolset.

Figure 5.1 shows the logical toolboxes as nonlinked entities. This chapter discusses each toolbox and its proper function in the software process and connects the toolboxes in a correct process flow.

DEVELOPMENT AND TEST TOOLBOX

The first chapter established the fact that coding and testing were among the very earliest programming activities. It is appropriate to begin our functional

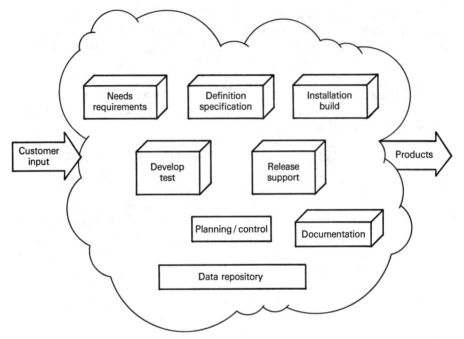

Figure 5.1 Domain of nonlinked toolboxes.

toolset with the development and test toolbox, which supports the following major activities:

- code creation and editing
- code testing
- system/application integration and testing
- change/version control
- configuration management
- optimization
- destructive testing
- performance testing
- other testing as required (functionality, integration, system)
- internal maintenance specification

The craftsperson could work well with module construction and testing and with system/application integration and testing. The actual toolbox that contained a full complement of tools for all activities on the list would be "heavy" indeed. Source-code creation and testing are very well understood and documented. There are hundreds of programming languages, and many modules were coded by crafters again and again in a wide variety of languages.

Development and Test Toolbox: Code Creation and Editing

Software began with the creation of the first code, and editing followed very shortly thereafter. As machine and assembly languages revealed their deficiencies, higher-level languages promised a general way for communicating with the computer, and there have been many successful technology transitions from second- to third- to fourth-generation languages. But we now understand that the problem we face today is not how to use algorithmic languages but how to translate real-world application problems into solutions. Textual, procedural languages have not proven to be well suited to this work.

If so-called third-generation computer languages attempted to generalize procedural methods, then fourth-generation languages moved toward specialization and problem specific areas. Fourth-generation languages are nonprocedural; they focus on what needs to be done to solve the problem rather than how to solve the problem. They tend to be much more domain-specific than their predecessors.

Recent languages support higher programmer productivity and generally have a significant reduction in the lines of code required to solve a problem. In one sense, some fourth-generation languages become a sort of specification language. Some implementations have produced high-quality programs; this usually occurs where the language has remained pure. Where there has been a marriage of second-, third-, or fourth-generation languages, there appears to have been an irregularity in the marriage ceremony that affects the social standing of the offspring in the community; the programs are not popular in maintenance and support circles.

Software engineering will not find the language solution in the domain of linguistics, philosophy, or communication. If advances in artificial intelligence allow the computer to deal with meaning and context, there will be hope for new computer languages to be used in software engineering. In the meantime, fourth-generation languages continue to excite the computer community, but third-generation languages continue to prosper. Part of the reason for third-generation longevity is massive investment in programs written in these languages. Part of the reason is that fourth-generation languages are less efficient (in many applications) when compared to third-generation languages; and part of the reason is that fourth-generation languages cover only a limited subset of application domains.

In addition to the fourth-generation languages, there are a number of very high level prototyping languages on the scene. With regard to software engineering

- Languages are, of course, essential to software engineering; they are the key element in translating the design for the computer.
- There is no automatic programming on the horizon.

- There is no one language (third-generation, fourth-generation, proto-typing, and so on) that will fully meet the needs of software engineering.
- Design and programming require a dialogue between the software engineer and the system.
- There will be programming in some form for the rest of our lives.

There are many who would disagree with the second point; they believe that automatic programming will make a significant contribution in the near future. We do not fully understand language or specification, and a major breakthrough is needed before we will have a significant technology transition.

The ideal language for software engineering will not be algorithmic; rather it will be well suited to specification of the problem and production of the solution to match the specification. However, it will not necessarily be an ultraspecialized language.

The idea of developing a specialized language has been with us since the beginning of computer programming. To select just one example, in the 1960s there was a rush to computer-assisted instruction, which included the development of numerous special computer languages to allow course materials to be programmed for student instruction. These languages failed because they did not meet educator or student needs, and there were thousands of hours of course preparation done that cannot be used today. It must be noted that computer-assisted instruction did not fail to meet its goals because of languages. It failed because we did not understand this new technology and how to make a successful transition to the technology.

Development and Test Toolbox: Code Testing

The lesson is clear. Computer languages are still evolving, and software engineering does not have to wait for them. Just as the majority of present-day personal computer users do not want to write programs, software engineers should not want to write programs, and most will not even have to be expert programmers. At one point people calculated square roots with pencil and paper; today it is not necessary. Software engineers will not have to be expert in telling computers "how to" solve a specific problem; they will become adept at analyzing the real-world needs, specifying and designing solutions, and verifying the results. They will be able to integrate and test large-scale systems.

The earliest code testing was done by the developer. This tradition has more or less continued to the present time because unit testing is usually done by the developer. There is a large body of testing knowledge and practice available today, and unit testing can be accomplished in a timely and efficient manner.

Code creation, integration, and testing have been naturally linked since the earliest days of software development. As soon as code is written, there is need to see if it works. There are numerous testing methodologies, but they are all based upon two fundamental types of testing. "White-box" testing is done with full knowledge of internals; full functionality is known to the tester. "Black-box" testing is done without knowledge of internals; tests are focused on what the box can do. In general, white-box testing exercises logic paths; black-box testing validates ranges and calling sequences.

Development and Test Toolbox: System or Application Integration and Testing

System or application integration and testing proved to be a bit more difficult. In earlier days someone was placed in charge of the "release account," and everyone submitted their software, such as it was, near the deadline. In worst cases the release account could be updated on a daily basis, leading to the "release du jour" practice. During the testing phase it was not uncommon for several programmers to revert to crafter practices; while the defective module was being corrected and integrated, other programmers took the opportunity to change their modules. This led to an almost endless cycle of defects; in some cases it led to a downward spiral over time. The spiral was noted by the integration team saying, "That's too bad; they should have released it several weeks ago when they had a pretty good package."

System or application integration and testing tools will support an orderly construction and test of the complete program. These tools and practices will allow modules to be tested and integrated; subassemblies (databases, networking, applications, and so on) to be tested and integrated; and the final program to be built, tested, and tracked.

Development and Test Toolbox: Change or Version Control

To this day the biggest deficiencies in software quality are the absence of change or version control and configuration management in many software companies. This is true for stand-alone collections of software tools as well as for CASE/IPSE vendors. CASE/IPSE product offerings do not all have configuration management, or they offer a less than fully functional version. Version control provides the first level of tracking changes and knowing when software modules were first used.

Development and Test Toolbox: Configuration Management

Configuration management fully tracks programs, utilities, documentation, and the like and monitors and reports on changes to allow management of a system. Configuration management is vital in large-scale software systems or applications because the complete software system includes programs, utilities, data and/or databases, documentation, and support tools. If software could be frozen and shipped in exactly the same way for a year or longer, there would be no problem. But such things as modifications, fixing defects, and changes by vendors cause frequent changes to the configuration.

The more complex the system, the greater the need for configuration management. However, simply buying a configuration management package will not solve the problem. If there are no changes to the input process, it is quite possible that the newly installed configuration management package may simply provide up-to-date information on the decline and fall of the system. If the system were better designed and if there were accurate documentation of the designs available, it might be possible to minimize the need for frequent changes.

The internal maintenance specification was intended to tell how things worked, the trade secrets, and other things needed to allow someone other than the creator to maintain the code. Without configuration management, there is a high probability that the internal maintenance specification will get out of step with the code. Quality assurance and sign-off procedures usually have a "to be checked off" step asking if the specification has been updated, but that does not mean that the specification has been adequately updated. The biggest danger to check-off lists is that the check mark becomes the thing to look for, and it is awfully easy to make a check mark.

Development and Test Toolbox: Optimization

Coding first and then attempting to craft or custom-fit the code modules together appears to be an easier way to build systems or large applications. To the extent that this requires a major integration effort, work is farther removed from true software engineering. If components were properly designed in the first place, they would fit together with a minimum effort and provide optimal performance. If major changes are required, then there is a design problem, which should not be corrected by brute force.

Code creation, integration, and test should include an orderly integration process and should simply be part of the development work. Modules to be integrated should all be known prior to development. Modules should be developed to design specification, and performance should be predicted accurately. Modules should fit together in a very precise manner, and performance should be within predicted guidelines.

Development and Test Toolbox: Destructive Testing

There is another testing variation, destructive testing, which focuses on breaking or defeating the system. Destructive-testing groups perform a very valuable function in that they try things that otherwise might go untried. Tests done by those who designed a system will be based upon "normal" operation of the system. But many users are far from normal, and in one sense the system must be protected from these users. Destructive testers are particularly valuable in testing the security of systems.

Development and Test Toolbox: Performance Tests

As final system integration occurs, there are performance tests, which are usually accompanied by performance tuning. However, a major portion of final tuning must be done after on-site system installation. Final performance tests on-site are also part of the final customer acceptance of the system.

Beginning at the module level, it should be possible to conduct a complete test series with every path and function fully tested. As system integration nears completion, it should still be possible to test normal functions and many error conditions. Regression tests which are part of the system test suite, are essential to assuring that the current version of the system is performing at least as well as the previous version.

Development and Test Toolbox: Internal Maintenance Specification

Code maintenance is a constant challenge and will remain so until software engineering provides a viable alternative. This toolbox should contain tools that provide the creation and updating functions for the internal maintenance charts, diagrams, and documentation required to support the software program.

DEFINITION AND SPECIFICATION TOOLBOX

The definition and specification a toolbox has always existed to some extent. It would be impossible to code without an understanding of the problem and some sort of definition of the solution. The main functional tools support the following:

- technical analysis of customer's needs
- problem definition
- requirements definition
- structured analysis and design
- system/application/architectural specification

Definition and Specification Toolbox: Technical
Analysis of Customer's Needs

The weakest point in the definition and specification toolbox is the technical analysis of customer's needs. In many larger companies the analyst has never met the customer, has never visited the customer's place of business, and has never worked in the customer's environment. This is not the case when the product is system software that is to be used by system developers. The situation of analysts failing to understand customer's needs began to occur when compiler developers could not program well in the language they were developing. A specific example might be an RPG-compiler designer and developer who cannot code more than a few lines of RPG. The problem definitely occurs in applications software development, where many of the developers come directly from college to the development lab, bypassing the environment of the application's user. This is analogous to the early vacuum tube television sets. No one who designed one of those sets ever tried to change the tubes. Design criteria did not include supportability.

The main point here is that the best design meets the customer's needs fully. There were early attempts to validate the design by showing selected customers copies of the external reference specifications. These documents listed all the user screens, parameters, databases, and so on. Given a 6-inch-thick document, it took a customer of unusual comprehension to read the document and pronounce it fit to be a product. There was always the danger that the customer would read too much into the document and pronounce it fit when it was really not fit. Reviewers of a document looked for completeness of function; they did not get a feel for how the product would work.

Definition and Specification Toolbox:
Problem Definition

The key to success in programming is to meet the customer's needs fully. Good problem definition ensures that the needs are understood and documented in such a way as to be useful in a structured analysis of the problem.

Definition and Specification Toolbox:
Requirements Definition

There are requirements that may not be reflected in the user's needs but that must be included in structured analysis. These include safety, regulatory, security, and company guidelines. Good definition of requirements ensures that the requirements are properly prepared for structured analysis.

Definition and Specification Toolbox: Structured Analysis and Design

Two of the most well known techniques in the definition and specification toolbox are structured analysis and structured design (believers will also look for real-time extensions). In the structured analysis phase, the definition of the user problem is translated into requirements and segmented into levels according to process flows. Graphic representation is done by data-flow diagrams. But there have been significant improvements since the days of the hand-drawn flowcharts. There are automatic consistency checks based upon rules of the specific methodology. These checks support a complete analysis.

Structured design translates requirements into solution flow. Design includes process control, information flow, and data structure flow. At the lowest level, detailed design approximates actual code; in some cases, it is almost a one-for-one translation.

There are dozens of structured analysis and design tools that could be used in our software engineering definition and specification toolbox. In general, the structured analysis tool should have data-flow diagrams, process specification, and a data dictionary. If there is a real-time component, it should have control-flow diagrams, control specifications, and an extension to the data dictionary. Structured design should produce structure charts and module specifications or their equivalent.

Upon completion of the structured analysis phase, you should have defined the application or system that is to be implemented. Structured analysis output includes

- a clear, nonredundant model of the application or system;
- a graphical picture of processes and data flows;
- definitions (including textual) of all components and parts of the model.

Upon completion of the structured design phase you should have a structured solution for the application or system. Structured design output includes

- a decomposition of the problem into hierarchical components;
- a structure chart (graphically representing the application or system), which shows modules, connections, information flows, control flows, and communication between modules;
- rule checking of the design.

There are many sources of information about proven methodologies and tools for structured analysis and design. These tools have been the main focus for some companies; they are a staple for almost all companies and they are the main tools in this toolbox.

Definition and Specification Toolbox: System Application and Architectural Specification

System application and architectural specifications state needs for system functionality, support services, and other utilities that are needed to allow implementation of the design. In many cases this tool was not used or needed because the newly designed system was installed in the existing computer system. Consider a primitive computer that had no compare or move instructions, and then imagine designing a complex file system that would include key file searches. It would be much easier to develop an efficient file system if the microcode were enhanced to include the move and compare instructions. There are similar situations for utility services, communication services, and the like. If it were possible to understand trade-offs, performance degradations, and added costs to enhance the system, it would be possible to make good decisions. Until just a few years ago, this was not practical in many development environments. Today there are competing methodologies and tools galore to fill this box. The good news is that you have a choice of structured analysis and design methodologies; the bad news is that there appears to be a new game in town. Unfortunately, the new world of structured analysis and structured design may be too deeply rooted in the past.

Structured analysis and structured design have advanced the trade, but they may be subject to the adage that each new medium adopts the content of the last, nearest medium. Early horseless carriages had buggy-whip holders on the side. Early movies used books for their stories; later they began exploring the visual potential of the motion picture. Early television showed a lot of old movies; in recent years it has taken advantage of live around-the-world coverage potential. Early attempts at computer-assisted instruction used programmed learning texts. Perhaps history will record that early attempts at definition and specification used "electronic paper" flowcharts. The use of structured analysis and structured design has been challenged by the arrival of object-oriented design and programming. There is a lot of good debate and controversy here; one side says a new event has taken place, whereas the other side attempts to do object-oriented analysis and design in a manner similar to structured analysis and structured design. We revisit this controversy in a later chapter, which discusses the linkages between the toolboxes.

There is no doubt that we must have a thorough analysis of the problem and design of the solution to be members of the engineering community. There is also the fact that we must begin by advancing from the last, nearest medium The caveat here is that while there have been dramatic strides in structured analysis and structured design, there are also many critics with legitimate objections. One should understand the pros and cons before making large-scale investments in this toolbox.

NEEDS AND REQUIREMENTS TOOLBOX

The needs and requirements toolbox should have existed from the very beginning, but in fact it was almost nonexistent until just a few years ago. To this day there are heated arguments between customers and software suppliers centering on the fact that the customer deems a certain feature to be necessary, but the supplier says it is an option. The customer concludes that the software product has a defect, whereas the supplier scores it as an enhancement request. If the software is directed to a newer area of systems or applications, it tends to be difficult for the customer to completely describe the requirements. If the software product is built to a standard, there is less chance of this misunderstanding.

Waiting until the external specification is complete makes it difficult to change the project and awkward to understand what and how to change. The needs and requirements toolbox supports the following:

- user's business and environment
- international and government regulations
- market research
- simulation and prototyping
- product positioning

Needs and Requirements Toolbox: User's Business and Environment

We have already discussed the importance of understanding the user environment. This includes such factors as the physical layout, environmental factors, user interactions, and level of user understanding. What problem is the customer trying to solve? How would the customer like the problem to be solved? The customer is supreme in this regard; the customer is the only reason to be in business; the customer is the only reason for this book to be written. Everyone has a customer, even if it is oneself. Thus the primary need is dictated by the customer. If the customer is oneself, we usually make certain that the customer is satisfied. If the customer is someone else, we usually make decisions for that customer in direct proportion to the number of layers of organization between us and the customer. The greater the number of layers, the greater our willingness to decide what is best for the customer without asking if the customer agrees with our decision.

Needs and Requirements Toolbox: International and Government Regulations

There is a secondary need that can supersede the customer—that is the need to satisfy government regulations. If the software does something that violates regulations, then the customer's need must take second place.

One example might be a government regulation regarding lot tracking for materials used in pharmaceuticals. In this situation the user might not wish to have all the lot-tracking features, but they are necessary. Another example might be a foreign country's requirement that all user screens and reports that pertain to the safe operation of the system must be in the local language. A third example might be the requirement to provide printer support for all the characters in the NATO languages in order to be able to sell to any member country.

These are examples of regulatory requirements that could result in a significant loss of business if they were not included in the original requirements document. These requirements are different from the safety requirements for computer operation and fault tolerance. Software defects can cause errors during operation, and these are controlled by the use of fault-tolerant techniques, information redundancy, and software-recovery techniques. These techniques are applied during the definition and specification phase. However, requirements should state the level of reliability needed.

Needs and Requirements Toolbox: Market Research

Market research has been the neglected area of early computer development. For many years the systems were sold on a price or performance basis. This is still true today for a large portion of the market. The other main selling approach is support, security, and peace of mind. In some selling situations certain vendors play to the fact that their systems will fail. The customer is told that it will happen—probably often—and is asked to think about what happens to his or her career when support is not instantly available. In such cases, the customer signs the support contract. In some cases, the customer will actually pass over a superior computer system just to avoid risk.

Many salespersons approximate peddlers. They never really understand products or customer's needs very well. They simply want to move hardware. There is no time to match product to customer need; there is little need to understand competition or marketplace; just talk price and deals.

Lack of knowledge about the competitive situation leads to development of product features and enhancement lists. If there is no true market research, then product managers will want a complete set of features and all enhancements. This will lengthen development time, increase product cost, and not necessarily increase sales. In selected situations there are customers who will say, "I will not buy your product because it does not have features X and

Y." The fact is that they will never buy your product under any circumstances. Features X and Y were excuses to justify their purchase of another system; they did not really require those features.

Market research would not fall victim to such a deception. Proper studies would indicate not only required features and enhancements for today but also those required for tomorrow. This leads to user requirements planning. If you are in business for the long term, you must know

- where the user is going, what the user's problems are, what it takes to meet user's needs;
- where the industry or profession is going;
- where regulatory and safety requirements are going;
- the limits of expandability and adaptability of present design.

Needs and Requirements Toolbox: Simulation and Prototyping

Simulation and prototyping are coming into their own in this toolbox. For example, it is possible to simulate all screens for a shop floor–control system, an on-line banking system, or a hospital intensive care unit system. Users can then be brought into an amazingly realistic approximation of the actual environment. They can, in effect, "fly" the application. After just one or two sessions, they will have very informed opinions about functions, screen layouts, ease of use, and probable productivity of the product. Simulations can also be used by human factors and human engineering researchers to determine the effectiveness of the product. When this is compared to reading a 6-inch-thick external specification, one wonders how we ever got along without simulation. Prototyping is the practice of building a first or original model (sometime scaled down, but accurate) of a system to verify the operational process prior to building a final system. When applied to chemical engineering or power transmission, the practice is well suited to good engineering procedures. When applied to software, it requires some modification. In one sense, a complete software prototype would be the product.

As we have discussed in software differentiation, there is only one software program, which is duplicated many times. But it is possible to create prototypes of databases and their operation, user interfaces in draft form, and many system operations. We can create prototypes to permit validation of customer's requirements and develop the frameworks for functional and behavioral specifications.

Prototyping should be conducted in the needs and requirements phase. There is great promise in the rapid prototyping concept, which provides continuous feedback during the prototyping process. Some advocates of rapid prototyping place it in the analysis and design phase. While rapid prototyping can also be used effectively in this phase, it will have maximum impact in the needs and requirements phase. It is quite possible that although the prototype works to customer specification, the prototype looks nothing like the final product and is very large and inefficient in operation. It may take a very large computer system to prototype a program that will ultimately run on a hand-held computer.

There are special prototype languages and applications to support rapid prototyping of both computer systems and end-user applications. These languages support modularity, adaptability, rapid modification, reuse, and requirements tracing. There is also support for object-based prototyping; objects are very valuable in allowing the localization of information. An explanation of the object-oriented methodologies is contained in Chapter 7.

In general, any software project that will produce more than several thousand lines of code should be prototyped. The user should be able to try the prototype. Recommendations for changes should be translated to prototype changes continuously, and user needs should be met prior to beginning the analysis phase.

Needs and Requirements Toolbox: Product Positioning

Product positioning is vital but often ignored. If the product is properly positioned for the main body of users, it will have a normal life expectancy and require only normal changes. If the product is positioned as a compact car and then sold to customers who want it "upgraded" to a luxury car in subsequent releases, there will be endless difficulty. Product positioning is also important with regard to other products in the line. One example might be a shop floor–control system that features bar-code readers at workstations on the shop floor but does not support bar-code printing because the existing operating system does not support bar-code printing.

Determining needs and requirements is a very important product-positioning step because it allows an initial estimate of the risk and investment involved in committing to a project. The first of two key go/no-go decisions is made during this phase. This decision looks at the overall worthiness of the project and alignment of the project with overall goals. (In an earlier era of computer technology, it was common practice to develop an innovative solution and then search for a matching need.) The second key decision point occurs in the definition and specification phase when the investigation is complete and a decision is made to proceed.

LOGICAL ORDER OF THE FIRST THREE TOOLBOXES

The three toolboxes are shown in logical order on Figure 5.2; normal product flow moves from left to right. Feedback loops and other connectors are shown

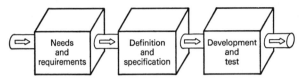

Figure 5.2   First three toolboxes linked.

in later diagrams. If the toolboxes were hardware boards filled with chips, they could be shown plugged into a computer. This chapter is discussing the logical flow of the software engineering process, and there are fewer conventions for showing "software boards or toolboxes." Here we are connecting them by showing the information flowing through logical network ports. In actual use the design, code modules, documentation, and such are stored in data bases, and then accessed by another tool in the same toolbox, or another toolbox, as needed.

INSTALLATION AND BUILD TOOLBOX

The installation and build toolbox can be very deceptive. If viewed from the perspective of a personal computer, it seems to be a trivial step that requires few tools. Users are able to install new software on their systems with apparent ease, as long as the software is known to be compatible. In many personal computers you simply insert the disc, select the install command, and wait less than 1 minute. As computer size grows to megaminicomputers, mainframes, and supercomputers, the installation and building problems (opportunities) grow at an exponential rate. This opportunity continues to increase when the user has selected a networked system that involves 10, 100, or 1000 computers.

In larger systems and networks, the computer hardware and communications can be thought of as the lot upon which a new home is to be built. The software can be envisioned as all the component products that go into the home. When we moved into our present home a few years ago, the builder's literature informed us that there were more than 3000 different components in the home. Subsequent repairs and service calls have convinced me that the figure 3000 is correct and that the permutations and combinations of things that can go awry is awesome. The largest computer systems and networks are "assembled"—some will even say "manufactured"—on site. The installation and building toolbox is the one of the most poorly equipped in our software shop. There are many tools already in the box, but they are of poor quality and often were not designed to work together. Computer companies spend small fortunes and field engineers spend thousands of hours overcoming this problem. There is help on the way, and the newest computer systems have made significant strides.

Figure 5.3 positions the installation and building toolbox, which supports the following:

- distribution and software installation
- interconnection
- security
- diagnostic tools
- sizing and tuning (performance)
- system/network version control and configuration management

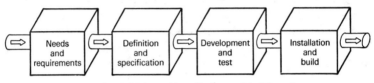

Figure 5.3   Addition of installation and build toolbox.

Installation and Build Toolbox: Distribution and Software Installation

Distribution of personal computer and small-system software is relatively easy. A small disc holds the software, and a typical installation consists of reading the disc and ignoring the manual until trouble occurs. Larger systems use a variety of media for software distribution. The classic medium is magnetic tape, with multiple reels needed to hold the system. The classic installation has the field engineer visit the customer and install those portions of the system that the customer has ordered. Fancier versions have attempted to make a customized tape for each customer in order to automate the installation. Newer media include discs and CD-ROMS.

The difficulty begins when one software product requires the upgrade of other software products in order to function properly. Newer configurations will monitor all the software modules and advise the installer, but even the best configurations do not allow for variances in other vendor's software that has become an integral part of the system. There are some very promising artificial intelligence configurators now being used, but networks seem to be growing at faster than the coping ability of rule-based artificial intelligence systems.

Installation and Build Toolbox: Interconnection

Software interconnection involves knowing when databases, network parameters, and system parameters must be changed. In many cases this becomes a specialists' world, and only a few very skilled persons can manage the network. These experts are a vital link in the process. They are serving in a crafter function. They will be very difficult to replace with software engineering tools.

Installation and Build Toolbox: Security

There are two viewpoints regarding security. The first is internal security of the software engineering system, including the network; the second is the security that must be designed and built into products. The customer's system can be vulnerable during enhancements or upgrades, especially if they are done on-line. Tools can be used to analyze the system and plan upgrade sequences. Tools can also be used to manage the upgrade. This includes a contingency plan to restore the system to its original condition in the event of a mishap.

These plans can include a small test upgrade to one computer or one node; they can also include the upgrade of a test system at the customer's site. Any plan should have intermediate checkpoints and constant monitoring. The point to be made is that customers should not require protection from the vendor. Today the vendor can unintentionally threaten customer security; someday the customer will not have to know that the system is being upgraded. The customer will not have to develop or acquire special tools or testing processes in an attempt to maintain system security.

The system should, of course, be secure during operation. Irregularities in system function should be properly reported; critical irregularities should sound the alarm. There should be protection against viruses as well as protection against unauthorized access. Do the software engineering tools in our toolbox allow us to design and implement these levels of protection? Are some of these same tools available to our customers? Are there diagnostic tools available? Security can likewise be very good at the single-machine level with no outside network access; security is another matter at the network level. When it is necessary to provide greater protection, users pay the price in terms of greater difficulty in accessing the system. Conventional wisdom was that we could not bring the system back to the lab; we could not duplicate the network in the lab.

Perhaps there is a new conventional wisdom. With the latest tools in our toolbox, with communications standards, and with large-scale modeling and simulation, it should be possible to guarantee security. Automated analysis tools, often using artificial intelligence, can model the external network to allow verification of system integrity.

Although we are concerned about the user system and network, there should also be procedures to ensure the security of software engineering tools and networks. Many software development companies have very lax security procedures. Software engineers tend to disregard or bypass security procedures. This has allowed flagrant security violations. These types of security violations have happened and will continue to happen. In attempts to prevent these violations, some system managers install multilevel passwords. Engineers are often offended by these security measures; most engineers are very trusting of their colleagues, and they are correct in noting that most security measures slow work on the system. There should be tools to monitor and guarantee system security. There should be restricted access levels, and there should be automatic encryption and decryption devices wherever necessary on the network. Software security tools and procedures should include tools for

- designers who approve specifications and who validate, inspect, and control changes;
- programmers who write, access, and modify code that has been secured, who use locks, passwords, encryption, and other security tools and practices and who are responsible for making the system "hacker proof";
- testers to ensure proper functioning of system security, which should attempt accidental accesses or deliberate break-ins;
- administrators who require record retention.

There should also be tools to support security due to natural disasters such as earthquakes or floods. These tools include dispersion of records, duplicate on-line records, and off-line backup and storage.

The bottom line to the security requirement is that customers demand total system security and integrity. This must be included in all phases from installation to upgrade to audits. There must be software tools in our engineering system to provide this security. Major accounting firms are now auditing computer system security. Many companies conduct their own internal computer security audits.

Installation and Build Toolbox: Diagnostic Tools

Diagnostic hardware tools (including software that analyzes hardware) can be similar to the finest medical tools in the hands of a medical internist. Discs, computers, and peripherals can all be quickly and accurately diagnosed. Hardware technicians are very good at the single-computer level; they have greater difficulty at the network level.

Installation and Build Toolbox: Sizing and Tuning

We used the house-building analogy. Perhaps we should now use the expensive-sports-car analogy to describe sizing and tuning. You must have a large-enough engine, and you must have the horsepower to attain desired performance levels. This requires a careful analysis of present system capabilities and an understanding of data flow throughout the network. The difference between mediocre performance and sizzling performance is often based upon the skill and effort of field engineers. If customers attempt their own performance tuning, their results will cover the spectrum of possibilities. Some application and systems specialists can do a better job than the vendor; they understand their business and their needs and they can see how to tune the system to those needs. Others will do much worse. Until the vendor is certain that the customer can handle the job, it is better to err on the side of having the vendor supply tuning.

Installation and Build Toolbox: System and Network Version Control and Configuration Management

There is a pressing need for system and network version control. If you do not know or cannot quickly find out what exists on systems and networks, then all attempts to find defects and to tune the system will meet with less than optimum results. The same is true for system and network configuration management.

The biggest single problem with this toolbox is that it is used by a different set of software engineers, those who live in the field. Thus the plight of field engineers is often not realized by development engineers. In many cases the field is working around things that could be fixed or just improved by software development teams. If these limitations were known, it is possible that software teams would

- minimize interconnections and dependencies between software products;
- consider installation and build needs during specification and design;
- work toward automated installation and self-tuning systems.

SUPPORT TOOLBOX

The support toolbox is still not fully equipped, but support engineers deserve credit for saving computers from early extinction. They use the tools at hand and overcome all sorts of obstacles to keep the system up and running. They achieve minor miracles in recovering from seeming disasters.

Figure 5.4 positions the support toolbox, which provides the following:

- defect analysis, repair, tracking, and reporting
- customer training
- field engineer training

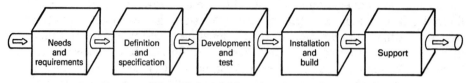

Figure 5.4   Addition of support toolbox.

Support Toolbox: Defect Analysis, Repair, Tracking, and Reporting

Almost all computer companies have some sort of defect tracking and reporting system; the most primitive track defects after the fact in a batch mode; the more advanced can do on-line reporting and interactive defect correction. In all such systems developers become involved. There is also a hierarchy of defects levels and a variety of ways to deal with defects. In some cases a specialized patch is sent to a specific customer; in other cases a general patch is sent to many or all customers. The classical defect tracking and reporting systems have had a great deal of difficulty in spotting duplicate reports of the same problem and in ensuring that everyone receives fixes in a timely manner. The classic *patch tape* concept has probably done more to undermine the "get it right the first time" guideline than any other concept. Software release is a complex process, often characterized by low quality and late delivery, with the misguided confidence that patch tapes will make everything right.

The next major hurdle is to be certain that all fixes contained in the last release will be incorporated into the new release. Users are most irritated when something that they finally had fixed 2 months ago reappears in the new release. Please note that this toolbox is, of necessity, linked to the development lab, whereas the installation and building toolbox is usually a stand-alone toolbox. Perhaps a better linkage could help to solve this problem.

Support Toolbox: Customer Training

The customer must understand the proper operation of the computer system. The support team must understand customer needs and how the system can meet those needs.

Many potential problems can be avoided by the support team having the right tools and being able to deliver information and training to the customer. One of the greatest dangers to any large computer system or network is a poorly trained operator or local support person. When something does go wrong, an improper move can often make the situation much worse. Consider the operator who discovers that some device is down and decides to take the entire system down in order to bring the device up.

Customer training must teach proper operation, safety, and mastery of the system. The operator should understand system tools pertinent to operation. In many situations a clever operator learns the use of some of these support tools by watching the service engineer, but the operator does not fully understand the complete functioning of the tools. Remember that skills required for successful operation are not necessarily the same as those required for good support.

Support Toolbox: Field Engineer Training

Technical support is another issue. The vendor's customer engineers must understand a great deal of the system operation; they must have mastered many of the same tools used in final stages of system testing and in installation and build. This implies a need for this toolbox to logically connect to other parts of the software engineering system; the field engineers are part of that system.

Larger customers pose a special opportunity. They often have technical personnel who are equal to or better than the best vendor's technical personnel. If these customer personnel know how to use support tools properly, they can be very effective in solving problems and in tuning the system. If they are forbidden to use these tools, the burden falls upon the vendor. The reality is that the customer's technical personnel will attempt to work with the system anyway; trying to keep it closed to them only frustrates their ability to succeed. There must be some clear-cut division, since some of the tools are proprietary to the vendor and others have not been well enough documented or supported for general release. In our software engineering world, the tools should be well designed and documented to allow general use. The only reason for keeping them from customers should be proprietary considerations.

The point to these support examples is that the customer considers the entire system and network as being the responsibility of the company that sold it. It does little good to have the most efficient software written in the latest language if the system and network are not sized and tuned properly. It does little good to have the customer down because there was no training available for the latest software product or because the documentation did not match the training. The present-day trend is to buy an entire solution; all components of the solution are viewed as one. Thus it would not be sufficient to fill all five toolboxes with the finest tools; there must be linkages and connections.

Figure 5.5 links the five toolboxes to a data repository. The five boxes are shown in normal left-to-right flow. There are other toolboxes required for our software engineering toolset, but these additional boxes will connect to all five boxes. Let us examine them separately and then consider the linkages later.

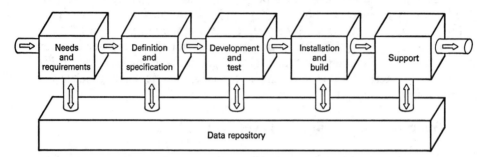

Figure 5.5   Addition of data repository.

DOCUMENTATION TOOLBOX

Documentation is cited as one of the most important elements in a successful system. Technical writers and documentation experts have suffered much criticism, although they have managed to develop some effective techniques for helping engineers and users to understand systems. In most cases they have not had the benefit of a complete documentation system. The documentation toolbox contains the following documents:

- documentation plan, to include a list of the manuals for the system or product objectives, requirements (including staffing), and assumptions   (*Note*: A single manual could require less planning than multiple volumes.)
- requirements definition
- design (including detailed design)
- software module input/output, interconnections, and networking definitions
- testing plans and results
- user documentation and on-line help texts

Documentation Toolbox: Documents

Crafted documentation has grown to the point where the total collection of operation, user, system, training, and support documentation can outweigh the hardware. Earlier documentation was often circular in nature; each manual would state that you should have read two other manuals prior to reading this one. The documentation made sense only after you understood how the system operated. Complete software engineering systems require an integrated documentation plan.

Earlier shops also had the outmoded notion that technical writers were crafters who lived only in one corner of the marketing (or other nondevelopment) department and that they would somehow take care of all documentation needs after the product was almost completed. In some situations technical manuals became the only current documentation, as software teams allowed their documents to slip into obsolescence. Technical writers labored in information darkness, working from documents that were updated on an irregular basis. They were not directed by a documentation plan.

There have also been ongoing debates over the proper qualifications for technical writers. One view would have them all be fully qualified engineers who have some degree of writing skills; the other view would have them be skilled writers who have been exposed to software. The best solution depends upon the level of documentation and the user's knowledge. User documentation should be easy to understand, but software engineers will find it easy to understand things that baffle the average user. There are several layered or nested approaches that seem to be working. User documentation should be very easy to read and examples should be easy to follow. Technical documentation is geared to the technical level and organized so that it is easy to find things quickly.

There are also a number of new developments including on-line help text, indexed error analysis messages, and CD-ROMs, which contain the most used documentation. All these things are helpful, but they do not solve the very large problem of keeping up with programming changes. This is another example of a stand-alone toolbox being awkward to use without knowledge of the changes, modifications, and enhancements going on back at the lab.

The existing documentation process includes a preliminary release to development, a release to testing at unit and system testing time, and a release to production (ideally prior to first customer ship). The documentation plan should describe all these activities and should be completed prior to design.

The documentation toolbox contains the following tools and services:

- a full set of software publishing tools
- full network services, including electronic mail, file and database sharing, and electronic bulletin boards
- localization of all appropriate documentation

Documentation Toolbox: Software Publishing Tools

Most companies will have to make major changes to have documentation be an integral part of the software engineering process. Technical writers should be full-fledged members of the team. Documentation plans, rough drafts, final drafts, and illustrations should appear at appropriate stages of the software development process. Proper documentation tools should be an integral part of software engineering toolboxes; they should not be some sort of add-on tools or afterthought. There is some risk in having technical writers be part of the development team. Writers must retain the user perspective; they must not lose their user focus.

Crafters did not worry about documentation. Many technical writers developed their own technical approach. The documentation tools are usually on another system; often the system was located in another computer room. During this time systems became more complex, and technical manuals increased in number and weight.

Even if systems were easy to use and highly automated, technical writers would still need to describe internal functions of the system. Consider the automobile owner's manual. This compact booklet describes the proper operation and some routine maintenance procedures. It contains all that the owner need know regarding the safe and proper operation of the automobile. There are additional volumes of material to describe engineering functions, parts and service, and regulatory compliance. In the computer system environment, there will always be need for higher-level documentation and training to include the best and most efficient ways to install, optimize, and use the system.

Documentation Toolbox: Network Services

Full network services are the key to successful documentation. One of the primary causes of documentation errors is the failure of the technical writers to keep the documentation up-to-date. In many time-critical situations the programmers change software, and the writers are unaware of the change. In other situations the programmers did not review the revised documentation.

Full network services provide the communication support required to allow the timely distribution and review of project specifications, documentation, release notices, change notices, and all other relevent information. In addition to having the network services in place, the software life cycle must include processes that include the generation and review of documentation. This is an area where the tools and methods exist today, but many software development organizations fail to use them.

Documentation Toolbox: Localization

The documentation toolbox will need some new and innovative tools to support localization. Some manuals, user screens, help text, and other documentation relating to safe operation must be available in local languages in some countries. Much of the present-day translation is done by hand in the destination country. This is time consuming at initial installation and maddening when upgrades and new releases occur. In many cases the system is on display or being used at one or more sites in the country prior to localization of the software. There has been some success with tools that provide automatic language translation, but at this time they do not provide a total solution.

Integrated documentation systems will allow localization to begin earlier in the process. New tools and new methodologies are required to make localization part of the software engineering process. Localization should not be an afterthought; it should be the result of deliberate engineering thought.

The bottom line on the documentation toolbox is that it has been used at a distance from the other toolboxes and has not always been part of the mainstream process. A complete software engineering environment must reduce the logical and physical distance. The perfect system would have little or no documentation; it would be easy to use and would do what customers wanted it to do.

MANAGEMENT PLANNING AND CONTROL TOOLBOX

Proper management is essential to successful completion of software projects in a timely manner. Proper management of many software projects has been only a dream. There are exceptions, but the original "waterfall" life cycle did not support a fully informed and understanding management. This brought about a climate where many first-level managers and programming staff were not certain that they wanted management informed. This is somewhat analogous to the arrival of on-line interactive shop floor production management systems. When these systems were introduced, many first-level managers protested vigorously. The reason for their protests was that they had developed their own unique management styles based upon the use of red tags and expediting, in which they waited for a bottleneck to occur and then descended upon the shop floor with clipboard and red tags in hand.

A similar situation exists in software. Managers have been used to receiving "creative" reports, and they have become accustomed to modifying progress reports and cost estimates according to the correction factors that have proven themselves over time. Our management toolbox is supposed to span all five software toolboxes, but in fact it rarely does so today. The management toolbox should support the following:

- modeling the project or product
- project planning
- project estimation, scoping, and costing
- project schedules and milestones
- project quality objectives
- project tracking
- project change, reestimation, rescoping, and rescheduling
- project integration
- productivity control

Management Toolbox: Modeling the Project or Product

The idea that an on-line system would allow upper management to know what was happening at all times would be terrifying indeed to this form of crisis management. It took a massive selling job to convince those managers that the on-line system with capacity planning and input/output analysis would enable them to spot capacity problems in advance and solve the potential problem by redistributing job flow and resources through the system.

Management Toolbox: Project Planning

It is important to have a plan for software development and be confident that the plan is being implemented. In many cases estimates are guesstimates at best, and the best way to come close to making a schedule is to double the number of the original estimate that is submitted. If several levels of management follow the doubling rule, the project can take years (in some cases this turns out to be true). What is wrong with this picture? Why does it usually get audiences to shake their heads or stare in disbelief? The answer is that crafted software is very difficult to manage on a large scale. Even if you acquire some sort of project management software, even if that software can be used to sum all the projects, you still get inaccurate estimates. The best course of action is to master best techniques for project management given today's situation and defer more sweeping project management tools and methodologies until such time as there is a repeatable, predictable process to manage.

Management Toolbox: Project Estimation, Scoping, and Costing

Many software projects would be considered to be well managed today if accurate estimation, scoping, tracking, and costing could be performed. Project managers need to begin with an accurate set of estimates and an understanding of project flow and critical paths. They should be able to monitor the project continuously or at least monitor it at numerous checkpoints to compare actual data to estimates. This can be done with available stand-alone personal computer software; it is easy today because many of these packages allow engineers to enter their schedules, submit them to management, and have overall project schedules automatically calculated. Project concatenation can be continued up to the program level.

Management Toolbox: Project Schedules and Milestones

Project planning and scheduling were among the very first software management activities. Originally the plans were based on guesstimates; later they were based on generous (allow plenty of time) estimates. Today there are many vendors offering programs that plan and track schedules.

Setting milestones is very important to accurate project tracking. The milestones must be clearly defined ("60% of the coding complete" is not a clear definition). One of the best techniques is to set functional milestones (functions can be tested and verified).

Some of the project planning and scheduling tools have been linked to tools in other toolboxes. Even if the tool is used in a stand-alone mode, it will prove to be beneficial to management. Stand-alone is acceptable; linked is better.

Management Toolbox: Project Quality Objectives

Management must set clear and measurable quality objectives that include products, performance, usability, supportability, and so on. Simply measuring defect rates will not ensure quality; lack of defects could be the result of poor testing.

Quality objectives should be monitored by tools in this toolbox, but they should be in accordance with quality goals established by top management. The specific goals should be defined in a quality plan that is based on achievable results, as demonstrated in earlier projects. Quality-control practices should be used to ensure compliance.

Management Toolbox: Project Tracking

Most present-day tracking tools do not provide good on-line tracking of actual project work. They tend to be better as historical tools. There is difficulty in changing schedules and very little simulation of productivity and schedule impacts caused by schedule changes.

Present-day tools should have a good graphical interface, and they should be able to do on-line analysis at the detailed project level. The tools should provide some way to validate data; this could be done by providing an on-line easy-to-use data verification procedure. Few present-day tools are driven by automatic data collection. In this sense the very professional-looking charts and graphs can be misleading. Their professional appearance and the inference of razor sharp accuracy make believers of most of us. If data were gathered by hand and based on personal estimates, they have a high probability of error. Data gathering should be guided by established project management rules. The data required should be specified in advance, before tools are selected. The project manager should not attempt to work only with the data at hand, unless the project manager has all the necessary information.

Management Toolbox: Project Change

The ability to change project plans dynamically is one of the biggest paybacks for using software management tools. Projects change, plans change, priorities change, and resources change—and they can all change at the same time. Tools that allow reestimation, rescoping, and rescheduling are essential to controlling cost overruns, delayed schedules, and the like. If management does not have timely project information, project variations can go undetected. If management does not have tools to make project changes, project variations can be inadvertently magnified.

Management Toolbox: Project Integration

When the project is a subsystem in a larger program, management tools are necessary to ensure timely completion and successful integration. Many companies use software project planning tools that allow individual project estimates to be "rolled up" to obtain a program estimate. Fewer companies use management tools to control project integration.

Management Toolbox: Productivity Control

As software technology transitions occur, they should be managed. The toolbox should be able to support tracking actual productivity and comparing actual data to estimates. It should also support postrelease work to ensure that apparent prerelease gains are not erased by expensive support costs.

Project management tools include standards for monitoring, scheduling according to types of resources and availability, on-line collection and reduction, automatic monitoring, and simulation. However, the first step should be to get control of today's projects using today's tools. Do not wait for the ultimate project management solution. This point deserves repetition throughout this book. Try to make the commitment to get control of your present projects; you will have taken the first step toward project management.

This lack of a complete set of integrated project management tools does not mean that we are powerless today. There are some near-term steps that will help to get control of today's software projects; these are covered in the last chapter. Understanding the coming software technology transitions involves developing the software engineering model and showing why we must be moving to make that model a reality. Today's remedies are necessary; tomorrow's software engineering is vital to survival in the computer industry. After completing the entire scenario for software engineering, we will revisit today and place it in a perspective that will allow today's detection and correction processes to be aligned with tomorrow's prevention processes.

SOFTWARE ENGINEERING DATA REPOSITORY

The software engineering data repository is supposed to be a storage box only. This will be true if we have a database that is well integrated with and supported by our software engineering system. A complete description of the connection and support tools, services, and "functional databases" is given in the next chapter. The point to be noted here is that we speak of a "repository" that fully supports the software engineering tools and platform. The database is fully accessible throughout the company and will be able to connect to external databases, which will be described shortly.

The term repository implies one large, heterogeneous collection of all the data needed for the software engineering system. If this book had been written a few years ago, there would have been a long list of discrete files and databases required for software engineering. There is a list of all the types of data that must be maintained for software engineering. There is also a major problem with the lack of database standards for software engineering. Companies are developing all sorts of tools and associated databases. There are few interconnections and many promises, and most conversion programs are designed to go just one way (to the vendor's tool). Rather than attempt to deal with this confusion, we will assume an integrated database (perhaps relational; perhaps an object management system) that fully meets all the software engineering system needs. Such a database is well within the existing technology, and leading vendors already offer integrated database solutions (generic solutions, not software engineering in particular). The user services offered as part of the database service classify it as a toolbox.

Software Engineering Toolboxes

The eight software engineering toolboxes are shown in Figure 5.6. The connections serve to illustrate the concepts of management throughout the process, documentation throughout the process, and an integrated framework. The implied left-to-right flow is used only to place the toolboxes in logical order. The software engineering process will not flow one time only left to right. The process will require a new life cycle, perhaps a new paradigm, to describe the actual process flow.

There are major transitions to be accomplished here. The toolboxes, documentation, management planning, and data repository all require transitions. A new paradigm will require transitions in both conceptual thought and actual development process.

If each of the eight toolboxes that have been described was filled with

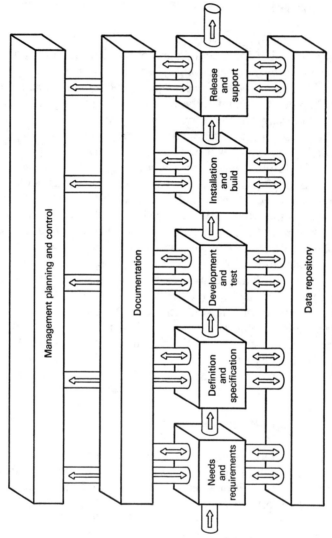

Figure 5.6 Software engineering toolboxes.

a complete set of tools, it would still not solve the crafted software problem. Selected tools can help today, but Chapter 4 outlined the evolutionary steps that inevitably lead us to the integrated and then automated world of the next millennium. Thus it is almost a mandate that tools, toolboxes, and methodologies must be linked. The complete toolboxes could allow us to "tool" software to specification, but the specifications would remain rudimentary indeed. The next step is to define the linkages required and the platforms that are needed to turn toolboxes into engineering enclosures (the term "software factory" gained some acceptance in the past, but shop floor analogies do not accurately represent software engineering). The transition to software engineering will require linked toolboxes and toolsets.

6

Transition to Linked Software Development Tools

NONLINKED TO LINKED TOOLSETS

Linkages are a series of connections that allow tools to function as a system. The first linkages have already been completed; some linkages are more than 20 years old. We have already mentioned the compile, link, load, and run sequence. Older existing linkages are almost without exception within one of the toolboxes discussed in the previous chapter. Linkages between the tool-boxes are still in the formative stages. In general, the newer the tools within the box, the fewer linkages existing between the tools. The development and test toolbox has the best linkages today, with the support toolbox second. Program compilations, linking, loading, and running were some of the earliest programming sequences to be linked. Decks of job-control cards supported early programming linkages; today's file modifications happen automatically, with directory entries, opening and closing, and file conversions becoming almost transparent to the user.

Why do we need linkages? The process reason is to eliminate unnecessary manual shifting, thus providing a sort of "automatic" transmission. One example is compilation, linking, loading, and running. The practical reason is to allow all the tools to be invoked and used with minimum overhead and confusion. Toward that end there are a number of "front-end" interfaces that allow the toolboxes to be logically accessed as one unit. Figure 6.1 illustrates a basic front-end interface. In this straightforward example, information from five of the toolboxes is presented on five individual windows on the workstation screen. The tools have not been linked; the information is "logically" linked only in that it is presented at the same time. In this example the project manager is examining the impact of a design change on the project schedule. The project manager is able to look at the present situation and determine the level of effort required to modify the design, make coding changes, and prepare a special patch tape. The estimate even includes the time required to make changes to the maintenance specification.

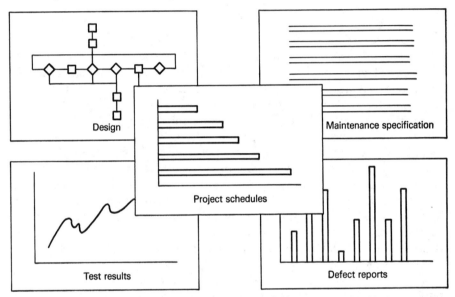

Figure 6.1 Example of nonlinked reports.

Even though tools are not linked, there is significant value in having this system available. There is much greater potential value in having linked tools and reports. The optimum linkages will evolve over time and there will undoubtedly be a lot of trial and error. One of the premises of this book is that we will begin with themes and variations on the manual nonlinked toolset and then move toward the fully linked and integrated versions.

LINKAGES FOR QUALITY AND PRODUCTIVITY

Linkages for quality and productivity are needed as part of an overall drive to improve quality and productivity of software development and delivery. The definition of quality is to meet customer's needs fully at the lowest possible cost of ownership. Quality and productivity are linked to the extent that for a given process, you could move very slowly and produce an expensive crafted work of art, or you could move very fast and produce a low-cost, low-quality version. The ideal is to improve productivity while at the same time improving quality. Thus, improving linkages could allow us to produce software faster, but it does not necessarily allow us to produce better-quality software. Quality and productivity have a linked dependence because a higher-quality process requires less rework (fewer defect fixes and releases), less testing, and less support.

SOFTWARE REUSE

Automatic linkages should not focus on making the existing system work. The new linkages should be directed toward the software engineering process. The process change that will produce the highest-quality software in the long term is increasing reusability of software. Today many attempts at software reuse are in fact "contributed libraries" in which a catalog of items is provided. These software-reuse libraries lack standards, testing, certification, and maintenance. While some reuse libraries have selected functions, others place users at the mercy of the crafter who submitted the module. If we look at hardware chips, we note that pins are positioned in rows according to a standard; boards accommodate the chips according to a standard; voltages and connections are governed by standards. Hardware engineers do not redesign every chip on every board every time they produce a new board. There are some new chips and some hybrid chips from time to time, but reuse of standard chips is an accepted engineering practice.

But we do not have software chips or software chip standards. There are language, database, data communication, and other standards, but much software is still crafted. What are the odds that you and I could sit at a table and design by hand and then look in a contributed library and find software components that would fit into our design? Even if we attempted to design to the components, they would have to have some sort of standard interfaces, standard input, standard outputs, and so on.

SOFTWARE "CHIPS"

A very practical solution would be to have software "chips," much in the same way as we have hardware chips. Then we could have electronic catalogs of these chips and begin to increase the level of software reuse.

Software chip quality is essential to the success of software reuse. Any sort of contributed library or catalog of software chips that have not been fully tested and certified will have limited success. Part of the reason programmers do not use other programmers' software is that they are not certain about the quality. They also are not certain who will fix the software module if a defect is detected.

There are many companies that have attained software reuse levels of 60% or greater in some small portion of the company. It is not surprising that these groups report significant gains in software quality and productivity. Most of these successes have come in applications software areas, where the application does not change significantly. But it should be possible to have software chips attain high levels of reusability in system areas; the key to success is to define chips at the right levels. Key ingredients in the successful chip recipe are

- to develop standard interfaces;
- to use those interfaces in design tools;
- to provide full chip support;
- to provide full chip documentation;
- to follow a standard methodology for using chips.

DESIGN REUSE

The same criteria can be followed for reusable designs. If we start with the notion that a chip catalog would have individual chip designs that are in a standard format, then the designer could examine the listing of available software chips. If there was a likely match, the designer could then look at the documentation and the standard design and include that software chip as part of the design process, being confident that the software chip would fit into the new design and work as documented. There is one group of pioneers who believe that the future will see code generated from designs, and thus we will need only design libraries. For the moment let us assume that both code and matching design documentation will be required for software reuse. We deal with code generation in a later chapter.

It was necessary to introduce the concept of software design reuse in order to establish a firm foundation for software toolbox standards. If we developed only the front-end interface described in Figure 6.1, the crafted techniques would continue to be honed, and many craftspersons would still be overcome by the increasing size and complexity of software systems. Software engineering involves harnessing knowledge power and putting that power to work for humankind. Engineering uses principles of science and mathematics; it does not rely on trial and error by the user. Trial and error properly occurs during the design segment of the engineering process. After the design has been selected, an established set of standards will permit solid linkages of toolboxes, with tools being well connected. This will permit reuse of software chips. Craftpersons are very creative, but they cannot escape the trial-and-error aspects of their craft; they do not practice reuse.

The software craft has brought us to this point, and we owe a great debt to all these pioneers. However, if we allow the linkages of software tools to be pragmatically developed according to present need, we will guarantee a 5- to 10-year delay in arriving at the first level of software engineering.

CONNECTION AND SUPPORT

If we view the toolboxes described in the last chapter as generic processes, then Figure 6.2 describes process connection and support services. This is a far more important step than simply providing better linkages between the boxes and special cross-linkages as required. The main elements of process connection and support are

- full network services, both local area and wide area;
- electronic mail, bulletin boards, and service information;
- software component libraries (code, designs, quality, and so on);
- standards;
- metrics that include productivity, quality, process, and product.

Many companies already have the wiring in the walls to support full network services; some have library support for software reuse practice. Anyone who tells you that the same type of service can be approximated in a local area by disc distribution or file transfer has not experienced network services. Many companies have electronic mail, but electronic public bulletin boards are not as widely used. Bulletin boards are vital tools, but they still need formatting and optimum implementation before they will be most effective. When five programmers are working on a project, they exchange bulletin board information on a verbal ad hoc basis. When five thousand programmers are working on five hundred projects that must come together in a final application, they find it difficult to be aware of the latest updates. The process connection outlined here must allow instant communication to all team members; configuration management should help, but there must be some orderly way to prioritize and disseminate information.

Some electronic mail systems use first-, second-, and third-class mail to address this problem. Wide distribution of first-class mail is limited to messages of high priority; second-class covers less important business messages; third-class includes personal messages, concerns, and low-priority communications. A similar system might be used for large software programs. Such a system might also use local distribution lists for those messages that are not of general interest.

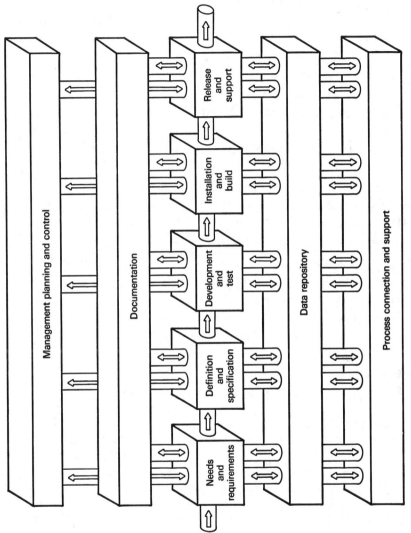

Figure 6.2 Software process connection and support.

Libraries and databases containing software engineering and metrics are vital, but once again they can increase in number and size to the point where it is difficult to locate pertinent data quickly. This is solved by having a hypertext system that brings order to potential gigabytes of information. Requisite items include the following:

- customer needs
- customer surveys, ratings, service requests
- regulatory requirements
- code modules and documentation
- design libraries (including existing prototypes)
- testing scripts, results, and requirements
- defect tracking (including service requests and status)
- program and project schedules and costs
- program and project deliverables and milestones
- personnel information (skills needed and available)
- simulation programs and status
- prototyping programs and status
- programming tools: compilers, editors, debuggers, and such
- version control programs and status
- configuration management library
- installation and building of programs and documentation
- support programs and documentation
- project schedules, costs, deliverables, and metrics
- defect tracking and reporting
- office systems (to support software engineering).

Ideally, customer needs would be understood by communicating with customers regularly and by having connections to up-to-date market analyses and market-trend projections. Even if some of this data are gathered by hand today, it should be formalized and entered into a system that permits on-line access and rapid analysis. There are many spreadsheet-type tools that would serve well in this application. Yet this is one of the most neglected areas because we think that we know what to do. In reality, we know what we would like to have if we were the customer.

Customer surveys should also be on-line for further analysis and study. The surveys are needed to corroborate customer's needs. They can also be used to track outstanding customer issues. We need to know how we are rated; we need to know where we have opportunities to improve software products. If we do not, then we are working in isolation, and even a roomful of state-of-the-art software engineering tools will not win customer approval if they produce products that fail to meet one or more customer needs.

The regulatory needs have been discussed in several chapters, and they should be on-line and current. The rapidly changing marketplace of the 1990s is causing constant changes in regulations; usually they are becoming more stringent. An elaborate but out-of-date regulatory information system could be worse than having to consult an expert every time there is a design or engineering change.

Many companies claim that they have most of these data available within their company. However, it is not possible to get all the data at the same time or to access all data from the same personal computer or workstation (even if you are authorized). Some advanced companies have on-line information systems. Tools and technology are available for all engineering personnel to have this service.

Even if all these items are available in the company, there must be linkages to make it easy to access, use, and interpret data. If programmers are needed, the project manager should be able to locate them quickly. If a program module is being modified, the project manager should be able to locate all other modules affected, all supporting documentation, and all related test scripts.

SOFTWARE SUPPORT PLATFORM

A complete and well-integrated set of connection and support services is already under development in companies around the world. Several labels have already been coined and applied to some of these pioneering efforts. There is a rush to be the first to develop a successful platform that ideally would be adopted and become a standard. The rewards for the company that develops the winning platform are obvious. Thus far, many of the platform efforts are specific to UNIX, MS-DOS, or other environments. Specifics are important; incremental changes are important. The increments must be planned and controlled, or the platform could collapse.

This platform pressure is part of a larger pressure that is driving the entire CASE/IPSE movement. As we have illustrated with earlier examples, major technological changes usually take place only when an existing technology comes under very heavy pressure. Vacuum tubes could not sustain color television; horses and buggies could not sustain Los Angeles today. In this instance there are some major engineering feats planned for the coming years, including permanent space stations in orbit, supersonic transportation systems, global banking systems, and fiber-optics communication networks in every home. Houses of the future will use chips to run all areas of the home; automobiles already contain chips and local-area networks.

When we begin to think in terms of very large scale projects, the idea of providing some additional linkages to the myriad software tools in the software toolboxes will be too little, too late. It is somewhat analogous to 1945 telephone seers who determined that one-half of the population of the United States would be needed to serve as telephone operators in 1960. When 1960 arrived, technical linkages and automated switching had reduced the number of operators required. It will take thousands of engineers working in a well-organized consortium in order to develop and implement a permanent space station using present software tools. As the corporate giants began to contemplate the often sad state of software today and the exploding need for software tomorrow, they came to the conclusion that major changes would be needed in the software process. The software platform concept appeared to hold the promise of a technical linkage and automated development process, but thus far it has fallen short of the need for tightly coupled computer systems. It will require another generation of software engineering tools and platforms to allow very large scale project development by less than thousands of engineers. The platform alone will not solve the problem. The next generation requires a linked methodology and linked tools.

LINKED METHODOLOGY

The companies engaged in the legitimate development of software tools responded to the need for integrated solutions, and leading thinkers began to develop the CASE and IPSE concepts and linkages. The only problem is that we do not have a generally accepted linked methodology to support the leading thinkers. To illustrate the importance of this missing link, it helps to examine a few other examples of methodology.

Although it is true that tools sometimes come first and winning methodologies are derived later, it is also true that leading thinkers can outpace tool builders. One example is in structured analysis and structured design. The first visionaries and writers were bringing the concepts into focus in the late 1970s and early 1980s, but it was 5 or more years before they were available on a large-scale commercial basis. Many larger computer manufacturers began the development of SA/SD tools and are still using some of the homegrown versions today.

Other examples of methodology coming first are in materials management and production management. APICS, the American Production and Inventory Control Society, described methodologies for shop floor control and material handling before there were commercially available systems. It was almost a decade before the first offerings appeared.

An example of tools coming first occurred in compiler design. There were compilers and utilities long before the development of well-recognized compiler methodologies. The pressing need for compilers and high-level languages outpaced the ability to get processes into place.

Although it is possible for tools to come first and methodologies to follow, the sheer size and scope of software engineering indicates that tool linking will occur within the toolboxes, but linking across the toolboxes will be difficult without a successful guiding methodology. Well-linked toolboxes and an integrated methodology are prerequisites to making a successful transition to software engineering.

CASE AND IPSE PHENOMENA

An example of the difficulties inherent in a "tools come first and methodologies follow" philosophy occurred in the early 1990s. A variation of the tools come first and methodologies follow caused the current CASE and IPSE excitement. Aerospace and defense establishments recognized the need for these integrated toolsets and had begun to make their needs known. Software tool companies who had developed some good, solid tools within the individual toolboxes responded, and the race was on. This led to the use of the new term *vaporware* to describe the promises of software that existed mostly in the minds of the promoters. All software engineering functions were going to be available in the fabled second release.

As the CASE/IPSE merchants began to promote their products, they generated much interest. Everyone wanted to know about the tools, and everyone wanted to be able to say something about how these tools would be used in their own shop in the near future. Consultants began seminars to bring CASE/IPSE information to the programming masses, and companies began to install the new tools.

The obvious problem was that tools were not developed, and linkages definitely were not in place. The less obvious problem was that a linked tool methodology was not evident; there may be leading-edge methodologies in local circles, but there is no declared winner. The reason for stopping the software evolution description and focusing on this gap is that it is essential to understand two fundamentals before we continue with the technology:

1. A collection of tools does not make software engineering.
2. CASE/IPSE as proposed may or may not be in the mainstream of the certain move to software engineering.

The excitement of recognizing the need for all these tools and the specification of all the software development and support phases masks the need for the methodology. Imagine the following promotion of these ideas: "Then you see the value of all of the tools we have described?" "Yes, I certainly do." "And you see that if we had them all readily accessible it would make things better?" "Oh yes, I see that." "Do you see that it will make software development more productive and result in higher quality software?" "Yes, yes, yes!"

But how would you use the tools? Would you simply invoke them one at a time? Supposing that we were shoemakers each working in our little shops in the same small town. We use wooden mallets to pound the shoe leather, softening and shaping it before completing the sewing. A wise old shoemaker devises a new vision and goals for making shoes; the vision will be based upon the assembly line. The idea will be to have ten shoemakers in the town come together and form a shoe-making consortium. Two of us will cut the leather, two of us will pound it, two will treat the leather, two will sew, and two will do the final polishing. The wise shoemaker also discovers that wooden mallets do not do well for pounding leather. They are uneven in applied pressure and sometimes leave small splinters in the leather. The wise shoemaker creates an iron hammer, which does a superior job.

Then the shoemaker calls the other shoemakers together and gives a seminar on the merits of the iron hammer. Demonstrations convince everyone, and before the day is over nine hammers have been sold. The normal course of events is that each of the nine other shoemakers will take the iron hammer back into their cottages, use it successfully, and say, "This new hammer is superior; I have gotten a 5% increase in my productivity."

The only problem is that the wise old shoemaker did not simply want to sell hammers. The shoemaker wanted to form a consortium and get a 50% productivity increase in the shoe-making process. The shoemaker had visions of branching out to sell in other towns and of franchising the new process all over the country. The problem is that the shoemaker understands the vision and the need but is not able to get the other shoemakers to understand the requisite methodology. Even if the shoemaker did succeed in selling the methodology, it would have to be technically possible to develop all the new tools and processes, measures, and training and put them into place. The wise shoemaker is a visionary who does not understand how to accomplish a technology transition.

This points out a weakness in showing the connections between the software engineering toolboxes. There is an implied information flow from left to right, beginning with needs and requirements. We have discussed the need for a new development cycle as well as the fact that the cycle may take some sort of iterative or spiral form. The spiral cycle supports the trial-and-error nature of the engineering design process. Toolboxes are intended to show functions and tools; they do not accurately show information flows.

The largest upcoming engineering projects have enormous needs for software engineering; the toolmakers have only some tools in the toolkit and only some idea of how the entire process comes together. There is an automotive example with Henry Ford and the development of the automobile assembly line. He did not attempt to put an entire production line into operation in one step. A little research revealed that Mr. Ford determined that magnetos were a production and quality problem, and he developed a miniassembly line, with specialization of labor, to solve the magneto problem. When the miniassembly line proved to be successful, he moved on to other areas and worked his way up to the full assembly line.

The difference in this example is that automobiles were still a new form of transportation in Ford's day, and he did not have the pressures of space stations, high-definition television and information distribution, or local-area networks in cars to produce a pressure for change now.

There is a rush to market CASE/IPSE tools. There is an unfounded fear that companies who fail to implement software engineering today will lose their chance tomorrow. The rush to implement software engineering solutions will have two likely outcomes.

1. There is a CASE/IPSE "winter" in which many software developers become disillusioned and retreat from their attempts to use this technology; The signs of winter may already be at hand.
2. The transition to software engineering will continue, and those who follow an orderly process of technology transition will successfully implement software engineering and prosper.

In some places the winter, or at least a "severe frost," has already started. There are two major things to keep in mind when analyzing these events:

1. In many cases the failure was caused by other elements; the software tools never had a chance. The other elements are discussed in the technology transition cycle chapter.
2. There will be a "springtime," or renaissance, which inevitably follows a cold snap. Those who persevere with the transition to software engineering will reap the rewards.

There are many historical precedents to illustrate these points. The late 1960s saw a great deal of enthusiasm for computer-assisted instruction (CAI). Many of the large computer companies rushed to get into the CAI business as the federal government poured hundreds of millions of dollars into this new technology. The result often was small children wearing 5-pound headsets and reaching above the tops of their heads with light pens to touch a screen. During this time, all educators simply had to know what CAI was about and to have some plans in place. Educators were more enamored with the sizzle of CAI technology than they were with the educational benefits. They believed that computers could somehow do wondrous things to educate children. There was—and is—a very legitimate need for computers in education, but it was not to be those early systems. Perhaps they were necessary as an evolutionary step, but they certainly contributed to a CAI frost, which lasted for at least

5 years. It should be noted that a major factor contributing to the CAI frost was the government's withdrawal of support for CAI research and development. It must also be noted that CAI did not meet customer's needs.

Closer to the present time there has been a sort of frost on artificial intelligence. A few years ago some extravagant claims were made, and many small companies sprang up in Silicon Valley. Today there are fewer companies. Although the truly legitimate ones have always been responsible and are now reaping the benefit of renewed interest in artificial intelligence, it was a time of sadness and loss for many investors and hardworking researchers. It is to be hoped that a prolonged downturn for software engineering can be avoided.

The ultimate success of software engineering is not entirely dependent on CASE. If the CASE winter is severe, it will almost certainly slow the transition to software engineering. The best way to ensure success is to have a successful transition to linked software tools. A proven methodology will support this successful transition.

The last few pages of this chapter have been more subjective in nature. They are based on my "judgment call" of the observable facts. Although there are recognized experts who also agree that the transition to software engineering will be slowed by a CASE winter, there are others who disagree.

There is a legitimate need for software to join the engineering community. Even if we develop a good linked tool methodology, it will probably be but an intermediate step in the process of implementing engineering. Let us go on to examine some of the workings of an integrated software engineering environment.

7

Transition
to Software Engineering

FULLY LINKED TOOLSETS

The integrated nature of software engineering toolsets is shown in Figure 7.1. The software platform is now fully connected to all major functional areas; let us assume that a proper methodology exists and is in place. The overall objectives for creating this software environment are

- to achieve the highest possible quality and productivity in software products;
- to establish a standard software development environment that is hardware independent (or at least minimally hardware dependent);
- to promote software reuse; to minimize duplication;
- to have well-trained and well-equipped software engineers;
- to establish a new baseline for the total engineering changes to come;
- to produce software products designed to be an integral component of a well engineered system.

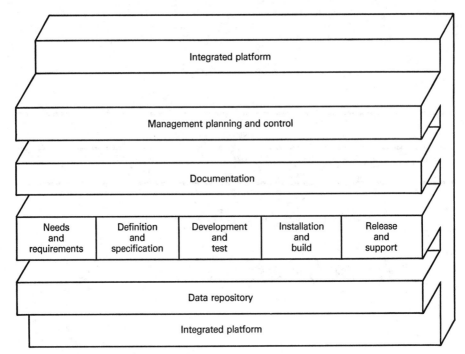

Figure 7.1   Toolsets installed on integrated platform.

THE DISAPPEARANCE OF COMPUTERS
FROM THE USER'S VIEW

Considering the elements of the preceding section, software becomes an integral component rather than something that is added to the system. This parallels the evolutionary integration that is causing computers to disappear from public view. They have already started to vanish and will in the next 20 years be only a memory in areas where they are dedicated to solving a particular class of problem. Computers are really engines, and as such they belong in a knowledge or control vehicle. You do not go to a store to purchase an automobile engine, then go to another store to purchase an automobile body, and so on until all the pieces have been acquired. In a similar fashion, the central processing unit is literally disappearing from view when you consider the size of a chip that holds an entire 32-bit microprocessor. Customers are thinking in terms of purchasing an entire shop floor–control system, an entire transaction processing system, or a home word-processing system. They are less inclined to purchase components and assemble them in the home, office, or factory.

AN INTEGRATED DESIGN EXAMPLE

To continue the automobile example, let us consider an integrated design system that has well-known, well-measured automotive requirements and operating environments. The system allows the designer to experience the user's point of view. This allows precise simulation of almost all the driving and operating conditions for the proposed vehicle. Figure 7.2 shows the proposed vehicle dashboard without communication equipment. (Line drawings are used here. The three-dimensional, full-color workstation could show the vehicle frame or any stage of design up to the complete automobile in full color.) The designer is going to try a radio that has been selected from an available parts catalog (shown in a window on the bottom of the screen). The deluxe radio is included in the dashboard design, and it is possible to run simulations to determine that it meets all safety and regulatory requirements in this country. The engineer then checks to see if the radio is available in options that meet requirements in all other countries where the vehicle is going to be sold.

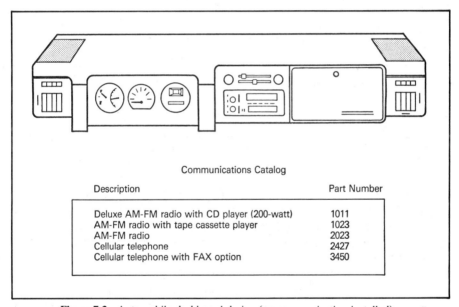

Figure 7.2   Automobile dashboard design (no communication installed).

Figure 7.3 shows the vehicle, with communications, and a spreadsheet that shows the material costs, production costs, and all warranty and support costs associated with the radio. In this case the engineer can see that it will add $1000 to the final cost of the vehicle. This is a very large cost, and the engineer then checks the catalog to try another radio. Once again, the second

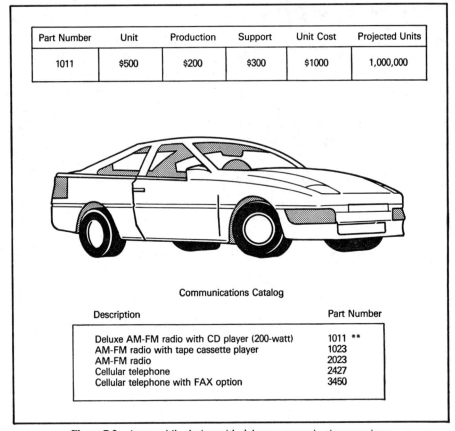

Part Number	Unit	Production	Support	Unit Cost	Projected Units
1011	$500	$200	$300	$1000	1,000,000

Communications Catalog

Description	Part Number
Deluxe AM-FM radio with CD player (200-watt)	1011 **
AM-FM radio with tape cassette player	1023
AM-FM radio	2023
Cellular telephone	2427
Cellular telephone with FAX option	3450

Figure 7.3 Automobile design with deluxe communications receiver.

radio is checked for regulatory and safety requirements, and once again it passes. The spreadsheet in Figure 7.4 shows that now the final cost is only $150 added to the selling price of the vehicle, but there is a loss of 10% of the potential market because this radio is not as attractive as the first set; it does not have the power or features of the first set.

The point to be made is that the engineer can now consider the trade-offs that involve sales, manufacturing, and support during the design phase. In earlier days it was not possible to consider all these trade-offs and still get closure on the design. It was, in fact, necessary to keep the marketing, manufacturing, and support people at some distance in order to complete the design. Also, it was not possible to get accurate information regarding the sales or regulatory impacts. Even if the engineer attempted to listen to comments, the advice was often based upon hearsay.

Architects suffered a similar need for seclusion during the design phase and did not allow feedback until they had presented the model and completed

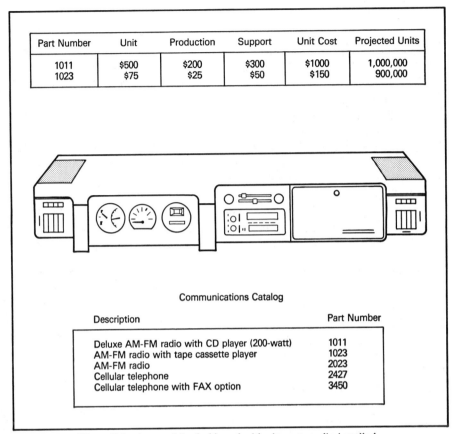

Part Number	Unit	Production	Support	Unit Cost	Projected Units
1011	$500	$200	$300	$1000	1,000,000
1023	$75	$25	$50	$150	900,000

Communications Catalog

Description	Part Number
Deluxe AM-FM radio with CD player (200-watt)	1011
AM-FM radio with tape cassette player	1023
AM-FM radio	2023
Cellular telephone	2427
Cellular telephone with FAX option	3450

Figure 7.4 Automobile dashboard with alternate radio installed.

plans. Architects or their assistants used to spend hours calculating the stresses on all beams and support structures in proposed buildings. Today most of these detail calculations are automated, and the architect is free to concentrate upon building design in relation to the customer's needs.

Granted the communications example was set in a well-known environment with known performance parameters and known standards and regulations. But many software products being developed today fall into similar categories. However, designing state-of-the-art systems and experimental software may require a new approach.

A known and defined environment could permit early successes in the use of structured analysis and structured design. Often selected claims of success are made in business environments but proof of performance is not shown. In any event, an unstructured and ill-defined environment would only make success a remote possibility.

AUTOMATED IDENTIFICATION OF REUSE

Consider another linkage. In Chapter 6 we spoke of the evolving concept of software chips and gains in software quality and productivity that could be made with high levels of reuse. In the earlier example we considered the use of a software chips catalog during the design phase. At this stage of software engineering integration, we can now consider the example shown in Figure 7.5. Here the busy designer has begun to sketch a new module that will perform an accounts receivable transaction. With only a portion of the module completed, an asterisk begins to flash in a newly opened window in the upper right-hand corner of the screen.

The asterisk indicates that while the designer has been busy working on the new design, the system has been checking existing designs in the library and has found one that is very close to the new one under development. Two other possible matches have also been identified. The system is now asking

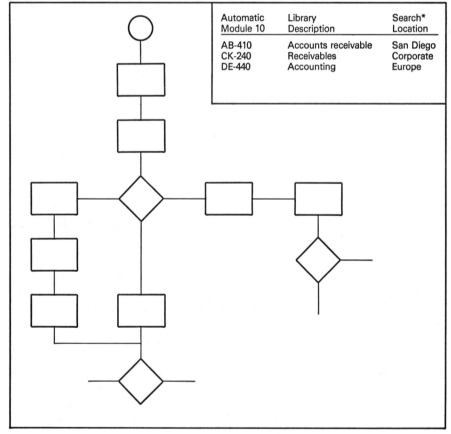

Automatic Module 10	Library Description	Search* Location
AB-410	Accounts receivable	San Diego
CK-240	Receivables	Corporate
DE-440	Accounting	Europe

Figure 7.5 Application design with automatic identification of similar modules.

the designer if it is appropriate to stop and consider this already-existing design, or if the designer really wants to press on. This level of sophistication begins to approximate fingerprint identification. It presumes that a sophisticated design classification and storage scheme exists and that the analysis program can correctly classify the partially completed new design. But the example is used here to illustrate the power and potential of an integrated design system. The identification program could also be instructed to detect duplicate submodules and algorithms that have already been designed and tested.

The example also reinforces the idea that we have to develop some intermediate steps and stages before we can move to this level of sophistication. If present-day CASE/IPSE developers were to consider such a design identification system, they would almost surely become bogged down and find it extremely difficult to get a product released. In this situation we probably want to grow with the flow. It would be good to have software chips and some sort of catalog before we had design identification.

There are four reasons for doing these examples.

1. It is good to have some sort of idea of where we might go in order that our steps will take us in that direction.
2. It might inspire one of you to make a bold move in that direction.
3. It is fun.
4. It demonstrates the need for software engineering.

Even if some of these glimpses into the future do not show exactly what will happen, the overall need for an integrated engineering environment is the wave of the future. Successful technology transitions require an understanding of the integrated environment and automated reuse practices.

PRODUCTIVITY LINKAGES

Productivity spreadsheets allow us to gain an understanding of times required to design, develop, build, and support various types of software. Today many of these are guesstimates; tomorrow they will be based upon data and models. We will be able to know which software groups require the most time, relative risks associated with any given scope of project, and the impact of unanticipated changes. If there are problem groups, it will be possible to identify and help them. There are studies that indicate that the average half-life of a software engineer's knowledge is in the 5- to 8-year range. This means that half of the technical knowledge that should be known is not known. In many cases this is due to new knowledge, tools, and methodologies coming on-line. There are things that can be done to better support software developers who are affected in this way; the point to be made here is that it will be possible to identify groups that might need assistance.

In a similar way linkages will also help us to understand quality problems. Are there chronic pockets of problems? Are there systems and modules that require reengineering? What are the risks associated with the release of new software? To what extent have those risks been reduced through structured testing? Engineering practices include risk analysis and management.

CONFIGURATION MANAGEMENT LINKAGES

Configuration management can also be linked to the design library in order to understand the effects of module changes. Consider the following hypothetical example. Hundreds of millions of dollars have been spent on a project to put a permanent deep-sea monitoring station in place. The station is up and running and performing all its functions. The designers had the foresight to anticipate the need for software changes, and they allowed modules to be replaced as necessary. A new series of experiments has been developed, and the new code will require the replacement of four modules and the addition of one new module. This will require removing something from the existing system.

The 32 software project managers who are involved in this large project are assembled and told of the need to remove a module. They return to their work areas for 30 days of analysis and study, as this is a very important step that must be taken with the greatest of care. When they reassemble, one project manager suggests that they remove the module that searches for new communication frequencies in the unlikely event that the present frequency becomes unusable. The existing frequency has performed well for over 1 year, and they can always put the module back if needed. Everyone agrees that this is a likely candidate and they return to their work areas for further study.

They meet again and agree to remove the frequency-scanning module. No one remembers that the selected frequency is stored in the data portion of the scanning module and that the frequency-selection module uses that information to set the receiving channel. As the module is replaced, the frequency-selection module switches to a frequency that cannot be transmitted efficiently through water, and the entire project shuts down.

This scenario could happen, because it is impossible for project managers to remember all dependencies between modules and actual functions performed by all modules. The scenario also has its origins in the memory-saving practices of leaving data in the originating module rather than duplicating it in another module. Also, in the unlikely event that data were legitimately changed, the other module would still be up to date if the data were shared from one source. If we had the integrated system described in this chapter, one of the linkages would allow us to know that the module we proposed to delete had another module accessing data from it. An alternative plan could have been selected. An even better scenario would have an integrated design review tool detect the data coupling between the modules and require that it be changed before the program code was generated.

CODE GENERATION

Figure 7.6 illustrates a code-generation example. The detailed design level of the new software module is completed. The language is selected, and code is automatically generated from the design. There is an almost one-to-one correspondence between detailed design components and code statements, but there is still advantage in having the code generated; it minimizes errors, guarantees that the design matches the code, and saves time.

An improved linkage would allow us to make a correction in a line of code. Let us assume that there are three conditions in the design: The first branches to A if X is greater than 99; the second branches to B if X is greater than 50; and the third is supposed to branch to C if X is greater than 25; but unfortunately the designer omitted this step in the design, and consequently

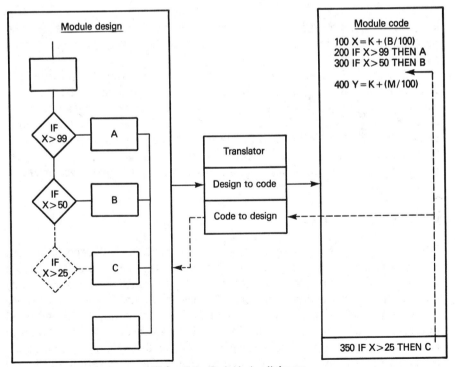

Figure 7.6 Code/design linkages.

there was no code statement generated. In this case the code would look like the following:

```
X = K+(B/100)
If X>99 then A
If X>50 then B
Y = K+(M/100)
```

There is no statement for the condition where X is greater than 25 but less than 50. In this case the improved linkage would allow us to simply add the following statement directly to the code:

```
If X >25 then C
```

to produce

```
X = K+(B/100)
If X>99 then A
If X>50 then B
If X>25 then C
Y = K+(M/100)
```

Not only is the program now correct, but when we return to the detailed design, the design has been updated to reflect the changes that have been made in the code.

The deep-sea example was hypothetical, this two-way design/code linkage has been demonstrated at two Japanese computer companies. As far as we know, they are not able to support automatic code linkages above the detailed design level, but it surely is an advantage to be able to keep coding changes in sync with design documentation. They also are able to flag higher-level design modules that are affected by this change to permit the designer to determine if it is necessary to make any changes in higher-level designs.

DESIGN SIMULATION

We consider one more example of design verification and synchronization. The Japanese are also able to use a design interpreter to examine detail design modules in a running condition. With the detail design on the screen, they open a window that contains run-time database elements. Then they set those elements to the starting conditions and initiate the module. The design is interpreted into code and runs in slow motion. As each of the little boxes in the design is executing, the box flashes and the data elements change accordingly. This allows the designer to watch the design in action and to see if it is performing as expected. Of course, any changes in the design can be immediately interpreted to allow testing of the completed module and/or program. Some of the newest Silicon Valley tools can execute a design at the data-flow diagram, state transition diagram, and minispec levels. These systems can also do simulation based on data-flow diagrams.

TEST SUITE LINKAGES

One traditional testing technique is to develop sets of test suites, which are then used to test modules and programs. The test suites are often based upon simulated uses of the program; in many cases they are actual applications with known results that are run in the testing lab.

Figure 7.7 shows a set of test suites that have been loosely linked to the development and test phase and to the support phase. Traditionally, test suites are updated and maintained by a crafted process. One of the biggest dangers to the use of these suites is complacency. Because tests have proven effective in the past, there is a very high confidence level placed upon them. The increasing functionality and other changes cause each new release to be significantly different. Without a linkage, it is possible that the suites are not

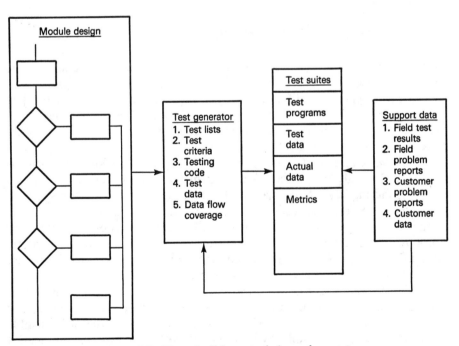

Figure 7.7   Test suite linkages to design and support.

updated to test all enhancements. In the linked mode, there can be two basic validity checks. The first can occur at design time; as a module is enhanced or a new module added, the appropriate test suite can be examined and updated as required. The second can occur as field-reported defects are corrected. The defect can be checked against the test suite to see why it was not detected. If the test was flawed, corrections can be made. If the test simply omitted this check, it can be added.

In this way test suites should become better and better over time. There are several cautions that should be noted regarding test suites used in this way:

- It will still not be possible to test all permutations and combinations in larger systems and applications.
- If design test suite verification is not used to update the test suite in initial design, it will be much more painful for the customer. It is true that feedback from the support group should eventually get test suites in line with the program, but users will be discovering all flaws in the test suites. Better to use both the design and support loops.
- Do not stop testing; there are other very good testing techniques that can also be used, and they will prove to be a very powerful force in the engineering environment.

PROJECT MANAGEMENT LINKAGES

Project management tools have for the most part remained stand-alone tools that are used in parallel with actual software engineering tools. However, there is a very great need for accurate project estimates and accurate project tracking. Figure 7.8 shows one possible set of linkages between project management, structured design, complexity metrics, and cost-estimation packages.

We have already discussed structured design. Stand-alone cost-estimating tools generally have several dozen parameters that are initialized and then begin gathering key estimates and facts about the proposed software project. In some cases the cost estimator asks for estimated lines of code in the completed program. The estimator then calculates the cost of the project and proposed schedule times. When input data are valid, estimates are pretty good. But what if you are not certain about lines of code? What if you are not certain about the project because it is a new application?

Figure 7.8 takes the structured design output and uses it as input to a complexity-measuring routine. There are a number of these routines, and they have varying points of view. The general principle is that it is possible to calculate relative complexity of a module based upon its size, number of

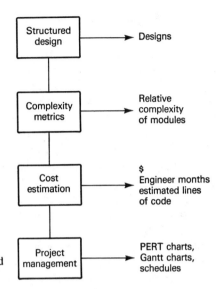

Figure 7.8 Design, complexity, and project management linkages.

data transformations that take place, number of input and output parameters, and so on. The routine usually generates some sort of complexity number for each module; ideally it compares similar objects for all modules.

The complexity number for each module is used as input to the cost-estimation program, which has been recalibrated and tuned to this use. The cost estimates for each module are now based upon complexity; one of the outputs could, in fact, be the estimated number of lines of code for each module.

Cost estimates and complexity can now be used as input to a project management program that also has been appropriately tuned. This program can now generate schedules, PERT charts, GANTT charts, and the like. The power of this linkage is that a well-tuned set of modules can provide an accurate set of schedules.

The real power of this combination comes when it is necessary to reengineer some portion of the program. This could happen during the development phase (assume that we do not have code generation yet). In any event, immediately after design changes have been made, another set of cost estimates and schedules could be run, and an updated schedule could be put into effect.

There is also the possibility that this combination could be used to study design trade-offs in order to find the optimum schedule. This would be similar to using "what-if" simulation techniques to do optimum shop floor scheduling. As actual schedules are collected and a baseline is developed, it should be possible to tune this combination to a high degree of accuracy. All these pieces exist today; the linkages are still in the pioneering stages.

STARTING CASE/IPSE POSITIONS

At this point we might step back and try to put this chapter into perspective. We are supposed to be moving toward software engineering, and yet the linkages seem to be all over the software map. They are, we hope, interesting and useful, but why are they developing in this way? Part of the answer is the various immediate needs and starting positions of various software development interests. Figure 7.9 shows the basic starting positions. Traditional programming development teams began in the development and test phase, and they have been reaching out to the platform, to analysis and design, and to software management tools. There is still a great deal of interest in the proper language, and there is even greater interest in the potential of object-oriented programming. There is also the need for better diagnostic tools, testing tools, and language support tools.

Megaprogramming environments have an urgent need for project management and control. There are project management tools in this area, and technical managers are pressing for linkages to allow complete management of all phases of the software cycle. Companies that are developing CASE/IPSE tools for this environment will almost always have such tools as cost estimators and project tracking and reporting in their standard packages.

Megaprogramming environments include aerospace, large government projects, and some networking projects being done by the largest companies in the world. These groups need software engineering for their megaprogramming; they are providing the impetus for it to happen.

A small group of software development companies and some selected labs in the very largest companies are also working to produce software development platforms or data repository platforms. These groups generally have different starting positions, and they are in competition to see who will prevail. The platform development teams are operating in the crafter phase.

Many companies start with structured analysis, structured design, project estimation, or project management tools. There are established methodologies and practices in these areas; the computer community speaks their jargon; and most of the companies who have started with these tools promise much more in the very near future. They really all seem to believe that they will have the time and the money to develop full software engineering solutions. All but one or two will not.

The starting positions are therefore all over the software engineering domain. There are many informed opinions, some heresies, occasional truth, and much confusion operating in an environment with no unifying paradigm, life cycle, or methodology.

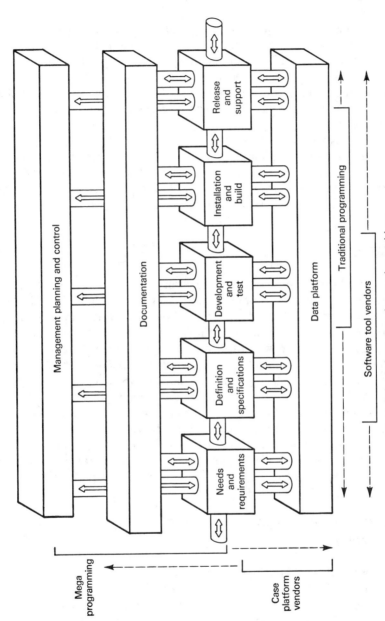

Figure 7.9 Software vendor starting positions.

NEEDS AND REQUIREMENTS SIMULATION

Some of the large government contractors have done very exciting work in the needs and requirements phase; they have simulators that can accurately show the finished products without one line of code being written. In general, they still have work to do on the ways to decompose these simulations to allow an accurate analysis of the problem. The simulators are greater than the reality in some situations. They lack linkages to analysis and design in most implementations.

Companies who hope to be major players in needs and requirements toolsets and some smaller companies who hope to set the standards are working on platforms to support software engineering. The work is very promising, but thus far there are no standards; needs and requirements are still in the early stage. Transitions will be coming in the next few years.

TOOLSET STANDARDS

How do standards come to be? In general, the standards committees of national and international computer societies and professional organizations do not usually set standards; they recognize those that are already self-evident. Standards are initially set because the majority of the users voted with their money or because one or two of the largest players simply announced that a standard is now in effect. The U.S. government is in a very strong position to cause a CASE/IPSE standard that includes needs and requirements, especially one based upon the Ada programming language. There have been and are presently such initiatives underway. Based upon history, some will work but others will not. If the technology is sufficiently mature, the standard will probably stick; however, in the case of CASE, it will probably be an interim standard at best. This is not meant to be discouraging. There are advantages to having someone cause the movement to align itself.

APPARENT RANDOMNESS OF SOFTWARE
TOOL LINKAGES

Software tool linkages appear to be all over the software map. Figure 4.1 outlined the basic progressions in software evolution. Because there is no defined standard and, as we concluded in Chapter 6, there is only the glimmer of a linked methodology, the crafters have moved in and are beginning to make the software engineering linkages between the toolboxes and the platform.

The crafters are meeting the immediate needs and they are usually linking via the shortest possible path. Of course, the longer they work, the more cross connections we will have and the more difficult it will probably be to convert to a true engineering platform. It may simply be a necessary part of the software evolution to have the first platform handwired.

Or it may also be that crafters are wiring the last of the manually operated telephone switchboards. As the development of object-oriented methodologies, tools, and practices emerges, there is a strong indication that we may want to wire the platform to support this exciting new concept. There are some excellent books being written on object-oriented programming, and there are some emerging sets of design and development diagrams, languages, and techniques. The optimum language and the ideal form of that language will probably elude research teams for a few more years, but the power of objects is becoming very clear. Here is a brief description of the world of objects, but the serious student should refer to one of the books listed in the bibliography. The beginner's version is necessary here to allow a discussion of object linkages.

OBJECT-ORIENTED LINKAGES

Object-oriented practice had its origins in SIMULA (the original source of present object-oriented languages), LISP, and SMALLTALK; it therefore reaches back to the 1960s. This new programming technique is supported by specific linguistic features (with variations) in programming languages that have been modified to support object-oriented programming (Objective C, C++, PASCAL, extensions to LISP, and so on).

There are several distinguishing characteristics that place objects in a class by themselves. The first is, of course, objects. An object is typically created from observing a class of things. This permits the creation of objects whose data and data transformations are hidden. Perhaps a comparison to the microcode of most computer systems, which is generally treated as a black box. You know what it does but you are not allowed to see inside. In this case, the closed property of objects allows clean interfaces between objects. Objects form programs; objects represent designs; and objects represent both functionality and data.

The second distinguishing characteristic is inheritance, which allows the original definition of an object to be extended, with the original properties inherited by the offspring. Another way of looking at this property is that we can specify a new class by defining only the incremental changes while retaining the original properties in our new creation. Inheritance is a way of reusing common attributes; inheritance is the keystone of reusability in the object environment.

The third major distinction is polymorphism. Object-oriented modules are polymorphic in the sense that they can dynamically select the code to be executed, depending upon the type of object. Polymorphism allows messages to produce different results when directed to different objects.

There are other characteristics such as encapsulation, data abstraction, and information hiding (these are not necessarily object-oriented concepts; they can be done with conventional programming; object orientation is simply the latest vehicle). The problem is that there is no general consensus on exactly what these characteristics and attributes mean, and there are no standards. Object-oriented languages are in the pioneering stages of development. We do not have established object-oriented development systems at this time. Let us return to the user's point of view to understand object-oriented design.

In an earlier example of integrated design tools, we portrayed an engineer selecting a radio for an automobile. In this example there were a number of radios that could be used, and the design engineer was able to make an informed selection thanks to linkages within the engineering system.

The design engineer was meeting the functional requirements communications reception in an automobile and was able to take other parameters into account. This is one of the fundamental approaches to functional design.

Object-oriented design takes a different approach. A problem is viewed as interrelated classes of real objects, which are characterized by common attributes. Automobile objects could include the body, bumpers, tires, radio antenna, and windows. Attributes might include brake horsepower, weight, turning radius, and acceleration.

The modern automobile, as well as many modern appliances, conceals a great deal of information. It is not necessary for drivers to understand the type of engine, the firing order, fuel, braking system, and electrical system in order to use a car. Information hiding works to the driver's advantage.

In an object-oriented design system an engineer could design the entire automobile, including communications, by inheritance. This assumes that earlier versions of the automobile were designed on the object-oriented system or that the engineer had somehow been able to get the attributes and objects from earlier models.

Figure 7.10 shows an automobile with information tables containing attributes and abstracts. The designer is still responsible for making the decisions that say, "I want it to be like this, but with these changes." In this way the designer is adding value and improving, not simply scaling up an existing design.

The classical design linkage, which had the engineer trying radios from an existing catalog, works well if one of the radios happens to be a good fit. It also presumes that the radio manufacturers are improving their designs over time. It does not work as well if communication requirements now include a cellular mobile telephone and earlier models did not feature cellular telephones.

In the object-oriented world the designer could come up with the optimum communication design using inheritance of earlier communication sys-

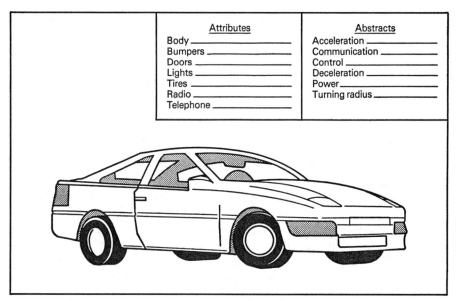

Attributes	Abstracts
Body _____	Acceleration _____
Bumpers _____	Communication _____
Doors _____	Control _____
Lights _____	Deceleration _____
Tires _____	Power _____
Radio _____	Turning radius _____
Telephone _____	

Figure 7.10   Object-oriented automotive design.

tems and then see if the radios exist or can be built. In traditional functional design, organization is by function and data are evident. In the object-oriented approach, organization is by data, and the data structure is hidden.

Object-oriented design is most promising in graphics design and in physical real-world problems with complex interfaces. It really would work well for radios, navigation, hospital systems, office systems, and the like. It is well suited to applications software with large, complex data structures. There is great potential for supporting software reuse.

There are other features and advantages, but this example will allow us to consider linkages and the potential impact of object-oriented methodologies. There are some areas of opportunity (potential problems to be solved):

- There are almost no standards; this is a very new programming concept, and we do not fully understand the technology.
- Object-oriented practice does not seem ideally suited to all types of problems; it does not scale up well.
- Thus far object-oriented practice is a resource carnivore.
- Thus far changes in one part of an object-oriented system are not automatically correlated with all the other objects that have to be modified.
- There is a need for a proven object-oriented analysis and design methodology.
- This is a leading-edge technology; we should continue to tinker.
- Object-oriented technology is a candidate for technology transition.

The potential for reuse using object-oriented methods appears promising; the modularity of design and construction would allow a foundation for software chips. There is a need for standards, but they will almost surely appear within the next few years. One of the most promising linkages for object design could involve the use of an object "viewer" or "browser"; there are several in use today.

The viewer would be used in the design stage and would present an easy-to-understand "view" of the objects that are candidates for reuse. The designer has determined that there is an object-oriented module having almost all the properties desired at this point in the design. The viewer presents the object-oriented module in such a way that the designer does not have to examine the code or surrounding documentation. As the designer makes changes in the viewer window, the object-oriented module will undergo changes to produce the "new" module, which will be a perfect fit. If this type of reuse were combined with code generation, the designer could be certain that the inherited module would be correct when coded. This approach is somewhat analogous to customization concepts used to modify user screens in some applications. The customizer allows screens to be modified, but the application code still performs the same functions. In the example cited here, the object viewer becomes an easy-to-understand and easy-to-use interface. It also allows the designer to place a name on the inherited module, and the design has closure during the design phase.

Consider the primitive alternative. If the programmer has to read the design, examine the list of object-oriented modules, attempt to perform the inheritance, and then find that it is not a perfect fit, design becomes difficult. The design would have to be reworked, and there is always the possibility that the programmer did not understand the designer's intentions.

We have now raised the stakes in the linkage game. The original problem was that we were trying to hook the software tools together to begin the development of an integrated toolset. The crafters were the first to begin the connections, and this meant a pragmatic selection depending upon the most pressing need. There was the possibility that these linkages would reveal some fundamental weaknesses in the tools and that it would be necessary to replace some of the tools with yet-to-be-developed tools. There was also a need for some sort of architecture to bring stability and clarity to the platform. However, these problems have been overshadowed by the advent of object-oriented languages. Now there is a real possibility that the reuse properties and other properties will propel object-oriented languages into becoming the new linguistic backbone of the integrated software development environment.

It will not be necessary to stop and ponder the problem. Both groups continue working feverishly. Governments will press for solutions now, and the Ada platforms will no doubt come into full blossom. Meanwhile, there will be enough serious research and development projects using object-oriented platforms to allow a complete evaluation. The only danger is to the company, research facility, or university that feels a decision must be made in the near future. Such a decision might result in the major investment in a software platform that will not endure over time.

PRESENT CASE/IPSE CONNECTIONS

There are several different developments happening concurrently. One community of software tool developers is making genuine progress in development of CASE/IPSE platforms for the information systems community using many of the existing technologies and focusing on COBOL or other business languages. Other groups are attempting to develop workstation platforms, often UNIX-based, that will be used for aerospace and other industries requiring very large and well-integrated applications and systems. Pioneering groups are pursuing the evolutionary trend to develop platforms that use object-oriented languages. These developments follow two paths: The pragmatic path attempts to bend and mold the existing structured analysis, structured design, and other methodologies and tools into object-oriented packages; the newer path attempts to define an entire new set of object-oriented tools, platform, methodologies, and support structures.

While the academic and advanced industrial groups are searching for the best answer, crafters are hard at work making connections, molding tools, and doing all the necessary groundwork to find some solutions. This serves us well. Crafters will learn which things work and which things do not; they will also determine whether the existing tools can be modified to serve in somewhat integrated CASE/IPSE platforms.

The danger posed by crafters is that they will keep making quick and expedient connections that will not only complicate the workings of the platform, but will also make it difficult to gain modularity, which is essential to having "plug-in" tools and software reuse. Figure 7.11 shows a top-down view of the platform and some of the areas that have already been connected by crafters. Most of the connections have been made within major functional areas such as analysis and design, but they have also extended connectors to other areas. To illustrate the problem of crafted connections, only the connections between toolboxes are shown. This is analogous to early attempts to develop language monitors that handled all editing, compiling, linking, loading, and other functions. Connections were made in such a way that it became difficult to replace linkers or other modules at a later date. It also made it difficult to have relocatable modules that could be used on systems with similar architectures but slightly different operating systems.

Figure 7.12 illustrates a "cleaner" block structure, which would allow the use of plug-in components. The major functions must retain their integrity and must remain physically isolated from the other functions. This requires considerable modification to the tools so they will operate through local

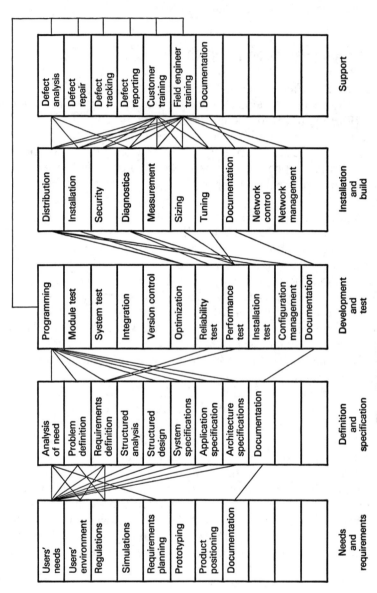

Figure 7.11 Top-down view of crafter connections.

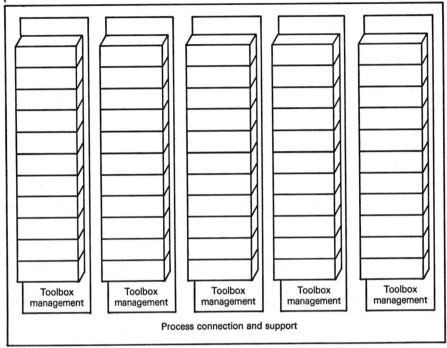

Figure 7.12 Toolbox management connection and support.

toolbox management platforms with standard linkages. Recalling our earlier example of a code change causing an update of the design, it would require some sort of checking and synchronization mechanism to ensure that the design module knew when to modify the design. This is a straightforward problem, but it will require that the design module be invoked at the time when the code module is "closed" after being modified.

If you have had prior experience in this area, you have probably read the last paragraph and decided that you could solve the problem in another way. The real problem here is that unless some standards develop for these interfaces, the many software programming teams will solve the problem, and we will again have an abundance of solutions. Everyone should come to general agreement about the following:

- It is important to have standard process connection for the platform.
- There must be a clear definition of the modules, their functions, the user interfaces, and the formats for the designs, code, documentation, and so on.

However, not everyone will agree on who is to create these standards and who should recognize them as standards.

The interconnections that follow normal development flow are essential; other interconnections to documentation, project management, quality, testing, and other essential activities must also be made in such a way as to preserve the integrity of the system. The biggest danger here is that even if we have developed some workable standards for the development flow, other activities will be cross-wired into the system in a way that limits the potential of the engineering platform.

All these functions should have plug-in tools that can be removed and replaced without causing the system to lose its ability to function. This requires the definition of a base set of functions that must be supported by all tools and an understanding of the optional functions that are available with selected tools. Base-set definitions have been accomplished at the PC level, where you can purchase a personal computer with a built-in hard disc or you can chose to operate with removable discs. If you take the less expensive option of removable discs, the system will function in the same logical manner, but you will be asked to exchange discs as the system requires different application and support modules. If you purchase the removable disc system and then decide to add a hard disc, that is usually permitted. The same underlying philosophy should permeate a CASE/IPSE platform.

This architecture will support a variety of structured analysis, structured design (with optional real-time extensions), and support tools for the analysis/design phase. Each of us might have a specific tool that is preferred for some technical reason, and our tools can all work together with full software engineering platform support.

There are also connections to project management across the full range of product development functions. The full integration of these tools implies that project planning, tracking, and control tools can use the engineering databases. If proper standards were established and observed, then it should be possible to have a variety of project management and control tools, with each tool able to work with standard databases. All this could be accomplished if the database standards were defined and variances were allowed to occur at a "higher" level. It would be possible to have one project management tool provide information on actual progress compared to estimates; another tool would perform sophisticated extrapolations of actual data to provide warnings of pending problems, especially problems involving complex interactions within the development schedule. This would include tracking critical program paths and allowing simulations of proposed changes in the schedule. Proper management practices will be required here. If proper practices are not used, project managers could become project dictators, and developers could become drones with no privacy and muted genius.

In a similar manner, there should be a standard interface to all documentation activities. Here it becomes more difficult to predict the possible connections because the look and feel of documentation is changing. This is another example of the phenomenon of the new medium adopting the content of the last, nearest medium. There is no doubt that the original style of documentation is stretched, and it is often difficult to find the necessary information in a timely fashion. There have been many interesting experiments with on-line help text, with interactive training and documentation, and with CD-ROMs to contain the volumes of information. The problem is that we have better and more standard ways of doing project management than we do of documenting systems.

There are also various levels of documentation to describe system functions and system internals, to describe application functions and application internals, and to describe the best ways to use the application. In general, the farther we move from system and specific application documentation, the more difficult it is to automatically track changes in documentation. This becomes very important in actual development and installation of large, networked applications. Consider the situation where an advanced user manual tells the insurance company programmers to use the file system for communication and even for some types of process control. Although this is technically feasible, it could result in poor performance due to the overhead added by the file system. There are better approaches to process control.

The point is that either documentation writers or engineers—or both— might have contrived a way to use an application to control parts of the system, but this is not the most efficient use of the system resources. If this happens, then the customer will spend a lot of time and money to develop applications that use the system inefficiently. Even if the original approach to applications were correct, then in our preceding example, if a subsequent release of the system included an extremely efficient process-control mechanism, the documentation might not reflect the changes. Users who had used the file system to control the processes might find it difficult to adjust their thinking and modify the application to use other forms of process control.

The only defense against these and other documentation misunderstandings will be to have very knowledgeable technical personnel participate in the writing and critiquing of manuals. At programming levels closer to the system, it will be possible to have changes in the system modules accompanied by automatic markings of documents to be changed and perhaps even some indications of what to change.

As the products become easier to use, there should be less need to tie documentation to system-specific features and machine internals. Users will operate in a machine-independent environment. As mentioned in a previous chapter, internal documentation will become more important. One of the reason for this internal emphasis will be the linkages that must be accurately documented and must adhere to system standards. Software engineers must understand how to use the internal linkages correctly.

There will also be a need to explain the product linkages for the installation and building phase; this includes sizing and tuning. Documentation informs software engineers not only about actual linkages that exist but also of virtual linkages that can be used to develop an optimal solution.

In many large programming areas today, the documentation personnel would be more than happy just to find out what is being changed (including linkages) and when. An integrated system could certainly keep them informed by automatically tracking design and program modifications; proper documentation system and linked tools would undoubtedly make documentation modifications easier to perform and much more accurate and timely.

Quality and product safety are two very important measures that should be included in the interconnected system. Just as changes in modules should allow evaluation of whether the documentation must be changed, the change process should also allow for an evaluation of whether the test suites, design and code inspections, and other quality-assurance activities should be changed. This is also subject to the guideline that the closer we are to the system or application, the easier it would be to mark affected areas. Higher-level implications will be more difficult to determine.

Product safety is definitely included in these connections. The analysts and designers must know what is expected by law, and they must in some cases be able to prove that they have tested to guarantee that the system or application performs as advertised. This is certainly true in areas such as air-traffic control and financial transactions. It is also true in materials-management systems that advertise lot control; in this case, the government may demand proof that lot control really works. If a bad batch of aspirin is manufactured and it becomes necessary to do a recall, the software company and the aspirin manufacturer could be liable if they suddenly find out that the lot tracking did not perform as promised. We will revisit product safety in a later chapter on quality, but the connections will be needed and they are therefore noted here.

The final connection is to the "front" of the software engineering platform and tools. The user interface must be

- consistent;
- friendly and easy to use (and forgiving);
- efficient (from the standpoint of human factors);
- localizable;
- customizable.

Consistency is a generally accepted concept today, but it should extend to all tools and functions in the software engineering environment. This includes a consistent "look and feel," and all software suppliers would adhere to look-and-feel rules. The user interface would include the following:

- screen formats, appearance, and organization
    justification (right, left, center)

protected fields and data entry fields
text (including free-running text)
tables, lists
graphics
abbreviations
windows
- dialogues
forms
menus
commands
queries
graphics and icons
functions and function keys
natural language
localization
- input/output
auditory levels; digitized speech
gestures
keyboards (standard keyboards and beyond)
mice
joy sticks, track balls, light pens, and the like
touch screens
printers
portable input and output devices
- visual
shapes
brightness
colors
lines
documents
motion (television)
- user help
error assistance
status (system and application)
interactive help
automatic error recovery
- system consistency
familiarity
consistency of screens and windows (*Note*: Too much consistency can
   be a disadvantage; in some systems you get lost in layered nests of
   windows and menus because they all look exactly the same.)
messages
response times (and advisory messages during delays)

Friendliness and ease of use are also generally accepted concepts, but there are still fundamental differences in agreeing what these terms mean. To some they mean very cryptic shorthand sequences with highly efficient communication; to others they mean icons, pointers, and easy-to-understand information flows; to still others the present-day solutions seem to be a trade-off between confusing control sequences and confusing icons. This may require a synthesis of the ease of use with the consistency guideline to produce several levels of consistent, easy-to-use interfaces. If this is the proper solution, then engineering sequences will probably be a bit more cryptic, whereas project management will use icons, charts, graphs, and be more complete in nature.

In any event, the entire environment must be efficient and easy to use at every level. Probably the best way to design these interfaces at each level is to do extensive simulations for each of the engineering, management, documentation, and support levels, using experienced professionals from each of these areas. The most important point is that interfaces should be designed to be user-friendly and not simply constructed after databases are in place.

The ability to localize the computer system to meet specific country needs becomes very important if this is to be a multicountry system or if it is to be sold and used on a worldwide basis. Localization usually includes translating part or all of the screens, manuals, and such into the local language. In some countries it is necessary to localize all screens and information related to the safe operation of the system. In other countries it simply is good business to localize. The software engineering environment should be designed so that the system is as close to 100% localizable as possible. Localization also means allowing the foreign country to customize the system and to add local applications and services as required.

Customization allows the users to create their own screens, to change existing screens where allowed, and to add their own code modules, which could then be controlled according to the system standards for operation. Note the overlap in the concepts of localization and customization. If the environment were designed to be customized, then it should be easy to localize. However, the discussion of localization implied that the developer or supplier would provide an already-localized version.

Customization would allow the user to change the appearance of the screens, to add fields, to delete noncritical fields, and to link locally developed modules into the system. The usual problem with customizable systems is that subsequent releases of the system require either a recustomization of the system or the loss of old customization upon installing new screens. A typical scenario is that we may have selected an available line to add one of our fields, but the next release uses that line for a new field that is part of enhanced functionality. There are checking programs that examine the old and new screens and alert the user to conflicts, but the inconvenience factor is still there.

The solution is probably in some sort of automatic customization by which you make your preferences known to the system (left-justified, double-spaced, input fields directly beneath questions, and so on), and the customizer then observes these rules in upgrading your screens for a new release.

But hold that screen change; did we not make the point that consistency was a guideline? Did we not make the point that users should know what to expect when they encounter a system? This may all work out if there are fundamental processes and screens that are defined as unchangeable and the customization is applied to user-oriented and user-specific functions. The debates over the boundary lines for user interfaces will be grist for several years of international conferences and nationalistic debates.

IMPORTANCE OF AN INTEGRATED
DEVELOPMENT ENVIRONMENT

This is all well and good, but just how important is it to achieve the level of integration that we are describing? What if there is a country that thinks it is sufficiently important to make it a national project? What if there is a country that plans to establish a uniform software development environment that is hardware independent and to construct a nationwide network for communicating technical information? Would it make a difference if that country has no proven track record in high technology; on the other hand, what if that country is Japan?

The Information-Technology Promotion Agency, Japan (IPA) organized the SIGMA System Development Office in October 1985. SIGMA (Software Industrialized Generator and Maintenance Aids) is the nucleus for the industrialization of the software development process through the development and promotion of a distributed software development environment. SIGMA objectives include

- improving software quality and productivity;
- consolidating development facilities and accumulating technology know-how;
- minimizing redundancy in software development;
- increasing the efficiency of specialist education.

SIGMA high-level features include

- a high-level language for software development;
- general-purpose programming tools to run on a variety of chips;
- all development on a consistent environment;
- strong testing and debugging support;
- a complete set of development and support tools.

SIGMA researchers realized that existing software development tools do not necessarily meet these stated objectives. They have, therefore, taken a two-step approach to development of the integrated platform. The first stage is to develop a prototype SIGMA system and get their users' reactions. The second stage enhances and improves the prototype system. When the production system is in operation, users will pay fees, which will then be used to help defray costs of the system.

There are well over 100 companies that have invested in this project. SIGMA employees come from many of the supporting companies, usually doing a several-year assignment before returning to their company. The more than 25-billion-yen SIGMA cost has been split between private companies and the Japanese government.

Earlier we discussed the need for consistency with some allowances for customizability. SIGMA recognizes this need and is allowing each company to pursue its own specific methodology. SIGMA is attempting to provide standard workstations and standard networking and plans to be a nationwide network.

The core of the system is UNIX-based, and software development tools must be able to use the UNIX file system. They will use a platform for interfaces to various libraries. There is a SIGMA center, which supports users by controlling the network and providing database services, part of the network services, and demonstration and promotions.

SIGMA has completed the workstation and prototyping; workstations are now being produced by several manufacturers. The workstations and the operating system constitute a de facto standard to assure portability of the tools. In this way the potential market for tools that meet the standard becomes very large and provides inducement for the best toolmakers to enter the market. There are separate tool groups for the requirement-definition process, design process, programming process, debug/test process, and maintenance process. There is also a data architecture group.

Recognizing that some important work has already been done on other platforms, SIGMA provides integration with existing development environments. SIGMA is also developing real-time support and automatic test support.

SIGMA's main functions include: project management support, documentation support, networking, resource management support, business application development support, scientific/engineering and process control support, and microcomputer support.

There are thousands of pages of SIGMA documentation, newsletters, and reports. The brief outline that has been given here is sufficient to highlight several key points.

- The Japanese are hard at work on software engineering.
- They have selected a UNIX-based environment.

- They are providing a standard workstation and a portion of a standard platform.
- They are not waiting until the final decision on object-oriented languages is in.
- SIGMA has enjoyed only partial success; the current project status is discussed in Chapter 16.

The major U.S. initiative is centered on APSE, the Ada Programming Support Environment. The one key difference is that this set of software engineering tools and the supporting platform is Ada-based. The Department of Defense "owns" the name Ada, and those that claim that they have software tools such as Ada compilers must be certified by the Department of Defense; validation requires passing a suite of over 2000 tests. There has been an initial slowness in the response, but this is changing as more and more government contractors move to Ada-based systems. There is also a growing commercial population that is becoming Ada-based, and this is moving Ada from the exclusive domain of the defense-related industries. Europeans have been developing their own Portable Common Tool Environment (PCTE), and they have been working to reconcile PCTE with APSE.

This platform is still a long way from claiming to be a complete software engineering solution. There is still only minimal support for the needs and requirements and analysis and design portions of the software development cycle. Linkages between tools is minimal, and databases are far from unified.

Europeans are also major players in the quest for software engineering standards, but European developments have taken a new twist with the emergence of a unified Europe in 1992. The original work toward a formal specification was started under PCTE, and it was to become an international standard for software engineering architecture and supporting environments. While this may prove to be a major contender in world software competition, there is now the realization that Europe will have such things as common sets of standards, common passports, and common currencies early in the 1990s. There is a very strong movement toward quality standards and certification, which is embodied in the work of the International Organization for Standardization (ISO). The ISO 9000–series documents describe the quality system standards and guidelines that will be used throughout Europe. These include quality in specification and design, production, testing, safety, and other areas. This work will no doubt influence PCTE activities, and while it may cause some uncertainty in the short run, there is no doubt that the "new" Europe will have enormous strength in determining international standards.

The drive for European standards had its origin in the 1979 introduction of British Standard (BS) 5750. The British government established an inspection and accreditation process by which businesses could be certified to be in accordance with the standards, have a plaque to display in their lobby, and be listed in the official accreditation guide.

Today there are well over 9000 businesses that have attained certification. Although some organizations originally doubted the value of certification, today it is the lack of certification that can bring a customer's attention.

In 1983 the BS 5750 standards were part of the impetus for a European standard. In 1987 the International Standards Organization 9000 series of standards was published. It is the ISO 9001 standard that is of interest here. ISO 9001 deals with quality specification for design, development, production, installation, and servicing. The standards are designed to ensure that the products perform as specified by customers.

These standards are becoming important throughout Europe, but they are most important in the government sector, where they are used by all major purchasing agencies who represent the public sector. There is a complete set of the ISO series, inspection teams, local offices, and the like.

But what can this mean to the rest of the world? It means that software is part of the certification process. It means that U.S.-based manufacturers who sell in Europe can have their California-based facilities inspected as part of the approval process. It means that certain statistical procedures must be employed and results returned on a periodic basis. It means great difficulty for crafters who attempt to gain and maintain certification without benefit of software engineering.

There are other software engineering platform projects underway in both public and private sectors. India has a very strong software community, including some of the largest "software houses" to do contract programming. These groups are developing tools and platforms. The Soviet Union and some countries of the Eastern bloc are also at work on this opportunity, and the dramatic political changes of the past few years will allow them to play an even greater role.

Finally, there are a number of U.S. companies who are working on their own versions of the tools and platform. Some of these companies claim to have the entire solution (usually in the fabled next release); others are making more realistic claims, but all are doing serious work and making important contributions to the field.

The importance of all these activities is that the majority of the major players agree that something must be done, and they have projects underway to do something. What are the prospects for near-term success?

- Crafters are hard at work connecting, innovating, and finding solutions. We need this activity to succeed in the long term.
- Toolmakers have entered the arena, and there are now some well-designed tools for specific tasks.
- In addition to connecting modules and functions, crafters have moved up to the network level.
- Government-directed projects manage to go beyond the crafter level,

and they have a track record (ARPA, for example) of being able to enforce network discipline. Governments have had mixed success at the language and database levels.

- There remains a methodology gap. As long as we are connecting without understanding and following a proven methodology, the chances for total success are limited.

- Prospects for near-term success at the full-blown software engineering level are very limited; prospects for major success with one or more segments of software engineering and a "thinly" connected network are very good.

As we complete the technology focus in the first major segment of this book, we have seen a strong technology pull driving events since the very beginning of computing. The technology pull is still very strong, and new technologies are continuing to emerge. While we are watching this phenomenon, we must also face the fact that customers are now telling us what they want, and we must meet their needs. This requires a blending of technology and customer inputs. It also requires a mastery of technology transitions.

How does one know when and where to begin? If one has already started, and had some success (or perhaps tasted failure), how does one know where to begin again? It is hoped that all that you have read thus far in this book and will read in the chapters to come convinces you that software engineering is going to take its rightful place in the engineering community. We are living in an age of technology transitions; they appear to be increasing in quantity with a corresponding increase in cycle time. The feeling that one is getting behind can promote a desire for action now, but what action now?

The next chapter examines the concept of technology transitions, the generic nature of transitions, and their use in helping us to understand where we are and what to do next. All technology transitions are following a well-worn path; let us shed some light on that path.

8

Software
Technology Transitions

CHARACTERISTICS AND PHASES OF SOFTWARE PROCESS TRANSITION

Chapter 4 began our understanding of technology transitions by explaining phases of the software engineering evolution and roles of the crafter, tool builder, and engineer. The technology transition curve has its origins in the constant parade of technological progress. Figure 8.1 outlines the generic cycle. We begin in the lower-left corner when basic or very early research illuminates a new discovery and pundits promise early progress. In recent years superconductivity has inspired dreams of magnetic levitation trains, very low cost power transmission, and much more. Cold fusion inspired even greater dreams of almost limitless energy. In all such cases it is simply too early to tell. Those who wish to invest in early research realize they are at high risk, but they are motivated by the promise of large rewards.

THE GENERIC TECHNOLOGY TRANSITION CYCLE

The generic cycle begins with basic research. In many cases this research is based on an existing practice. Someone sees the weakness of the practice and begins to think about a better way to get the job done. In other cases scientists

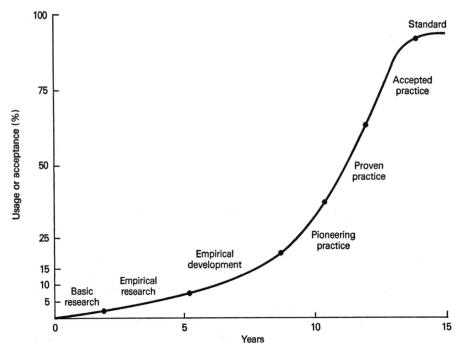

Figure 8.1 Generic technology transition cycle.

come up with an answer and then search for the matching questions. Computer scientists do not seem to develop good theory from the best practice. In all cases, in this very early stage scientists are excited over the fact that they know something new, that there is another avenue to pursue in the search for truth. In those cases where basic discoveries lead to legitimate applications, there is a long and winding road that takes years to travel. True software breakthroughs that result from basic research today will take years to become generally accepted software tools and practices. The average time for a Silicon Valley breakthrough to become a billion-dollar business is 15 years.

Many of our tools begin in the empirical research phase, where researchers earnestly seek to devise ways to apply discoveries to solve practical problems. This work is continued by empirical developers, who refine the tools and begin to use them to solve present and persistent problems. These developers have been using other tools to solve the problems; they are now willing to apply the new tools, techniques, or solutions. During these phases there are apparent leaps forward and often severe setbacks. These are also the phases with the greatest technological "sizzle": the promise of the new robot or automated factory, or the promise of the power of formal methods or neural networks. This sizzle can misdirect the investment of millions of dollars in the fruitless attempt to force unproven tools into a production process; dollars should not be spent on innovations that still must prove themselves in development and testing.

As development progresses, the new tool or technique becomes a pioneering practice. At this stage not everyone is a believer, but there is enough proof of performance to begin serious investment. In many cases we still are not sure exactly why the tool works in some areas and not in others, but we do know that it does work. Pioneering practice sites often make the decision to use a new tool or methodology primarily on the motivation to be innovators.

Things really begin to move when the tool or technique becomes a proven practice. At this point there is confirmed proof of performance, and general management can begin to speak in terms of return on investment. At this point the sizzle is gone, and many who would benefit from the use of these tools pass them by in favor of the newer offerings. They also pass by the opportunity to make the largest gains with minimum risk. Management allows this because it does not understand the significantly higher risk involved in adopting pioneering practices rather than proven practices.

The accepted-practice phase marks general acceptance of the technology by mainstream companies. There is no real risk other than not understanding how to make the transition or how to use new technology effectively. Accepted practices have full support, consulting, and all assistance necessary to succeed.

Finally, tools and techniques arrive at the accredited level of standards. Somewhere along the way, methodology, metrics, training, and a full complement of consultants have joined the practice. In many actual case histories, the recognition of the standard is an event that takes place after the fact. Many national and international standards committees are simply formally recognizing a de facto standard.

This technology transition flow applies to all areas of engineering endeavor. Consider the case of the large factory that manufactured clocks, watches, and wristwatches. Somewhere around the turn of the last century this company was founded as a high-tech venture to mass-produce timepieces in a world that had been dominated by craftspeople who were unwilling to concede that you could make clocks on an assembly line. The factory developed special tools and processes and became very successful. As development of the pinwheel movement occurred in the 1950s, the company began to feel the pressure of technological change. Subsequent transition to digital watches and to analog watches using digital-timing technology proved to be too much for the company, and today the factory sits empty.

This company, which had successfully made the transition to mass-production techniques, could not make a successful transition to digital technology. Although it might be true that crafters would do well to stay with their original products and survive, this was not the case with the clock factory. It was simply put out of business by its failure to be able to switch to the new technology.

The companies that dominated vacuum tubes continued to make large research-and-development investments in vacuum tube practices and thus failed to move forward with new technologies, including transistors and integrated circuits. Thus the technology transitions discussed in this chapter are intertwined with the engineering evolution phases discussed in Chapter 4. Understanding these evolution phases and transitions and knowing criteria by which you can determine where you are now and where you want to be are the keys to making successful investments in new technology.

Another way to understand the cycle is to look at a very exciting television technology, high-definition television (hdtv). The original television standards were developed in a time when glass technology did not promise screens larger than 7 to 10 inches, and engineers did not think in terms of movies at home. The pioneering engineers realized that you could attain a much higher quality with additional scanning lines, but they also knew that it would take up much more of the broadcast spectrum. Thus they made the trade-offs and selected a portion of the broadcast spectrum that could support only about a dozen channels with any degree of transmitting efficiency. Those countries who initiated television after the United States did use somewhat higher standards, but they still were not suited to a 6- by 8-foot picture.

And now we trumpet the coming of hdtv with special demonstrations, much excitement, and the market potential that numbers in the billions of dollars, yen, or francs. Part of this hoopla is justified with the arrival of fiber optics to allow us to get many channels of hdtv into homes. Wiring of some selected towns with fiber optics is beginning. In any event, hdtv is now in the applied research and development phase.

Once again there are competing systems and intense competition to attain standards. There is also the question of backward compatibility to allow present-day sets to receive broadcasts. The problem is easy to understand as we all have a stake in the television business, and it is already a worldwide communication medium.

Knowing all this, would you rush to invest in any one of the proposed systems? If you owned a television station would you rush to install any of this experimental equipment, or would you upgrade to better equipment that uses the recognized standards of today? The answers are almost self-evident in the television business, and yet we often miss the facts in the software engineering business. Perhaps it is because we are in the middle of this software forest and it is hard to see anything for all these piles of program listings or perhaps it is because customers can see the television picture and express their needs and requirements.

Observations and Conclusions about the Generic Cycle

Figure 8.1 leads to several observations and conclusions.

- The transition cycle from applied research to standards takes years to complete

- There is a tendency to overlook some proven practices, which can be the best possible "medicine" for development problems.
- There is a tendency for some to believe that a technology is farther along than it is and to recommend full implementation of the technology before it is ready; this is coupled with love of the "sizzle" of new things.
- A software improvement program that combines elements of pioneering and proven practices can yield a leadership position.
- A software improvement program based upon elements of applied development and pioneering practices offers hope of a significant leap forward, but it also carries the risk of betting on the wrong technology. (Remember the promises of bubble memories, early voice-recognition systems, and domestic robots in the 1980s?)
- There is a very subjective element to this technology transition flow. What becomes a safe "jump" for one group is a very risky jump for another group. The fact that there are published papers heralding the success of a new tool does not mean it is right for your group.
- In general, the larger the scope of the jump, the greater the risk. A widescale implementation of an early pioneering practice becomes a frontier exploration.
- Technology transition flow is generic for all engineering progress. If we understand where we are and where we want to go, it is possible to develop and implement a leadership program.

CHARACTERISTICS OF SOFTWARE PHASES

There are several phases that new technologies must cross on the way to becoming standards. The characteristics for each of the phases are as follows:

Basic research.   Repeatable phenomenon, effect, or action/reaction.

Empirical research.   Application of discovery to various disciplines and specialized areas within disciplines to evaluate potential for further development.

Empirical development.   Application of the principle or effect to solve a known but previously unsolved problem or to solve a previously solved problem in a new and better way.

Pioneering practice.   Refining, tuning, tweaking the empirical solution; this marks the beginning of a process and perhaps the beginning of a methodology. This application occurs at one of the actual sites of final use.

Proven practice. Further application at final sites using commercially available tools, documentation, and training. Used successfully at three or more sites (in larger companies). Has a highly probable return on investment. Is a good fit. Users have objective data and good subjective vibes to support their claims of success.

Accepted practice. Application at other than leading companies. Is fully accepted at conferences, users groups, and so on. There are fully documented claims of productivity gains.

Standard. Recognized by: market acceptance; adoption by more than one company; adoption by more than one country. Becomes formally recognized by national and international standards organizations.

CHARACTERISTICS OF ENGINEERS AND MANAGERS

The characteristics of engineers and managers in each of these phases varies according to the risk and interest levels, as shown in Table 8.1.

It is important to understand who belongs in each of these levels in your organization. If you ask a dedicated researcher whether you should install a new technology across your entire development organization, you will probably get a different answer than you would if you ask a mover and shaker. There are some individuals who are renaissance persons by nature, and they not only could work at almost all these levels, but they would also give a consistent and objective answer to your question. Asking a cross section of

TABLE 8.1 Characteristics of Engineers and Managers

Phase	Person Involved	Descriptor
Basic research	Researcher who seeks truth	Scientific explorer
Empirical research	Researcher who seeks to apply truth	Problem searcher
Empirical development	Experimenter who searches for uses	Problem solver
Pioneering practice	Explorer who finds the first useable paths	Application solver
Proven practice	Movers and shakers who show large-scale results	Application provers
Accepted practice	Doers who go with the flow	Application leaders
Standards	Everyone	Application doers

persons from all these categories would be interesting, but it would not be the best way to make a go/no-go decision.

DEVELOPMENT SCENARIOS

In many development situations where quality becomes an issue, there is a mental panic that comes from the realization that the team is not using the latest software tools and techniques. This sense of panic is created when something goes wrong. Perhaps defects increase dramatically; perhaps development and support costs soar. The general manager issues a call for something to be done, and a very talented engineer with more guts than experience is assigned to make recommendations for new tools and techniques. The engineer conducts a 30-day research program by contacting the most prominent research institutes, universities, journals, and ad hoc experts. This nets a short list of the most promising tools, languages, and supporting technologies. The engineer then consults with others in the team and holds several review meetings before a decision is made. There are three major problems with this approach.

1. In many such situations the engineer does not really understand where the team is today (with respect to the true needs of the team). Thus the well-intentioned engineer sets out to solve the wrong problem.
2. It is easy for engineers to be blinded by the technology sizzle in the search for the productive software engineering solution.
3. The engineer does not understand that technology change involves a balanced program using methodology, tools, training, consulting, metrics, and more to achieve success. These are explained in detail in this chapter.

The worst scenario occurs when the attempt to use the new tool fails. In many cases the conclusion is that failure was due to selection of the wrong tool and perhaps the tool was really on its way to being obsolete. The quest for the latest tool begins again, when, in fact, the original tool might have done well if used as part of a balanced program.

GOVERNMENT SCENARIOS

Megaprograms, discussed in the preceding chapter, avoid most of these pitfalls by selecting a pioneering practice that is well on its way to becoming a proven practice. In the case of governments, countries, or continents, it may be possible to get the full weight of purchasing power and regulatory bodies behind the effort to enforce a standard. The hdtv system could be straight-forward; the U.S. government will decide the official standard. Officials and experts will, one hopes, select the best system, and broadcasts will be able to be received on existing receivers (with quality comparable to existing low-definition television). A lesser-known fact is that the U.S. government orig-inally selected an incompatible color television system based upon a seg-mented red, green, and blue color disc rotating in front of the camera and receiver. Part of the reason for this selection was the fact that the all-electronic and fully compatible system was not quite ready at the time. When it came time for a color broadcast, no existing black-and-white sets could even receive the color broadcast in black and white. The point to be made here is that just because a government is large and powerful, it is not always wise and thoughtful. The U.S. government has put considerable pressure upon industry to conform to the APSE standard. One hopes APSE is a well-considered choice for Ada software engineering.

Governments are better positioned to survive major wrong choices than those who compete in the business world. In the mid 1980s there was no clear standard for windowing. Several large companies invested heavily in the de-velopment of windows, support tools, and programming interfaces. With the advent of X-windows those same companies were forced to consider expensive upgrades. These included several of the largest Japanese computer companies, who had developed CASE tools and workbenches using their own custom windowing systems. It is not clear that the Japanese companies have agreed to recognize X-windows as a world standard.

TECHNOLOGY TRANSITION OBSTACLES

There are many obstacles to a successful technology transition. In many cases they are masked by the idea that technology is the operative word. The major obstacles are as follows:

- resistance to change
- management resistance
- technical resistance
- engineering resistance
- methodology mismatch
- the right process at the wrong time

Resistance to Change

In many cases there is a very strong resistance to change. With the "half-life" of a software engineer in the range of 5 to 8 years (at this point the discipline has progressed to the point where the engineer is lacking about half of the technical knowledge that is required, assuming no continuing education), those engineers who have been the backbone of the development and support efforts are also those who have suffered the greatest technical "slip." In many situations where software engineering is presented to them, these engineers will mask this technical obsolescence, since it causes them embarrassment. If someone calls for new tools and new technologies, the engineer will often object to the proposed changes. These objections can be overcome only by allowing the engineer time and opportunity to upgrade skills. This upgrade becomes part of the overhead time required for change.

Management Resistance

Systems development managers recognize the need for change; software managers admit that change might be good; users call for change for the better. Systems development managers are especially good at spotting hardware engineering productivity problems. Software seems to blindside many managers; some will simply state that it is a fact that software will always be late, over budget, and filled with defects. In many companies the biggest management obstacle to change is middle management. Project managers have been sold on the necessity for change; they are suffering the adverse consequences every day. Top management is sold on the idea because they recognize it is the only way to get a leadership position. However, top management forgets to modify the directives and grading system for middle management. The original dates remain firm; there is no time for change, and middle managers are expected to accomplish this technology miracle in addition to their already heavy load of tasks. Middle managers are accustomed to having solid control of their environments, and they resent being forced into changes that seem to be unproven and probably to be yielding unpredictable results. Thus many middle managers shun change and wait for some other middle manager to prove that a given technology transition is successful before agreeing to make the change.

The key to solving this dilemma is to have a genuine executive-level commitment to improving the software process and then have that commitment translated into goals and objectives that can be fulfilled by middle management. Although this commitment is beyond the area of influence for the individual programmer, it is not beyond the area of responsibility of software management. Software managers can make general and executive-level managers aware of their responsibilities and gain their commitment, which must be translated to the business plan that supports the change. Cost of the tools, training, engineers' time, support, and other necessities must be stated as part of the business plan, along with measurable goals and deliverables. This is best accomplished by adoption of proven practices where costs are known and where successful implementation will bring credit to the middle manager and team.

Technical Resistance

Technical change must make sense. If it reaches too far or attempts to prove a new tool, it should be approached with great caution. Unproven tools guarantee surprises. There is the danger of solving the wrong problem. If the code needs reengineering, then it probably does little good to switch languages, unless the entire program is to be coded in the new language. The biggest risk in the technical arena is that it requires a balanced program to ensure success in technology transitions, and balanced programs require analysis, planning, and careful execution. Technical resistance is usually encountered at the team level or higher.

Engineering Resistance

We have already discussed engineers who have become obsolete. They may also simply be too busy. This is another factor in sustaining their resistance. If an engineer is too busy to consider how new technology helps, then the engineer does not approach change with an open mind. In many cases there is also a belief that winning past positions will become winning future positions.

If engineers are still operating in the hacker or crafter mode, there is also the danger that they are using tools inefficiently or in the wrong manner altogether. This can often be overcome via workshops with a respected technical leader who discusses better ways to use the tools. Obsolescence resistance is usually encountered at the individual level; it rarely gains team consensus.

Methodology Mismatch

The methodology should fit, and it should be selected first using proper selection criteria. The methodology should be appropriate to the level of advancement desired this year, and it should still be appropriate 3 years later.

If circumstances warrant a revolutionary approach, then it may be necessary to reach into the applied development area and implement a very new technology. This could also be done to accelerate or force development of a new methodology; it could be done to gain the attention of tool suppliers in order to get them to support this new technology.

Normal circumstances call for an evolutionary approach to rely on constant and known gains using proven practices. The best methodology here would be one selected from the proven-practices category. A methodology mismatch could occur here if the selection process was biased to the point where it ignored the need for an orderly evolution and selected a revolutionary practice. If a group is not ready for near-quantum leaps and if it needs to minimize the risk involved in a wide-scale technology change, then a revolutionary methodology will snatch defeat from the power of proven practices.

Another form of mismatch can occur if a business program development team selects a methodology that is well-suited to advanced scientific areas. There are some excellent tools and methodologies available to business program developers, and a proper set of selection criteria should prevent methodology mixups.

The Right Process at the Wrong Time

The long-term winning course of action is based on the concept of continuous process improvement. Although it is very important to select best-fitting methodologies and tools, it also must be understood that there will be ongoing improvement in tools, best ways to use them, and best ways to improve the software product. Thus it becomes vital to select the right process now, but the process must be right for the foreseeable future.

The decision to reach out toward the quantum leap increases risk that the process may not be improved. A company that has made no major change in the last 10 years will probably have difficulty with quantum leaps. It is better for them to use proven practices. But if quantum leap is written in the corporate winds of change, then it should be done in planned phases with clear, attainable milestones and objectives.

The bottom line is that planned technology transitions require much more than the latest technology. Technical and business managers must know

- where they are with respect to software engineering technology, and where their competitors are;
- where they want to go, what problem they are solving; and the criteria that must be met by a successful technology transfer;
- whether someone who understands technology transitions is involved in the decision-making process;
- why change is being proposed (Is an obsolete process being replaced?);
- all elements of a technology transition and how to put those elements into a balanced program;
- that proposed changes will happen one way or the other—changes can be planned and controlled, or they will happen through the pain and suffering of errors and obsolescence.

TECHNOLOGY TRANSITION ELEMENTS

Technology transitions involve the following elements, and all must be present in proper proportion:

- The production process must be understood; then an appropriate methodology can be selected.
- There must be a methodology. If it already exists and is well understood, then it will provide a solid foundation for change. If it is not understood, the knowledge must be included in the training program. If the methodology cannot be presented clearly in a training program, then the tool is still in the empirical development or pioneering practice category.
- There must be a new tool or a new way to use an existing tool. The tool and methodology should be compatible with overall development objectives. In many cases a tool is selected; then management searches for ways to mold the development cycle and team to the tool.
- Training is essential; this includes discussion of the methodology, tool, metrics, and reasons for the change. If there are prerequisites, they must be taught prior to transition training. Teaching artificial intelligence without a firm foundation in logic creates problems. Teaching LISP-based artificial intelligence without a firm foundation in LISP yields artificial intelligence with too much emphasis on the artificial. It is often the best course of action to conduct initial training and then follow up with consulting and advanced training in the form of workshops and sharing sessions.
- Metrics, or measurements are essential to recognizing progress. Implementation of dazzling technology can often mask the fact that there is much excitement and little or no productivity gain. Liking the tool is an important plus only if the tool increases quality and productivity.
- Understanding organizational culture is essential to transition. There must be a quality and productivity gain that will be a return on investment. In many cases, the software culture is not directly suited to or interested in these gains. You must know where the development culture is and how it will react to change. Engineers and managers must understand what the transition program is, why it is important, and what it will do for them.
- If there is a companywide technology transition program, this transition should be part of that program. There must be an understanding of where we are on the engineering evolution and where we are attempting to move to on the technology transition curve.
- Management should understand the reason for and factors influencing the decision to make technology change; management should support change, and reward successful changes.

Technology Transition Caveats

There are also several caveats that go with the decision to make a planned technology transition:

- Do not replace an obsolete process with another obsolete process.
- As conventional wisdom says, if it isn't broken, don't fix it with a technology transition; do continue to improve the process.
- Do not initiate or improve pain-killing processes. Get to the source of the problem and fix it.
- If you look back and nobody's gaining on you, you may be dead last; if you are dead last, do not automatically select a revolutionary transition. If you determine that you are second with respect to one competitor, be certain that all other competitors are not tied for first place.

KEYS TO TECHNOLOGY TRANSITION SUCCESS

One of the keys to success is to know when to make a fundamental change to a process and when to simply continue improving the existing process. Consider the telephone center that takes all software support calls for its company. Upon analysis of phone usage, it is determined that a capacity problem exists for 2 hours each day when the system can handle only 75 calls per hour but 100 calls per hour are being attempted. If the manager conducts a study of the problem and announces that at the present rate the company can anticipate a maximum of 750 calls per hour in less than 5 years and the manager proposes to build a new answering center to handle a maximum of 24,000 calls per day, that may not be the right solution. Why not eliminate the software calls, or at least have a goal of reducing them to less than 75 per day? Of course it may be necessary to add some phone lines in the short term. The company wants to be able to take all customer calls but does not want to be overwhelmed. Putting programmers on phones is not the best long-term solution.

If the company institutionalizes the process, it may become difficult to see when to change. A similar situation could occur if an extrapolation of present software growth yields the conclusion that in 5 years the company will require ten times its testing resources to maintain the present level of customer dissatisfaction.

MOVING FROM INSPECTING TO ENGINEERING

Formal inspection of software design and code by organized teams is a most valuable technique, and we should not hesitate to use it. However, the idea is not to continue present-day team inspections for the next 10 years; the idea is to minimize or eliminate inspections because we have improved the software process and are now engineering software. We will be making specific suggestions for how and when to make process changes in the last chapters of this book. For now it is important to understand that these recommendations must be made in the context of the concept of technology transitions. You must know where you are and where you are going.

The following list sums up technology transitions.

- Changes take a surprisingly long time to occur; it takes years before applied research and development yield proven practices.
- If changes seem to occur very quickly, then you are being caught off guard.
- If you work in a very small company, especially a start-up company, it is very difficult to keep products coming and stay abreast of the latest developments.
- Understanding the concept of technology transitions allows you to calibrate the pace of change, estimate risks involved, know where you are and where you wish to go, and estimate the risk involved in your transition program.
- If you do not have a repeatable, predictable process, all bets are off; technology transitions usually become most difficult. A repeatable, predictable process is not absolutely essential to a technology transition, but without one, risk increases with size and scope of the transition.
- If you think you have a repeatable, predictable process and still experience difficulty, consider a second opinion.
- Viewpoints vary; one engineer's sizzling new applied development tool is another engineer's proven practice. One of the keys here is to ask what you would accomplish if you possessed this wondrous new tool.
- Experts will place technologies in different positions on the transition path; salespeople will place them wherever you are.
- Process changes should be well understood, well budgeted, well planned, and well executed. If something does go amiss, it is necessary to understand why it happened and how to prevent it in future attempts.
- Software is simply one part of the overall engineering process. It should not be subject to exceptions or special privileges.

During the consideration of technology transitions and how to use the generic flow, we have made numerous references to quality and productivity. As we have continued to examine the factors that influence the transitions to software engineering, it becomes evident that there are a number of critical factors, dozens of supporting variables, and complex interaction between all of them. Quality is one of the most important factors, and it deserves special explanation and examination. We now move to the quality dimension.

9

Software
Quality

THE TRANSITION TO QUALITY IN SOFTWARE DEVELOPMENT

There are some old-timers who believe that the words software and quality are mutually exclusive. There is historical evidence to show there are legitimate reasons for this suspicion and that all things being equal, the pioneers did a remarkable job of maintaining quality while bringing software to its present level. This book has discussed how size and complexity have outstripped the ability of current software processes to guarantee quality and performance of products. But what does software quality really mean? What does quality really mean?

In the 1950s and 1960s many adults proudly purchased a new automobile every 2 or 3 years. The new owners would always be pleased with their U.S.-made purchases, and it did not bother them in the least to take their cars to the dealer for first servicing with a list of the 20 to 30 items that needed attention. Automobiles were complicated machines, and nobody could build them better than Detroit manufacturers; almost no one else was trying to build them better. The proud owners enjoyed their cars, defects and all, and they would enjoy them even more as manufacturers began to improve quality. In those days conventional wisdom had it that when it was possible to build them better, Detroit would be there.

THE INTRODUCTION OF QUALITY COMPETITION

Of course, foreign competition took the leadership in building automobiles better, and the automobile business will never be the same. Part of the success of cars built with quality processes goes beyond the fact that you simply have the dealer fix whatever is broken when you bring it in for service. There are many books and articles written about this phenomenon, but the gist of it is that is it better, easier, and more profitable to get it right the first time. The original belief was that you maintained the production rate and allowed quality to vary; you could always fix little defects later in dealerships and small garages. The new belief is that you maintain quality, even if it means varying the production rate. At the most progressive automobile plants it is possible for any production worker to halt the production line to allow correction of a process problem. There are very few software facilities where a programmer is allowed to halt the production flow.

All this is good for the automobile business, but what about the software business? It should be noted that software is definitely and most intimately involved in the automobile business and that cars today have LANs (local-area networks) throughout the car. This makes it possible to plug in almost anywhere and diagnose problems. The software business is becoming part of everyone's business, and as such software should be subject to the same quality standards as other products. Besides, it will prove to be very difficult to find local software experts who can repair software applications at the user's site.

THE DEFINITION OF QUALITY

Quality means fully meeting the customer's needs at the lowest possible cost of ownership. Cost of ownership includes purchase price plus all ongoing costs of operating and maintaining the system. Thus lowest possible cost of ownership does not simply equate to lowest purchase price. There are variations to this definition, but they all say much the same thing. The customer is the only reason that we are in business, and it is the only reason for this book: to better understand how to participate in the transition to software engineering that will better serve customers. But "I do not serve customers," you protest. In that case you either have internal users whom you do not consider to be customers (when they are, in fact, your customers) or you are developing software for your own use, in which case you are the customer. Everyone has a customer. In any event, that customer deserves the best that you can provide.

There are still some problems with the generic definition of quality, and there are other definitions. Fully meeting customers' needs implies that we completely understand those needs and have the means to meet them; it implies that needs have not changed over time. It also implies that we are aware of the customer's expectations (which may go beyond actual needs). Part of the problem stems from the crafted origins of early software. There are different viewpoints when you differentiate between crafted and engineered quality.

- Crafted quality is well done according to the crafter's standards or the crafter's interpretation of your needs. It is true that some crafters will make a second attempt if you are not pleased with the first effort, but it is also true that you must like the basic style of the crafter in order to be satisfied with the product.
- Engineered quality is well done according to a well-designed and well-executed specification. The product delivers full value, and it is possible to predict accurately the average cost of ownership. Of course, the potential buyer might not like the specification, but it is usually easier for the potential buyer to understand what is being offered when it is accurately described and perhaps simulated.

ORIGINS OF SOFTWARE QUALITY

If we are to understand present directions of software quality, it will be necessary to take another look into the past to understand the origins of today's quality process. Software quality control has its origins in hardware quality, and we discussed some hardware and software differences in Chapter 3. Now we will overlay the quality dimension upon the original discussion of hardware and software differences.

The basic hardware development and production flow is shown in Figure 9.1. I hope quality historians will allow this simplified explanation, which has the origins of quality in those inspectors (gatekeepers) who stood at the end of the line and observed or measured the final product. In the hardware process, quality efforts have moved forward; the concept of getting the process right—and keeping it right—prevails. If the processes of all your suppliers were correct and controlled, you would not have to consider incoming inspections. If all your processes are correct and under control, you have to sample only the final product; perhaps you could even eliminate final inspections. Doing away with incoming and final inspections would be very risky if processes were not under control. Elimination of inspections is done in some hardware areas today; it should be done in software within the decade.

In any event, when software became a clear and present danger to the overall sales of systems, management turned to the quality community and asked that it ensure the quality of all software. Thus early software quality engineers were gatekeepers, and no below-standard software was to be allowed to pass. These early guardians of software were diligent indeed, and

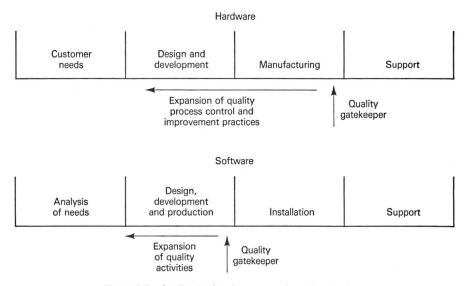

Figure 9.1 Quality in development and production flow.

they devised all sorts of ways to ensure that they tested functionality, documentation, and the like. These attempts were not without problems.

In some cases, software-testing groups reported to the upper-level software manager; this was a potential source of biased testing and reporting. In other cases, the quality group reported to the general manager, but that did not necessarily ensure objectivity. In many cases, the presence of a software quality group allowed the teams to meet all their deadlines. When the day to turn software over to QA arrived, the teams submitted the software in its current state. About a week or two later QA returned the release, announcing that it was unfit. The problem was that while quality gatekeepers were doing their job, no one knew how to isolate and fix software defects or control release versions. At this point software was sometimes released on the grounds that it had to be above the minimum level. Figure 9.2 shows a typical, large software system release. If design and functional modifications continue throughout the life of the software product, then there comes a time of peak quality when it would be best to release the software—somewhat analogous to the proper time to sell the wine. In many cases, continued QA testing time meant that the team was changing the design and function of software each time it cycled through the team for QA mandated changes, and this made it possible to release software when the quality had actually degraded from a prior high.

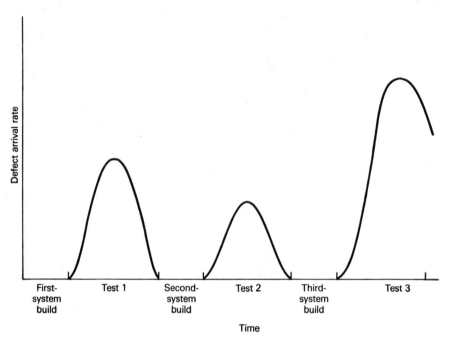

Figure 9.2 Instability of yesteryear large-system builds.

BENCHMARKING COMPETITOR'S QUALITY

In earlier days of hardware QA, one of the early analysis approaches was to see how hardware processes compared to those of competitors. Measurements included failure rates, specifications, time to produce, cost to produce, and so on. Thus one came to understand that a company's manufacturing took 30% more time and cost 20% more than its competitors' processes. The R&D took 25% more time. This did not say what was wrong about the R&D or manufacturing process, but it did say that something was different, and whatever it was affected the competitive position in the marketplace.

Software undertook similar comparisons, and various companies and consulting companies established baselines by which software development processes could be compared and rated.

These first measurements did not pinpoint where the problem was but simply indicated there was a problem. Later versions would indicate where a company seemed to lag others in facilities and use of software engineering tools but did not indicate exactly which new tool or office style would be the best solution. The baseline measurements did indicate when the company was using an outmoded process.

The quality approach is to fix the process one time rather than fix the product every time. If a process is in place and under control, there should be a quality program to constantly improve it. Continuous improvement implies

- the existing process is measured and relatively stable;
- the process is understood;
- the desired changes, and their effect, are understood;
- a feedback loop is present to continue improvement and guarantee system stability.

Continuous process control and improvement goes on until it is finally time to abandon the process by making a technology transition to a superior process. The danger that is inherent in approaching process improvement from a sudden need for quality improvement is that the company gets into a "we must do something" mentality and either solves a low-priority problem that provides no significant quality advantage or answers a question that was not being asked.

One risky tendency in software is to leapfrog technology and attempt innovations that are not necessary at this time. Hardware stories abound with process improvements that were almost overlooked or thought to be impossible. One Japanese quality expert developed a technique for turning around dies on large punch-press machines. This was originally a job that could take 24 to 48 hours. In many locations today, the job can be done in under 5 minutes with the same presses. This is analogous to running a 4-minute mile. In software, it should be possible to get at least a twofold improvement in quality and productivity of most software development groups without major investments in time or money. The trick is to know what, where, and how to change. Of course it will take a major transition to software tools and on to software engineering to achieve the tenfold and greater gains that will be necessary to be in business 5 to 10 years from now, but it should be possible to start on short-term gains today and have results within 6 months.

ELEMENTS OF THE SOFTWARE QUALITY ENVIRONMENT

Whereas hardware quality assurance is able to work with manufacturing and then engineering departments to improve the process, the software process is less rigid, and the development climate resists interference and change.

Early software assurance attempts by traditional quality teams met with limited success. As a result, the following occurred:

- Software testing became more entrenched. As we have discussed, testing can only go so far in the quality-assurance process.
- The chances of having well-understood, consistent software processes

were slowed. In general, those engineers working in the environment do not find enough time to think about how to improve that environment. Engineers also find it difficult to get an objective fixed viewpoint for analysis of their own environment.

- There seems to be less interest in improving the installation and building processes. Awareness of this has been increasing in the past few years, and more work is being done in this area. There is also some encouraging use of artificial intelligence tools for configuration and installation.

- In some companies, software quality assurance has become intimately involved in the analysis and improvement of software development processes. This trend will continue in the future. Quality is everyone's business; it should be an integral part of all phases of the production process. Toward that end, quality departments are working to make marketing, development, manufacturing, support, finance, legal, administration, and all other departments aware of the quality process and how to integrate it into their regular work routines.

Once again we return to the "what to do once you know" problem. Even when the quality department is able to help with or do the analysis of the software development process, someone must determine which changes to make. Someone must understand which methodology, tools, training and consulting, and metrics to apply. Someone must understand in what order to apply these elements of technology transition. Is this the proper work of the quality department? Is it the proper work of a separate engineering group dedicated to understanding the latest tools, technologies, and the process of technology transition? Or is it the proper work of the development groups themselves?

QUALITY METRICS

If a company is going to improve quality, it needs a consistent set of processes with the highest possible quality throughout the production process. Without some sort of organized review process, it is almost impossible to have consistent quality. This means having a review process that is documented and known by all. The criteria must be known and have been agreed upon in advance.

Quality review should be a formal process with all program elements reviewed. The idea is to get agreement that a problem exists; if there is no agreement about the problem, then there will be no agreement as to the solution. This is another instance where fascination with technology can lead us to make a software technology change that results in no significant change in quality.

The review must have global scope of responsibility. Perhaps the team is making a change that will cause a significant improvement in another department, such as support. Perhaps the change will result in significant improvement in the user interface. The long-term goal is to establish an orderly review process that will detect problems as soon as possible on a cost-effective basis.

Technology transitions should be part of a continuous software process improvement program. Having a formal review process and formal criteria may sound imposing, but it simply means understanding the situation in order to know what to do. Understanding implies measurement and the ability to analyze and interpret the measurements accurately.

Software Quality Metrics

Different approaches have been tried in different companies. In general, larger companies set up separate departments to specialize in these areas. Smaller companies attempt to have their development groups "cure" themselves.

All approaches require some metrics in the areas of product, baseline, and software process in order to have a high probability of success. It is possible to pick the correct answer and have it fall into place, but the larger, more established, and more successful the software group is, the harder it is for a technology transition to fall into place. In general, metrics are subject to the following variances:

Process changes. Unless there is an established body of results (as there might be in the case of a proven practice), it is difficult to know what process changes to make, what tools to use, and what results to expect. Even if a tool was successful in a similar development group, it might have problems in this group. The variation lies in the degree of crafted processes in the present development environment.

Timeliness. In general, product metrics are too late to allow precise process control. Baseline metrics are too coarse a measure. Even process metrics could be misleading if they are not directly relevant or are too late to be effective.

Focus. Metrics should measure a specific part of the process. One Japanese maxim is, "Beware of data collection; it can become a hobby." There is an implicit belief that we know a lot about a process and have it under good control simply because we have a lot of data about it. We should know why we are measuring each part of the process and what improvement to expect.

Effect on behavior.   If you measure something, you are causing it to change. This is one of the fundamental rules of physics, and it is true for software development. If you measure lines of code per group per week and publish results, you will in all probability see code production go up. If you publish known reported defects by product line or module, you will in all probability see the number go down. This may seem to be obvious, but consider a major investment in a new software tool where the measure that you select is lines of code produced per week. You may be missing the most important gains from the change.

Start-up time.   You may also forget to allow for start-up and transition time. This could result in a report that the new tool takes 20% more time when, in fact, it will take 30% less time and will have much higher quality by the second or third project. Again, this type of information will be known when you are making the transition to a proven technology; it will be much less certain for a pioneering technology.

Return on investment and overall benefit.   If a major new-product-development process is installed, major benefits may not be in the development process itself. If a new process resulted in a 75% reduction of problem reports, well-documented software that was significantly easier to maintain and enhance, and well-engineered software that could support enhancements, it would be a good investment even if it achieved only a slight reduction in development time or no reduction at all. The key here is to know what problem you are going to solve. If you do not know, then you should gather data in all potential areas of gain. If you do not know potential areas of gain, then data collection will expand to fill allotted disc space.

Stability.   If you make a serious attempt to analyze a crafted process, it will in all likelihood vary from project to project and from team to team. If you inject major changes into a varying crafted process, you might see significant gains, only to find that they were, in fact, anomalies that were due to uncontrolled variables. Conversely, you could see significant losses caused by variables that could have been controlled.

The bottom line is not to be goaded into making changes because something must be done. If it is not possible to give a reasonable explanation of the projected impact of a technology transition, then change should not be attributed to a pressing need for quality. Do not make quality the "scapegoat" and then attempt to use it as a ram for technology transition.

Statistics do not tell the whole story. If a person aspires to live to be at least 100 years old because statistics shows that only a very small percentage of the population dies when they are 100 years of age or older, that person does not understand the interpretation of statistics. Again, statistics show that 100% of the population who were born between 1700 and 1725 and ate vegetables are dead today. This should not lead to the conclusion that vegetables killed them. Finally, the people of ancient Pompeii (the city buried in the volcanic eruption) had a high degree of civilization. They had running water and central heat. They also died in their 30s, whereas those who lived in the country survived to much older ages. A statistician might conclude that the pressures of city living killed them, but in fact it was the lead pipes that they used for their water distribution.

Statistics and statisticians are absolutely essential to the success of our society. The examples cited here involved amateurs analyzing data and drawing wrong conclusions. This misinterpretation can occur on a higher level when someone who does not understand sampling techniques and statistical significance attempts to study experimental data and reach solid conclusions. In Japan, many major computer companies have all their employees take one or more fundamental short courses in statistics, significance, and how to read the charts that are posted. Employees on the shop floor can tell you the significance of production and defect reports, and they know how to read all standard charts.

Perhaps a better way to see how these examples could come closer to reality would be to ask, How do you know if your software engineering tools are meeting your needs? The answer "I will know" is probably not correct. What are the known problems? What are the expected results? How long will it take to measure the success or failure of the experiment? Have all variables been controlled? We will be revisiting this subject and making specific suggestions for measuring projects in a later chapter.

When defects were first being reported, someone came up with the metric that reports the number of defects per thousand lines of noncommented source statements (kncss). There are some weaknesses in this metric, but it serves to get things started. Today there are some companies who have upgraded this metric to defects per million lines of noncommented source statements, and they are planning to move to 10 million lines. The resolution at 1000 was no longer good, and defect numbers became too small to serve as a motivation to the engineers. If you move to 1 million lines of code, the number of defects is large enough to gain attention.

QUALITY AWARDS

Appreciation of quality is also essential to success, and it is always tied to metrics. The Deming award (named in honor of Dr. W. Edwards Deming) is the highest quality award in Japan. Winning the award is somewhat akin to winning the Nobel prize. The United States established the Baldrige award (named after the former secretary of commerce) to recognize highest quality. The importance here is that these awards result from best performance as judged according to stringent measures in a variety of categories. Inspection teams stay on-site for some number of days at each entrant's business site, and they verify results and conduct evaluations according to strict standards and guidelines. Even if you believe that you are not yet ready to enroll your company or group in these events, you can get copies of the criteria and evaluate your present performance against those criteria. There are also some private consulting firms that will perform this evaluation for you. It is another way of establishing the baseline that we discussed earlier in the chapter.

Winning a national quality award is not the ultimate goal. The process of preparing and applying for an award yields a significant return to all companies that participate. The preparation process causes a company to measure itself against a recognized set of criteria. Some critics argue that quality awards and quality do not always go together. There are few critics who would argue that the quality process does not work. Consider applying for a national quality award; you cannot lose; winning will simply be a bonus. If you do apply, you will be expected to have measured, controlled, and improved your processes, including software. You will be expected to have several years of data prior to submitting a formal application.

EUROPEAN CERTIFICATION

In Europe there has been a long tradition of government certification of quality; this included certification that your manufacturing processes were up to requirements. While these were often optional in many types of manufacturing, gaining certification had several benefits. First, you were able to post a notice of certification at your place of business and be listed in a directory. This allowed some measure of recognition and became of potential value when your competitors were not certified. Second, it seemed to have some implications for liability. Certification implied less liability than if you were noncertified. Today things are changing. The concept of strict liability, as in the United States, seems to be taking hold. At the same time, certification is becoming more important than ever, as the ISO standards are the standard for Europe. Once again, this allows European companies and multinationals doing business in Europe to establish a baseline for deciding where they are and where they will have to be.

There are basically two ways to approach these standards. A company can be reactive and rush to meet them just before the deadline, or they can be proactive and make process changes in advance of legal deadlines for compliance. No company should be caught with their reactive compliance down; all companies should be striving to be a proactive leader.

But what about software? The fact is that software is in no way exempt from these certifications and awards; it is an integral component, and the evaluating committees expect it to be up to standard and measured.

JAPANESE SOFTWARE WARRANTY

Several of the largest Japanese computer and software companies offer a lifetime warranty on their software. This seems to have its origins in the concept of responsibility; if software cannot change state and fail, then all defects must have been the fault of software developers. Therefore, it is the obligation of the company to correct those defects. In a similar manner, these companies do not follow the practice of making software obsolete. As we discussed in Chapter 3, this practice has occurred in the United States. This means the customer must upgrade to a newer version or risk the loss of support. Some Japanese companies support every line of code that they have ever released.

The important quality point is that they have institutionalized this way of thinking. When microcode is developed for calculators, or laser printers, or other hardware devices, the developers work on the principle of zero defects. You simply understand that you must get it right. Developers know that the burden and expense of a recall of tens of thousands of units to replace the microcode would be severe; they get their processes under control and deliver reliable microcode. There is a similar effect in Japan in those companies that expect to support a software release forever. It adds a sense of responsibility and it causes a different approach to all phases of software development.

SILICON VALLEY SOFTWARE QUALITY

Where do we stand on the issue of software quality? Several decades ago we were not certain what quality meant or why it was so important in a world dominated by U.S. products. Today quality is a very well accepted and pretty well understood concept. The problem is that quality is a generic idea. Employees want to do a good job; they want to take pride in their software and have it perform well. But in most development environments they do not understand what to do to attain the highest-quality software. In many cases, management does not understand either. Management posts clever posters exhorting the employees to do a quality job. The problem with the posters is that they do not say how to do a quality job. They do imply that developers are not aware of the importance of the quality concept, and in many cases this causes some resentments.

The following summarize the situation in regard to software quality:

- We all want to produce the highest-quality software.
- We want to produce it at the lowest-possible cost of ownership, we want it to perform as advertised, and we want it to be maintenance-free.

- We want to produce software with the highest quality in the shortest-possible cycle times.
- In most cases we do not know how to accomplish these noble objectives.

When a quality department is established or when an existing department announces that its members will also be responsible for software, there are four predictable reactions by the rank and file:

1. Great; let them ensure the quality of the software.
2. Great; let them work with me to help me to ensure the quality of my work.
3. Lousy; we don't need them; we have it under control.
4. Lousy; we don't want them (without regard to whether it is under control).

The correct response is the second one. Quality is not the job of the quality department; it is everyone's job. A large software-quality department or group should have the goal of putting themselves out of a job. Quality departments should basically audit quality processes much in the same way as the controller's department audits books of groups and divisions. If a financial audit reveals that the books are not in order, you do not fire the auditor; rather, you visit the division general manager and division controller to ask them about the problem and how they will solve it. You fire the auditor only for failing to do the audit or for doing a bad audit. In a similar manner, software quality groups should audit quality plans for software development and release. The plans are the responsibility of the development group.

QUALITY IN ALL SOFTWARE DEVELOPMENT PHASES

Plans for software quality should include quality at all phases of the software development process. For example, there should be a quality audit to see if customer's needs and requirements have been satisfied prior to beginning analysis and design; there should be an audit of analysis and design prior to implementation. If the entire software development process were fully quality audited, it would create the following benefits:

- Repeatable, predictable characteristics of the process would be supported.
- Final inspection and testing would be minimized.
- If your suppliers did the same, it would minimize need for incoming inspection and qualification; new releases could be integrated quickly.

In many companies the climate for software quality is not conducive to this permeation of quality throughout the process. Part of the problem is that most software development managers and engineers do not understand quality, process, or process improvement. Even if you acknowledge the concept of getting process under control and then improving the process, it is not certain that this will improve quality or will improve quality without having a negative impact on productivity.

When you get to the engineering level, quality and productivity are very closely intertwined; perhaps they are simply different measurements of the same thing. A well-tuned and well-running process that has product requirements matched to production resources will produce the best product in the most efficient manner. Doing it right the first time is the best approach. This includes using appropriate language, databases, development tools, and so on. Perhaps quality was viewed as a separate element only because it had been a missing element; it should have been part of the process all along. Perhaps attempting to inject the element of quality as a late arriver to the process created many problems and resulted in blame being incorrectly placed at the door of quality departments. Crafters have their own way of doing things and their very individualistic way of ensuring quality. Mass-crafters find it difficult to emulate crafters and attain quality in all that they do.

QUALITY AND PRODUCTIVITY IN THE DEVELOPMENT PROCESS

When quality and productivity become an integral part of the development process, as they should in a well-engineered development process, the following benefits accrue:

- The process naturally yields quality products.
- Enhancements to the process can be quickly tuned to increase the quality yield.
- Management can understand the process, evaluate competition and current technology, and know the optimum time to make process enhancements.
- Decisions can be based on return on investment; it is not necessary to take unknown risks.
- Financial controllers can understand what is happening.
- Technology transitions can be well planned over longer periods, and companies move into the proactive mode rather than making decisions under the pressure and strain of the reactive mode

These points will cause some readers to doubt the wisdom of having top management, including financial controllers, who are able to understand what is planned. The proactive mode is far superior to having to fight for every new piece of equipment or conduct some sort of chicanery in order to acquire new technologies. It is agreed that the size of some investments necessary to move into software engineering will cause top management to stare in amazement, but return on investment should be sufficient to convince them. If the return cannot be accurately predicted, then top management is probably wise not to bet the company on a massive upgrade. In these situations, it would be better to opt for a controlled experiment that changes one department and prove the effectiveness of new technologies before converting the entire company.

Quality is an integral component of software engineering; it should permeate all phases of the product process. Quality does not have a separate toolbox or place on the software engineering illustrations because it belongs everywhere. There are some special data gathering and analysis tools, and there is a place for a quality information system database, but these are used only for analysis, summation, and reporting of the quality data gathered throughout the product process. There may also be quality departments serving auditing, training, and consulting functions, but these departments do not have the primary responsibility for quality.

Every employee and every department should have quality and process measures and know how to use them. They should be able to tell you where they are now and where they plan to be in the future. They should know what their biggest challenges are, and they should have priorities. Where did these ideas come from? The committees who do visitations for national awards ask employees these kind of questions during interviews. A great deal of time is spent making sure that all employees can answer these questions and that they are working from the latest data. These interviews include software departments.

Quality and productivity are essential to software success. There are many excellent books, articles, and organizations dedicated to quality. There are far fewer books, articles, and the like dedicated to software quality. Process modifications are a minimum step to achieving software quality. Technology transitions should be an opportunity for major quality gains, but poorly planned and executed transitions become an excuse for quality setbacks. One of the major benefits in the transition to a software engineering environment should be the significant gains in quality and productivity.

Now that we have established the quality base, let us return to the advancement of software technology and take a glimpse into the next millennium.

10

Automated Software Engineering

THE TRANSITION TO AUTOMATED SOFTWARE ENGINEERING

The journey to the software engineering environment has already begun, and some research labs are making serious headway. The technology transition to automated software engineering is still in the planning stages, and we could be a few years into the next millennium before standards are in place. There will be some who will say that major components of this new process are already in place and that technology transition is well within reach. When you consider what it will take to have 85% to 90% of those who should be using this technology for software development actually to be using it, the journey takes longer. We are not close to automated software engineering for the following reasons:

- Software "chips" are still in the research phase; there has been some progress, but chips are far from being standardized and software "boards" are still in the earliest stages.
- Industry specifications for this advanced platform are not in place or universally recognized.

- There are no universal tool standards, and there are no universal tool linkage standards.
- There are no conclusive studies showing the productivity and return on investment for this technology on any large scale.

There is also a strong possibility that it will require a new software development life cycle—and perhaps even a new paradigm—in order to use these tools effectively. Recalling the trend of each new medium to adopt the content of the last nearest medium, it will take some fresh research and thinking to devise the proper ways to use this technology. This fresh thinking could be linked to the development of fifth- and sixth-generation computers. Although there are a variety of opinions by the best experts around the world on architecture and operation of these future generations of machines, there seems to be a general consensus that they will not operate on von Neumann serial processors. Rather, they will be information engines that will operate on knowledge and data transformations. Although this is very interesting conjecture, it will be very difficult to apply a new paradigm to a vaporlike architecture.

FIRST-RELEASE AUTOMATED TOOLSET

The most probable course of action will be for automated software engineering technology to begin as the latest, most integrated, and best set of tools that run on today's computer engines and then perform a sort of metamorphosis as it moves to the next generation of hardware. This will allow researchers and users to get some hands-on experience and come to know what it is that they really want. The intermediate software development technology may be analogous to chemical engineering, which focused on how to design and build the processes and plants that in turn produced the chemicals and chemical products used by the rest of society. In this case, the software discipline may develop one area of specialization for software engineers who know how to design and build software engineering systems.

Thus we begin with Figure 10.1, which shows the layers involved in an automated software engineering system based on the software engineering tools explained in Chapter 7. The logical linkage between major functions is complete, whereas physical linkage occurs through the platform. The front end presents a clean interface with very consistent system command and control. Major tool modules can be installed with the same ease as programs can be installed on personal computers today. In reality, there is a central library of tools, but they appear logically to reside on each workstation.

Figure 10.1 shows the personal computer or workstation accessing the needs and requirements toolbox. The database and platform, shown as sep-

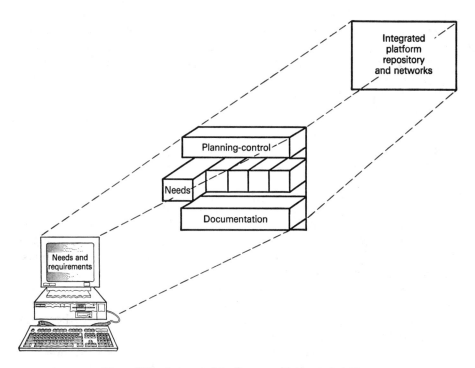

Figure 10.1   Automated toolboxes and integrated platform.

arate elements in earlier diagrams, are now integrated. It is possible to have more than one toolbox open using separate windows.

INTERDISCIPLINARY TEAMS

Although the development of this complex new platform may cause the creation of a new breed of software engineers, as previously mentioned, it may also tap selected other disciplines in the quest for the right blend of technical skills. Interdisciplinary skills have a precedence in some of the Ph.D. programs now in existence. There is also precedence in the fact that artificial intelligence has required the use of other skills, such as logic, philosophy, and linguistics. Interdisciplinary skills will be used as researchers come to grips with the concept of knowledge transformations and processing.

These new skills will also be required because the automated engineering platform will not be suited to traditional areas of engineering specialization. There will be some sort of rules for the transformations and dynamic connections required, and this will lead to the fact that the same problem will not necessarily have the same solution when designed by competing systems.

This is analogous to the automatic cameras that we have today. Different cameras will take slightly different pictures of the same scene, but all are good pictures. Thus far actual attempts at CASE systems that match traditional engineering specializations have not met with success, and critics charge that a CASE monolith will never be a viable approach.

EXPERT ANSWERS FROM AUTOMATED SYSTEMS

The verification of quality in designs produced using automated systems poses new challenges. Expert systems are rule-based, and they do not all arrive at exactly the same answer. The order in which hundreds of rules are evaluated and the exact positioning of the starting parameters influence the final decision. This is similar to human experts; a surgeon announces that you require major surgery. In real life you get a second and sometimes third opinion. If all three opinions agree, you have the surgery. Artificial intelligence–based CASE systems might not produce exactly the same software solution, but each solution should be one of a possible set of correct solutions. This becomes a very difficult challenge for traditional quality assurance departments; it is very difficult to test correctness of a solution and the relative merit of a solution as part of a complete set of solutions. There are other techniques for verification, and we will have to concern ourselves with them in the future.

There will be an appreciation of the beauty of the design at a higher level. Just as hardware chips have all but disappeared, both logically and physically, software chips will first appear and then disappear as the software professionals begin to see the beauty of the design at higher levels. At some point, there will be some groups of specialists who understand software chips, but they will work in the exclusive world of software design. If an earlier historical precedent would help, consider the early days of radio when everyone had to wire his or her own set or at least be knowledgeable in its theory and operation. As television first evolved, pioneering engineers and technicians operated the equipment. Later the broadcast business was taken over by those who specialized in programming and production; they do not understand how the equipment functions nor are they able to maintain the equipment.

Somewhere along this evolution there will probably be the development of the concept of software boards; these boards will provide higher-level functions and will be easy to connect. In the world of software tools, one of those boards might contain configuration management. If software boards come forth as predicted, there will be whole new toolsets developed to deal with them.

AUTOMATED LINKAGES

As we have already established, automated linkages will be logically dynamic in nature. They will be done in a way that enhances those functions that we already have today, assuming that we stay with the present paradigm. Let's revisit examples used in an earlier chapter and see what will happen to our engineering work.

In the automobile-design scenario that allowed us to try different sets of radios, the spreadsheet originally showed the percentage of the market gained or lost. In the automated system, it will be possible to have the consumer preferences known as part of the design process rather than doing a what-if trial-and-error sequence to solve the problem. In the automated system we can see the consumer preferences in the form of one or more optimal communication designs. The design of the front end of the automobile is also automatically changed to accommodate consumer preferences. After we have done some tuning of the design and determined what the optimum design is, we can then turn to the task of seeing what can actually be built and how much it will cost. The system will automatically search for the closest fit and will, upon request, work to the optimum cost. The designer makes design decisions and sets parameters.

The trend is from passive but automatic services to support the designer to active systems that not only make suggestions but also remember the designers' preferences and use them in the search for the best solution. This trend continues in the accounts receivable example, where the system recognized the possibility of reusing an existing module. In the automated system, there will be an automatic scanning of modules that are candidates for reuse, and recommendation will be made for the optimum module based upon customer need, performance, and country requirements. If a module is selected for reuse, detailed customization could occur automatically, based upon user requirements.

As we move into the automated engineering world, problems that used to be very difficult can become easy because they are now solved another way. In our undersea example, a software module was overlaid with a new module even though it still contained data that another module required for operation. Part of the problem was a lack of computer memory to hold the program. In this situation, memory will be so inexpensive and plentiful that it will take a very large program indeed to exhaust it. However, the problem can also be solved in an automated way by requesting a reengineering of the entire system in the underwater module. The reengineered and, ideally, more efficient and more compact code (due to improved algorithms and more efficient data handling routines) can then be remotely installed in the undersea unit.

Linkages extend across the entire spectrum of engineering functions. Before we had design and code linkages; now we have needs, design, production, test, and documentation linkages. It may be possible to interpret and simulate needs well enough to allow design generation from the needs analysis. In any event, it will be possible to have a much more accurate set of needs, which will be linked as input to the analysis phase.

Automatic test suite generation will occur during the design phase. These test cases will test logic and actual functions of design and production processes. Test cases will also test to see if the functions simulated during the needs phase are present and working. This is already being done to some extent today with the generation of test questions and test scripts during design. It will be the extent and nature of linkages that will make the difference.

Finally, costs, management schedules, and tracking of actual coding progress to estimates will be greatly enhanced. If there is a slippage in one area, the system will track the impact on the entire software development effort and will recommend optimal solutions. The system will also look ahead to predict where and when the most likely slippages will occur.

A word of caution is in order here. These connections will, of course, not all happen in exactly the way in which I have described them, nor will they occur in the predicted order. Crafters will again lead the way by making connections and seeing what happens. As the best and most valuable connections become evident, they will work their way into the accepted wisdom and start the journey to standards. The reason for recording these specific examples is to give some idea of the extension of the linkages across the evolving engineering platforms. There have been several public television series describing the continuity and connections that have marked technology transitions. Scientists and development engineers kept evolving rough ideas and inventions until they had achieved an adequate solution to a problem.

If you think in these terms, try to imagine what a historical television series 200 years from now would show when it dealt with the development of software engineering in our time. The series may record that the reason we abandoned vacuum tubes in computers was due to the problem of burned fingers from replacing the tubes or the high cost of electricity. Historians may also record that we abandoned the idea of writing software when the proliferation of competing software tools caused industry wide confusion. It is not certain that historians would reach the wrong conclusion and record these whimsical cause-and-effect relationships, but they would certainly trace logical connections in the ways in which we used innovative software engineering tools and methodologies to solve the software needs of society. Having the benefit of hindsight, they will probably wonder why we took so much time and effort to arrive at the optimal solution.

Automated software engineering is the result of many years of a continuing series of steps. It is the result of the quest for software engineering in the present generation of computer systems. Software engineering in the 1990s simply sets the stage for the next major technological advance. The shift to a major new paradigm, to future generations of computers, and to knowledge-based systems will occur in automated intelligent engineering.

Transitions should be made after the linkage has been proven. The risks involved in betting on a leading-edge process should be obvious. The important point here is to have established a solid technology foundation built upon proven linkages today. This platform will support the major transition to a new paradigm.

If this chapter provided a glimpse, the next chapter will take a wink at the superconnected engineering environment. It is hoped that this will provide final arguments that in some form or other, this software engineering business is happening and is going to cause dramatic changes. After establishing this concept and having it serve as a motivational base for change, we will return to today and get specific about the things that can be done to prepare for software engineering.

11

Automated Intelligent Engineering

THE TRANSITION TO PRODUCT-OPTIMIZATION TEAMS

The chapter title did not mean to say "artificial intelligence engineering"; there is nothing artificial about this software platform. Whether or not the new paradigm emerged in the previous stage, it will certainly emerge here. The transition to this level will be part of a larger engineering change that is happening throughout the world. Figure 11.1 shows the beginnings of this change. In an earlier chapter we spoke of the isolation of early engineering departments and how this was caused in part by the necessity to cut off change requests in order to get closure on the design. In this world, engineering is part of one continuous production process, and it is merged, coupled, and integrated with that process. All "walls" are down; teams with expertise in marketing, engineering, manufacturing, user interface, support, and finance participate throughout the entire production process. This is already happening in hardware engineering, where the new process is called concurrent engineering.

This merging is possible because operation of design, manufacturing, support, and other major company functions have been integrated and automated to the point that teams can understand and follow product flow. Team members do not have to become specialists in each detail area. The

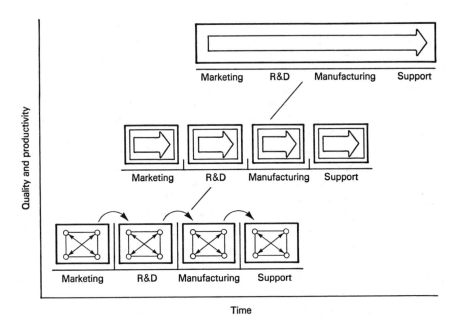

Figure 11.1 Department transitions to integrated product processes.

automated intelligent engineering platform combines components from disciplines of artificial intelligence, neural networks, fuzzy logic, chaos, and psychology to worry about all details of the production process. This does not mean that the system solves all problems; it does mean that the system automatically makes connections and resolves engineering details, freeing the production team to concentrate on goodness of product fit. This is supported by

- automatic checking and verification of connections at all levels;
- continuous modeling and comparing of actual performance to specified performance;
- automatic testing, self-correction, and self-improvement (the team is notified only when something is amiss);
- automatic presentation of customer needs and full and instantaneous simulation of all product functions;
- reuse at software board and software "appliance" levels.

THE LOOK AND FEEL OF INTELLIGENT ENGINEERING

How will intelligent engineering look and feel? Let us return to the car design of an earlier era. In that time it was possible to change communication equipment during design and make a decision based upon concerns such as customer's needs and preferences, safety, and cost. Now we have the entire product team seated at work centers that are logically connected. They all share the same visual perspectives and the same data. Perhaps they begin by looking at the exterior of the car from every angle. They can rate visual perceptions and compare these to customer and market preferences and trends. They can "seat" themselves in the car and examine the dashboard, the controls, and even the insides with an X-ray view. They can look out of the windows and see the countryside.

The best part comes with the test drive; they can all share the experience, or they can each take off in a different direction, with one trying the test track at high speeds while another takes a leisurely drive in the countryside and yet another takes a spin through the city. While they are driving, they can compare notes and decide to modify parts of the design, the shape, or size of the shock absorbers, frame, or other components. In all cases they will experience instant changes and be able to determine what the effects of their changes are. Product marketing can announce a change in customer preference or a new requirement, and it will be possible to modify the design in real-time.

While all this is going on, the final design takes into account the optimum design for manufacturability, supportability, and maximum staying power in the marketplace. The engineering platform remembers earlier attempts and improves its recommendations with each new design. It also remembers customer preferences and actual sales and satisfaction measures compared with projections. This is coupled with trend projections to allow the design center to become better and better at matching the customer's needs and requirements.

INTELLIGENT ENGINEERING OF APPLICATIONS

In the area of software applications it would be possible for a complete product team to participate in the design of an intensive care unit for a hospital. They would be able to see the layout of the intensive care unit; they would be able to see simulated patients and monitor medical procedures and treatment. They would be able to change medical instrument designs and see the effects upon patient progress.

If at this point you would say, "Just one moment; this goes far beyond software," you are correct. The automated intelligent design center does not focus on software; it takes the perspective of the entire product. It simulates and projects the complete product, and it will be possible to change all engineering components of the product and see the results. The system will also make suggestions for optimum design and product configuration. At each step it will be possible for the software specialist to open the software application and examine software boards and chips. This would be similar to consulting a broadcast engineer to examine some part of the camera and wiring technology in today's television studio and make recommendations for improvement. In a sense, the software specialist could go "off-line" from the simulation, work on a better solution for the equipment, and then return to the team with the solution.

Is all this going too far? If you think it is, conduct the following experiment. Take some fun money, take the afternoon off, and visit an electronic game parlor. Try some of the simulators that show airplanes in flight, automobile racing, or other activities. After you have enjoyed this experience, make an estimation of the chips and technology in those simulators, and consider the fact that these represent older technologies. If you are not convinced, visit one of the leading amusement parks; most of them feature very sophisticated simulators that provide thrills as realistic as a ride in the real vehicle. You can take a spaceship ride into outer space, or you can do some race-car driving. Simulators can spin you, roll you, or even flip you over. You will feel the bumps of the roadway. Then do a trend projection based on computing power in another 5 to 10 years; you should arrive at the conclusion that very sophisticated simulators will be available. There are major development programs underway today to create multimedia systems that tightly couple video, audio, CDs, and multiple processors to blend the best of information and entertainment techniques.

If you do not wish to visit theme parks but have friends in high technology, visit some of the simulators in the advanced flight training or ship training centers, and you will probably come away a believer. If the predictable technology shock happens, you will find the prognostications in this chapter to be on the tame side.

These automated intelligent design systems will consider all essential factors in the production process. There will be monitoring and awareness of product safety and regulatory requirements, and the system will endeavor to optimize the design for all countries in which the product will be marketed. There could be problems here as preferences for some features will be strong in one culture and weaker in another culture. Where it is necessary for priorities to be set, the system will ask.

The overall direction for this type of engineering has already started. There are forces stronger than engineering that will cause these changes. Figure 11.2 outlines the shift in product process flow for high-technology companies as functions become integrated into a continuous flow. The original corporate structure placed heavy emphasis on autonomy and control within each functional area. The marketing manager was almost totally responsible for all marketing and customer activities. In order to get something changed in another functional area, it required political skills, brute-force clout, or both. Most communication was within the functional department, and it was difficult to accommodate requests for change, especially rapid change.

In the integrated approach walls come down and there is much greater

Crafted	Tooled	Engineered	Automated engineered	Automated intelligent engineered
One of a kind; difficult to duplicate	Repeatable predictable discrete processes	Repeatable predictable engineering processes	Automated engineered processes	Automated intelligent engineering process
Project and lab span of control	Technical development span of control	Program level engineering control	Integrated departmental processes	Integrated environment and processes
Distinct project identities	Distinct department identities	Companywide R&D identity	Product team identity	Product team identity

Figure 11.2 Continuous product-flow evolution.

communication and cooperation between functions. Computers contribute to this change by making it possible to have up-to-date data used in decision making and by automated intelligent capabilities to accommodate change. Figure 11.3 shows the extension and logical integration of company databases to form a continuous process database.

Although there are quality and productivity benefits to be gained from sharing data, there is an increased security risk. Many existing networks and

Crafted	Tooled	Engineered	Automated engineered	Automated intelligent engineered
Project files and records	Lab files and records	R&D databases and records	Company databases and records	Company and external databases
Narrow band asynchronous communication	Wider band duplex communication	Wide band network connecting R&D	Integrated company network	Integrated company, customer, and regulatory network
Minimal product process improvement	Ad hoc product process improvement	Planned product process improvement	Continuous product process improvement	Continuous focus on company improvement
Minimal networking	File networking	Network database access	Hierarchical network access throughout company	Hierarchical network access; company to customers

Figure 11.3 Continuous process database evolution.

databases would be vulnerable in such a network. Companies do not want unauthorized access; countries will not tolerate unauthorized access. Database evolution must include security.

INTELLIGENT LINKAGES

The explanation of the product team earlier in this chapter made totally obsolete the automobile radio-selection example used in earlier engineering platforms. However, while the team is hard at work designing and enjoying the simulation of the latest sports car, the intelligent system is including requirements of all countries in which the automobile will be sold. It is optimizing the design to support these requirements; this optimization includes design for manufacturing, design for supportability, and design for ease of localization (with most parameters set automatically).

In the financial accounting example the same multinational requirements are included in the design; however, in this situation the intelligent system is using properties of our object-oriented development culture to put required options automatically in accounting modules and have them automatically selected based upon the specification of country by the financial accounting system.

Quality and productivity are greatly enhanced as the intelligent system is able to use linkages across the entire development process to anticipate potential running problems based on customer's needs. Today we are able to take real-time software needs into account during the analysis and design process. Tomorrow we will be able to spot potential "clashes" between all hardware and software components of the system being designed: the automobile whose center of gravity was affected by engine relocation; the hospital intensive care unit whose monitoring functions will not meet standards in Europe next year; the robots that work in explosive atmospheres and have a performance enhancement that generates a random spark.

The installation and build functions have not been forgotten. There will always be a need to get physical hardware installed, but it will be possible to install the system remotely and automatically. This has been done on systems of the 1980s, and it is planned for most future systems. However, it is the extent of the automation that will be interesting. The building requirements will be determined from the initial statement of customer's needs, and the installation plan will be part of analysis and design of the system. There will be no more of the "now that it has arrived, how are we going to get it installed" situations that have occurred in the past. Installation and build are part of the total product solution.

Quality extends beyond the span of company control; suppliers must meet quality standards. If you know that your suppliers have their processes under control as they deliver their products to you, then you can count on the highest quality in their shipments. This sharing can also be extended to having access (with permission) to the needs and requirements portion of your major customers' databases and to supplier databases. Figure 11.4 shows the connection to these databases and the logical connection of your product process to your customer's process. This connection has been going on in a more informal way for years. Companies routinely visited customers to better understand their needs and to measure how well the company was meeting those needs. Companies dealing with larger customers found it necessary to share longer-term product strategy in order to get large orders. You do not suddenly surprise your largest customers with the announcement of a new computer system and then expect them instantly to place large orders. They usually have planning cycles running several years ahead, and they must include your new system in those plans. The connection to suppliers allows on-line checking and verification to see if customer's needs can be met by your suppliers. It does no good to design a satisfactory system if one or more of the supplier components will not meet specifications.

During the course of our journey to automated intelligent engineering, we have periodically visited safety and regulatory requirements, noting that

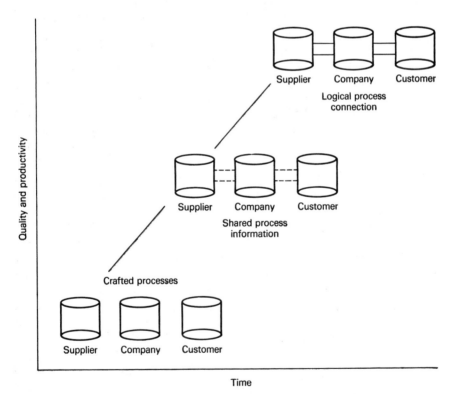

Figure 11.4 Company, customer, and supplier connections.

they are the only variables that can overrule customer needs and requirements. Figure 11.5 shows the extension of the product process system to have on-line access to the rules, regulations, and libraries that contain legal interpretations of these governmental dictates. There are two advantages to these connections to customers, suppliers, and governmental agencies:

1. The on-line nature of these connections allows us to be aware of the latest changes due to new customer preferences, supplier variances, or political forces.
2. The specific rules can be stated in a standardized format that will allow them to be picked up and used directly as part of the product process.

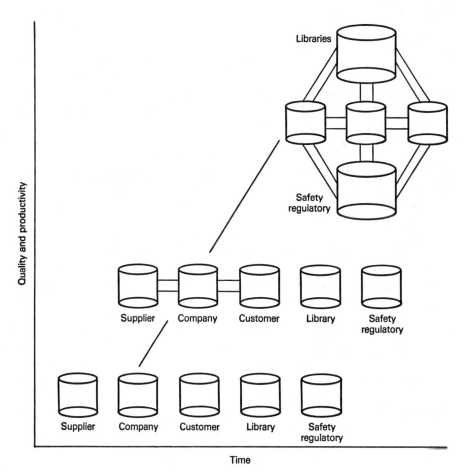

Figure 11.5 Company, customer, supplier, library, and safety/regulatory connections.

For example, radio-frequency interference rules could be used during design simulation and actual testing to ensure compliance. Rules regarding air-traffic control could be used during design.

If we step back and examine the preceding figures, it becomes clear that linkages are now occurring within and across company boundaries. The company becomes an integral part of a larger product process. If it fails to do so, the company begins to look like earlier crafters who preferred to stay in their own shops. These linkages include software development, which is really becoming chip development, with the difference between hardware and software barely perceptible. System design can be done first, and then the decision can be made about which portions to produce on a hardware chip and which portions to generate in software (using whatever software technique is prevalent). The driving force is integration of knowledge, of exact needs and requirements, and of knowledge of the optimum way to produce products to meet those requirements.

Knowledge is becoming the power of the next millennium. Knowledge engines will forge the future. The automated intelligent engineering environment will in all likelihood be the first engine of this new technology. Teamwork will be essential; teams will be interdisciplinary in nature; teams will transcend company and national boundaries.

In one sense these teams become the "crafters of the future." The original craftsperson was the consummate artist, with no two of his or her products being exactly the same. Production and assembly-line techniques all work toward minimizing variances, and the goal is to have products that are identical. Henry Ford's Model-T automobiles may have been the ultimate in consistency, including the color.

Automated intelligent engineering will work with standard processes, standard components, and standard software chips, but it will allow customization of end-user products with options and choices that will continue long after the product is purchased. These products will learn about their owners and determine how best to meet their needs.

What if this is not correct? If it is correct, what does it mean to us today in a world where software still causes executives to wince and wonder? If this vision were absolutely correct, I should give up working in software technology and take up investing in the market. The trends are clear; the exact path that technology will take is not clear beyond a few years. Science fiction writers of the 1940s and 1950s did not write about computers, because the technology simply was not on the table. When computers arrived, vacuum-tube models did not allow movers and shakers to dream about future tabletop and laptop personal computers. There are software methodologies, tools, and paradigms that are not yet available. The emergence of these new creations will undoubtedly affect the final outcome of this chapter. This book is not intended to be a monolith.

However, the trends are clear. Companies are definitely moving toward interdisciplinary teams, and old boundaries are coming down. Computer technology is already at the point where we can make many of the connections described; some companies are already making connections and database technology is still in its infancy.

There is the possibility that all computing to the present time has been analogous to spark-gap radio transmission. In the early days of radio the only way to communicate was by code transmitted by turning a spark on and off; the spark generated the impulse on a wide band of radio frequencies. It worked for ship-to-shore, and it was a major advance from the days of no "wireless." Consider a coffee session between several of the very best spark-gap design engineers of the time. One of them reports that it looks as if it might be possible to develop a continuous-wave transmission that could then be modulated. He explains that this would make it possible to send voice transmissions and perhaps someday to send pictures with the voice. After immediately dismissing the possibility of pictures (much less color pictures), the engineers turn to a discussion of why voice transmission would have value. The most obvious benefit would be the ability to talk directly to the ships at sea. This would make it easier to communicate and might even allow passengers to communicate with those on land.

But what else could you use this voice wireless system for? One of the design engineers suggests that you could produce receivers and sell them to people to put in their homes. What would they listen to? Perhaps transmissions to ships; well, not for long. Perhaps music; yes, you could transmit music live, the finest symphonies in the world. Another engineer responds that people already have recorded music in their homes and can listen to recorded symphonies at the time of their choosing. No one dreamed of the true possibilities; no one dreamed of receivers in cars; no one dreamed of personal headsets with full fidelity.

Computers were developed to solve mathematical problems, especially those that required lots of repetitive calculation. In the early days there were numerous stories about the experts of the time making predictions about only a few machines being required to handle all complicated scientific problems facing us. What if all our work thus far has been "spark-gap" problem solving and data manipulation?

The radio example is useful to allow us to get a proper perspective. When you are closely involved in day-to-day work on an existing technology, it is often difficult to find time to think about next steps or great leaps in scientific progress. This can be especially true in software engineering, which is very much in its infancy.

There has been much ado about the computer revolution in all manufacturing and business applications. In many cases, factories of the future have failed to meet expectations. Computers have often not been able to perform to hopes and dreams. When you consider the total time that computers have been available, it is only natural to expect a lot of investments that do not work as planned. There have also been some marvelous successes. The big payoff in the use of computers and evolution and integration of computers into business processes is beginning to be significant productivity gains. These successes will provide some of the directional information that will guide us into the "modulated" era of information technology.

The trends seem clear, and the direction is becoming clear. It is not possible to predict winners and losers because technology is changing. Those companies with flexibility and vision should be in good shape; those companies with rigidity should feel the pressure. Change is a fact, change will continue for the foreseeable future, and change will bring about automated intelligent software engineering in whatever final form it will have. The only way to ride the waves of change is to master the surfboard of technology transition.

Sitting in the present it is well to approach this in the airline-travel-guide mode. When you use an airline-travel guide, you determine where you want to go, and the guide tells you the various routes that take you to this destination. In our situation, the final destination is a level that we have never visited before, but it should be possible to understand the final destination from descriptions provided by researchers. The technology transition guide should allow us to select intermediate destinations with a high level of confidence that these destinations will move us toward our final destination and that we are moving in the right direction.

Change is a fact of technological life; we should approach it in a proactive way rather than fear it and be forced to change in a reactive way. As we move into the proactive mode, it is normal to wonder if those intermediate destinations are really moving us toward that final destination. Do we have a way of knowing that we are doing the right thing?

How do we know that our technology transitions are moving in the right direction?

THE ANSWER IS SIMPLE

As long as systems are becoming simpler to operate, as long as detail calculations, verifications, and dependencies are being handled automatically, making it simpler to concentrate on the solution, we are moving in the right direction. As long as the software portions of products are doing more and being seen less, it is the right direction. Simplicity embraces ease of use coupled with high productivity.

And now we have gone about as far as we can go. The spark-gap radio engineers would have had a very difficult time foreseeing high-definition television, fiber optics, and 200 satellite channels. The point to all this discussion and channeling is twofold.

1. It should convince you that there are very powerful forces at work that will certainly cause an integrated software engineering platform to emerge and be used. These forces are driven by fundamental changes in the production process and worldwide markets. They should serve as a powerful motivator to get busy on process control and technology transitions, which are described in the next chapters and which can be done today. These forces should convince you that this will not be wasted motion. They should also convince you that the movement will go forward even if one or more toolsets proves to be a "dry hole" in the software engineering drilling game.

2. It should get some creative juices flowing; there were no doubt visionaries who could foresee some generic forms of our present-day technology back in 1920. Today's visionaries should be able to guide us to the "simply correct" view of our future.

There will be new and yet-to-be new innovations, inventions, methodologies, tools, and practices, which will influence, reshape, and change the actual outcome of this chapter. However, setting an organizational structure and process in place to deal with these changes, no matter what they are, is a winning plan. Change is already here; change will continue; change will continue to be part of the software technology transition for the duration of our careers; change can be managed for success; successful change can give us the competitive edge by allowing us to outdistance our competitors.

This completes the second major area of focus. We have come to understand technology transitions, and we see that they will continue for the foreseeable future. We have also considered the marketing shift, from selling technology as fast as you can to fully meeting customer's needs and requirements. Technology transition must now go with the flow of customer needs.

This new stream of technology transition to meet customer needs while achieving the highest possible quality at the lowest cost of ownership is a management challenge. Winning management practices require harnessing technology transitions and integration of software in the total solution. Managing software technology transitions is the key to success.

12

The Software Engineering Transition Process

MANAGEMENT OF THE SOFTWARE TECHNOLOGY TRANSITION

Although change will be with us for the foreseeable software future, the process for managing and profiting from change can be put into place today, and paradoxically, it should not change significantly over time. The biggest obstacle to putting this process in place and getting started is that we cannot agree to an answer to the question, Who is the software technology transition manager? This is part of a larger question: Who is the technology manager?

One of the first answers that might come to mind is that general management and executives are technology managers. There is no doubt that they are responsible for the company and, therefore, for technology, and there is no doubt that they must approve, fund, and control technology transition plans. But they do not have the time and specific technical skills to handle line-management technology changes, especially selection and implementation of new technologies.

When it is time to decide that a new manufacturing building must be built to handle projected growth, there is a site-selection team, building-planning committee, financial process, and all the support structure necessary to get the building completed. Top management is familiar with building procedures and costs and therefore is able to communicate effectively with the teams involved. There is usually one manager somewhere in the organization who has built buildings before or has demonstrated skills in this area.

One of the reasons this building process is understandable is that buildings are almost always in the accepted practice category and occasionally are proven practice. The technology is proven and safe; the job can be accurately estimated and scheduled. There are exceptions and cost overruns once in a while, but these are usually due to some explainable cause.

We speak here of the problem of top management knowing when the proposed software change is a wise and safe course of action from a technological point of view. This would be akin to proposing a radical new type of building that had never before been built and was based upon some obscure principles of architecture. The irony might be that the radical building was proposed by a high-risk taker, while there was a very suitable and conventional building design that had been passed over by the risk taker. If top management had no basis for comparison, it could unwittingly follow the path of high technology risk.

The Technology Transition Manager

Who is the software technology transition manager? In some companies, it is one of the brightest and most aggressive young engineers. Or it might be a "gang" of several young engineers. In other companies the software managers decide upon a course of action. As we discussed in the chapter on quality, in some organizations the members of the quality department become members of the change team.

Special Change Departments

Among the foremost computer technology companies there is also an engineering approach that sets up special departments at the corporate level to focus on process changes. In these organizations there might be a department of engineering change, marketing change, or manufacturing change. The directors of these corporate technology departments are technology transition managers, although they do not have direct control over the groups they are changing. The idea is to have the best specialists in software, hardware, and manufacturing study technology directions and transitions and select the best course of action. These departments function in the role of technology transition managers as they use a wide variety of promotional, educational, motivational, and consulting functions to promulgate the right things to do. There is also a separate corporate quality department, which serves in an auditing and consulting role and works with the change departments.

It takes large companies to establish and fund this type of operation successfully. The need for a clearly defined technology transition manager who has been given the responsibility and proper authority to make technology changes is universal for all companies with more than 50 employees. This person or team must understand technology needs, skills available, and climate for change. The danger in large companies without a change-control authority is that local technology transition managers will fill a perceived void and appear in every software team location. These locals do not necessarily form a network. In many cases the local talent is a crafter by nature, who often is attracted to applied development or pioneering practices. A similar danger can occur in a smaller company where the one individual who becomes technology transition manager is easily fascinated by technology sizzle. The best and worst scenarios can be based upon a change dictator. A wise and benevolent dictator can be very efficient. An uninformed and totally technology-driven dictator can bring a company to its knees.

If we look to software project management practices, a similar situation probably would not happen. In a well-run software operation, when a software project is about to be started, the upper-level software manager selects a project manager who has proven, appropriate software skills and experience. The project manager, in turn, selects team members based on similar criteria. Junior team members are sponsored or supported in a way that guides them. The new project is supposed to have every chance for success. There are usually far fewer project managers and engineers who claim expertise in technology transitions. When the software manager attempts to select a project manager for a technology transition project, it is difficult to find the right skill set. When the technology transition project team is underway, it finds that it is harder to succeed in the transition environment than it would have been to succeed in the conventional environment.

Software Advancement Teams

Almost all these "SWAT" (software advancement teams) will have a stronger knowledge of software and a lesser knowledge of metrics, processes, and ways to cause technology change in other groups. They are crafters and pioneers by nature and often change project direction in midstream or become easily discouraged if they do not have initial success. The standard default criteria for selecting these teams is to find individuals who are very talented, very interested in the latest technology, and eager to see things done right. They usually have one or two near-term goals, and they often want to accomplish a major transition in 6 months or less.

LONG-TERM TECHNOLOGY TRANSITION CRITERIA

Earlier chapters have shown that software technology transitions go on for a long time and must work toward the long-term goal of software engineering.

The technology transition managers who work in this world must be able to meet the following criteria:

- They must be able to solve immediate software problems facing the company; they cannot exclusively focus on the long term.
- They must have a good understanding of technology transitions, engineers, and the best ways to effect change.
- They must understand levels of technology transition and know the risks involved in the planned transition; they must not be simply willing to take risk.
- They must have a vision; they must have a 3- to 5-year strategic plan that addresses their vision.

Remember, technology transition managers are responsible for implementing a technology change throughout an entire software operation, group, or company. They are building logical "software buildings" that support the company. This is not to be confused with pioneers, "wild ducks," and risk takers who start small-scale projects to try a new tool or technology. Many of these folks operate on intuition and hunch, and they often achieve surprising success.

Who are technology transition managers? They are technology transition experts who have mastered process change techniques. They understand when and how to initiate, monitor, and control process changes. They have fallback plans and alternate plans, and they understand that change will not always work. They are able to sell top management on plans and get funding. They are able to understand needs of their customers, and they are able to promote their projects and their successes.

But most engineers and engineering managers do not possess all these skills in balanced proportion. Exactly. This is not expected of successful engineers; it is also not expected of quality assurance engineers, manufacturing engineers, and so on. It is true that all successful professionals possess qualities in each of these categories, but many individuals have focused on an existing process and the improvement of that process. Here we deal with technology transitions and the associated process change. The ideal technology process model has a technology transition manager who understands processes and customer needs and includes the behavioral elements needed by engineers and engineering managers.

THE TECHNOLOGY PROCESS MODEL

The technology process model has three basic components:

Change program → production processes → products

These fit the quality methodology that says, "Fix the process, not the product." But the change program is not the principal driving force for the production process. While there is a very strong link and even a cause-and-effect connection between production processes and products, the change program is the "new kid" on the block that really has to find a way to work within this established model, shown in Figure 12.1.

The improvement of product processes is supposed to result in superior products; it is not supposed to interrupt normal business flow. With four major channels of input to the product process, it is difficult for technology transitions to be recognized. Technology transitions are also competing for time and resources with new buildings, new groups or divisions, and new products. It is small wonder that quality departments found product audits to be one of the most effective ways to cause production process improvements. Products are tightly linked to production processes, and discovered defects will be able to be linked to specific parts of the production process. This quality process of detection and correction is time honored, shows very near term results, and pleases top management. When we speak of technology transitions, we move from the immediacy of detection and correction to planned prevention. Companies with significant process problems today spend most of their time in detection and correction. Companies with processes under good control still have existing problems, but they are able to spend the majority of their quality time applying longer-term process improvements

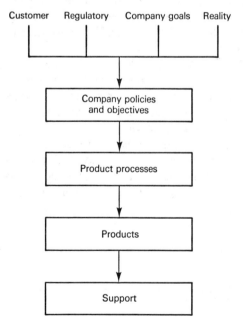

Figure 12.1 Established product process.

to prevent problems. There are also two types of process changes: the first solves a detection and correction problem; the second aims at prevention. This similarity between quality and productivity provides common ground for working together.

ROLE OF THE TECHNOLOGY TRANSITION MANAGER

The technology transition manager faces the problem of injecting process changes into the production process and doing large-scale technology changes or conversions on a well-planned and well-executed basis. To put this process change into perspective, let us recall an earlier diagram of technology transition. Figure 12.2 shows the technology acceptance over time as the technology progresses from basic research to standard. During the course of technology transition, the technology transition manager and change team must function in each of the following roles:

> direct change agents
> auditors of the process
> consultants
> advocates
> facilitators

The appropriate times for each role during technology evolution are shown in the figure. The change team can act as advocates and facilitators throughout the applied and practical phases. The serious consulting role begins with the emergence of a pioneering practice; at this point the usefulness of the practice can be shown. The auditing role can begin when a proven practice exists. Auditing activities ensure that plans are being fulfilled and having the desired effect. The role of direct change agent develops as the change team becomes absolutely certain that a technology is proven and is appropriate.

In Chapter 4 we examined the effects of technology change on quality and productivity and concluded that you can only get so much out of a given technology. Winning companies switch to superior technologies in a timely manner. For any given technology, the sizzle is created by the gap between acceptance and general usage and estimated return at that point in time. An emerging technology in advanced development and pioneering practice stages has the widest gap. As technology matures, everyone knows what it will do, and they know where to make corrections if it does not do it. The key measure of a well-established technology is that risk can be measured and managed. If a company waits until there is no risk, then there is no reward. If a company waits until there is no gap, then there is no possibility of becoming a technology leader.

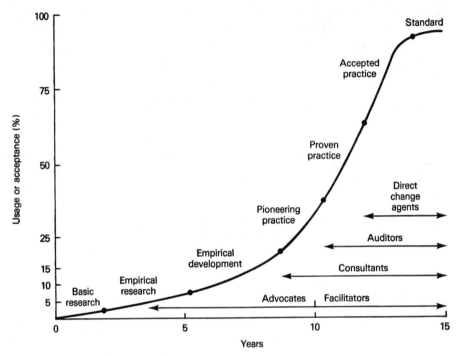

Figure 12.2 Change team functions during technology transitions.

OPTIMUM TECHNOLOGY TRANSITION

The optimum place to make a transition is at the leading edge of proven practice; not everyone is using the tool or technology, and it has minimum risk with maximum return. If a company wants to be a technology leader, it will appoint a technology transition manager who is able to follow one of the dotted lines that connects similar stages on the curves. Note that the angle of these lines is approximately the same as the leading edge of the composite curve that marks the beginnings of each of the technologies. You select a pioneering strategy that will give you high return early; you can select a proven practice that probably yields the optimum return; or you can select the accepted practice strategy, which minimizes risk. You also have the option of blending strategies; perhaps you begin with a conservative approach until your technology transition manager and crew are in place and then move to a more aggressive strategy.

In any event, this recognition of ongoing change is the reason why a technology quick fix, or even a series of quick fixes, will probably not keep you ahead of the game. When you couple the short-fix risk with the fact that most short-term fixes are driven by detection and correction pressures, it becomes obvious that those without a technology strategy are almost surely doomed to constant problems and final technological obsolescence. It also makes it difficult for those "on the line" developing products with ambitious schedules and tight resources to find the time to analyze these technology trends successfully.

When someone does step forward with the answer, management must wonder if:

- they really have matched the answer to the problem;
- they have validated the answer in some way;
- they know how to test the answer correctly in this environment and propagate the answer, if correct.

TECHNOLOGY CHANGE STEPS

An informal change model is characterized by

- ad hoc procedures and processes;
- crafters, wild ducks, or shakers who are either very high-tech, driven to change, or both;
- an informal methodology or no methodology;
- an external motivation of the detection correction genre.

A formal change model is characterized by

- a qualified and motivated technology transition manager;
- a realistic evaluation of the needs, resources, internal and external variables;
- a clear definition and prioritization of needs;
- an established technology selection criteria that will meet needs (lack of an understood selection criteria is one of the biggest reasons for internal bickering and ultimate failure of a technology);
- an understanding of change methodology;
- clearly stated, approved, and understood criteria for the change process (these are separate from technology criteria);
- a formal plan with strategies, goals, objectives, costs, schedules, and measurements;
- quality or productivity program involvement, or both.

The formal change model may appear to be formidable, but formal programs have been developed and put into place by one professional technology transition manager who uses outside consultants, university professors, and "captured but willing" workers from software teams.

Selection criteria are crucial and should be validated and agreed to before selection of any methodology and tools that will be installed on a large scale. In too many situations a well-intentioned technology transition manager makes selections based on too few facts and poor criteria and then attempts to force selections into software teams. Destruction, despair, and resignation follow.

Remember, software teams are internal customers, and to the greatest extent possible, their needs must be met. That is another reason why some sort of baseline evaluation, which was discussed in Chapter 9, can be of great value. The baseline provides a mechanism for understanding division software needs in the context of corporate goals.

Technology transition managers must also remember to select the methodology based upon proper criteria and then select the tool that matches the methodology. Another fatal mistake is to select the tool and then see what the underlying methodology might be. Without documentation, training, and support, it is hard to see how to use the tools effectively.

There must be stated objectives and measures. This seems obvious to experienced managers, but in so many situations the decision to start is based upon the promise of technology and availability of the equipment.

TECHNOLOGY CHANGE PLAN

To sum it up, there should be a full program. Another way to look at this requirement is to consider the technology change plan in Table 12.1.

The plan is completed by translating the vision into stated objectives for year + 3. Objectives are stated for each of the four categories shown in the plan framework. For example, a goal for year + 3 might be to have measurement be part of the culture and used in all software engineering

TABLE 12.1 Technology Change Plan

	This year	Next year	Year + 2	Year +3
Process				
Methodology				
Tools				
Training				
Metrics				

activities or to have all technical managers and engineers fully trained on software engineering. In any event, the planner then moves backward across the chart and fills in statements for each year. In the training example, a statement that all 1000 managers and engineers will be trained by year + 3 might be suspect if nothing was done in training for the first 3 years and then a training blitz was held in the last year.

The training objective is also suspect if the planner has not selected a methodology until year + 2. In other words, the completed plan must pass a sort of parity check in both horizontal and vertical directions. In each category the planner states what the objective is and what will be done to meet the objective. If resources or technology are not available in any given year, then the plan has problems. If resources or technology do not allow horizontal components to be completed each year, the plan is likewise in trouble. Key change elements (methodology, tools, training, and metrics) were selected for this example because they will lead to a balanced program. Other elements can be added; other ways to develop the framework and complete the plan can be introduced.

The important point is that the technology transition manager would do well to have such a plan in hand to convince top management that there is a long-term program and that the program will address today's immediate needs. While this seems like quite a bit of work to get a good plan together, there is a bonus for getting an approved plan. A successful plan will have stated and measurable goals for each year. When top management approves a plan, you do not have to resell them on the plan each succeeding year. They are already comfortable with the plan, and proven results for this year will gain further support for next year. Contrast this with the "plan du jour" approach, and the advantages are obvious.

As this and the next three chapters cover the proper way to approach technology transitions, there will be some who say that there is no way they can afford the time and effort to do all these things, even though they might be terrific things to do. A quicker implementation path will be given in each chapter. The quicker path is usually not the optimum solution.

The quicker path here is to find some other company, software team, or group that very closely resembles yours, find out if they have had success, and do what they did. It is always a good idea to visit other companies to learn more about software, and many companies willingly share a surprising amount of information in areas of productivity and quality. This is also shown in the number and content of papers presented at conferences. The problem with conferences is that it is sometimes hard to rate the quality of the papers. However, a visit to a company will yield a very good feel for what they have done and how successful they have been. This is also true for visits to other countries. I have visited many software companies and departments in the United States, Canada, Europe, Japan, Korea, and elsewhere and found that they are almost always gracious and very helpful. Productivity and quality data and successes can be shared in many instances without revealing product plans or strategies. If you present a calling card that says you are a quality or productivity professional, you will probably fare better than if you present a card that says software professional. (It is unfair to have two sets of cards printed.) In general, the closer a technology is to accepted practice, the more willingly others will share. If they have had a particularly bad experience in trying something, they also seem willing to share, especially if you lead by saying you have had some less-than-ideal experiences. In any event, visits do provide useful information.

Timing Variables

There are some external factors that can influence timing, both in planning and executing. First-timers have their biggest problem with the lack of a firm base upon which to build or change. While the final goal is not a rigid process with layers of bureaucracy, there must be something of a repeatable, predictable process before change can be planned and executed.

One indication of this process is the presence of a living life cycle that is understood and followed throughout the software organization. If you have a life cycle in name only, try reviving it by a new promotion campaign. If it cannot be revised, begin a new life cycle.

Transition Risk

The longer a group waits to start a technology change, the further behind they are—or believe themselves to be—and the further they believe they must move on the first cut. This belief often leads to risking a technology transition, which is not prudent. Risk is acceptable, but if one of the most important objectives is to get a permanent, viable organization in place for the technology transitions described in this book, then early successes are important. One way to accomplish this goal is to solve some of the most pressing problems in the detection and correction category. Many of these problems have very serious consequences but in fact can be solved by minor changes to existing processes. In the language of baseball, hit a couple of these over the fence, and longer-term technology transition funding will be yours. Do not pick one major long-term transition that will leapfrog a trailing group to the forefront of technology. This transition will require long-term support with no intermediate return and risk failure or limited success at the end of the multiyear plan.

Timing Variations

Study actual releases of software tools and platforms and prevailing winds of technology change. It was not so long ago that the accepted wisdom was to have a monolithic database with the marble platform; all data were in one physical location, supported by rigid data access mechanisms. Today we know that these have been less than totally successful, and flexibility is needed. Marble should become component, and monolith should become modular and distributed; data access mechanisms are customized to make access simple and efficient; distributed data allow rapid access from all points on the network. The first generation of monolithic database pioneers who put all these data into one central location are now struggling to make the transition to distributed databases. Large databases appeared to be the ultimate solution but were only part of the solution. This ties into the notion in the preceding paragraph; do not bet the company on a giant-leap-forward, single-package solution. To generalize, such a solution is probably the wrong time at any time.

Variations in company cultures can affect technology transition timing. Although companies can appear to be the same on the outside, the climate for change can be quite different on the inside. Age can also make a difference. In general, the older and more established companies will find it more difficult to change, but they probably have the advantage of stable processes from which to base the change. Newer companies have the advantage of fewer processes and commitments to those processes, but they also have more difficulty in settling into the discipline required for software engineering.

The last timing caveat is the changing customer and market. While investing heavily in your present language, you find out that your present language has limitations that prevent your meeting emerging customer needs. While investing in a single-project management tool, you now find that an advanced spreadsheet package is necessary to support future business. You cannot survey the world and then make a multiyear plan that will work without yearly modification. Although one of the advantages of a longer-term plan is the continued support of upper management, the plan must be modified each year to reflect these timing changes and other changes as well. If the plan has good long-term goals and objectives, these changes will not affect the fundamental direction or progress of the plan. You will have no problem in explaining these yearly "course corrections" to top management.

THE MIDDLE MANAGER

The middle manager deserves some of the highest praise for managing in software situations that have strained crafters to the limits. The middle manager was accustomed to having control of his or her domain, although there was not always order within the domain. Outside directives were usually issued at a high level, and most technical decisions were made at this level.

The middle manager in software development environments is the top level of technical "knower." Some general managers understand technical details to a degree, but in most instances they really do not have complete understanding. This is one of the reasons why top management is often much easier to sell on software engineering than middle managers. Top management understands benefits but does not understand what it will take to get there from here. You can almost hear the well-intentioned but nonsoftware executive saying, "If I order them to start coding everything with an object-oriented language, will that solve the problem?" The executive is frustrated when it becomes obvious that this question strains credulity among technical managers.

Conversely, engineers understand benefits and technology, but they do not understand or consider all the change factors we are now examining. Middle managers have very tight schedules, which allow no spare time; they must always attempt projects that use proven technologies because software variables will inevitably make the sure things risky. The last of the knowers in the management chain is also the last level of management to be able to approach the problem with a commonsense outlook. The software middle manager is, therefore, in a position to make or break the technology transition manager who attempts large-scale changes.

The technology transition manager must find a way to work successfully with middle managers. The technology transition manager should not issue directives unless he or she is in a direct-line management position. In any event, ordering middle managers will only alienate them, and technology change is a relatively fragile flower. Middle managers must be convinced that this is the right thing to do and the right time to do it. If the technology transition manager is also successful in selecting middle managers who are movers and shakers, then technology transition can be accelerated.

The middle manager must accept the philosophy and approach to change, the methodology and tools to be used, and the fact that it will require his or her full support to make a successful technology transition. Although top managers can be briefed, middle managers must be fully informed. (Some top managers are willing only to be briefed; they do not attend training. The agile technology transition manager will therefore schedule some "briefing sessions," which can take a day or two.) Middle managers also must understand how technology change solves an actual, or impending, problem. The technology change program must become part of their formal business plan. Productivity and quality improvements must become part of the culture if long-term defect prevention strategy is to work.

Middle managers must have a way to win. If all credit for change appears to go to the technology transition manager and team, but the middle manager is portrayed as a doddering doer who had to be pushed, the middle manager will not willingly participate. If the middle manager can get a project done on time—with higher quality—and at the same time be seen as a doer with vision, then the change manager has a winning combination.

The final point to be made regarding the middle manager is that technology transition must not create the impression that it is going to integrate, automate, and drone the software engineering process. Software design and specification have always been, are now, and will always be a human activity. The middle manager must understand that technology transition is simply automating the routine parts of the process and moving toward engineering in much the same fashion as the hardware engineering evolution. Middle managers must understand that their destinies are to become software engineering managers, with technology transition skills enhancing their possibilities for general management.

In many software operations the middle manager feels threatened and is basically afraid of change. This is often due to the fact that the middle manager is overextended and has little time to keep abreast of technology developments. The middle manager is still trying to cope with today's problems and the change manager advocates a transition that does not necessarily address those problems.

MANAGEMENT APPROACHES TO TECHNOLOGY TRANSITIONS

We start with the following choices and assumptions.

- Between an evolutionary or revolutionary approach, we chose evolutionary.
- Between people are basically trustworthy or devious, we chose trustworthy.
- Between willing or lazy, we chose willing.

We then want to show people direction, give them correct management support, and get out of their way. This is the best pragmatic approach because there are thousands of variables that affect success or failure of these transitions, and we need enthusiasm, drive, and talent of the engineers. This all sounds so obvious until one hears the horror story of a failed experiment in which engineers were told they would have to adopt a new technology, like it or not. They did not like it; the technology apparently could not stand being disliked and therefore died.

Successful Approaches and Philosophies

Given enthusiasm and trust, each of the following approaches or philosophies can be successful in creating technology change.

- The Johnny Appleseed model features one individual who goes about teams spreading good news, leaving literature, and encouraging new technology to take root. There are large companies where one dedicated individual has made an enormous difference. There are coordination problems as technologies take root, but that one individual has organized conferences and workshops that have allowed various teams to get together, share what worked, and agree on common future directions.

- The communications model uses publications, video, peer challenge, recognition, and reward. Elements of this model are used in other models, but it can also be used in a stand-alone mode.

- The franchise model has a larger group headed by a technology transition manager, and that group gets teams to buy into the franchise. The teams do exactly what they are told, follow the proven formula, and have a guarantee of success.

- In the middle-of-the-road franchise model, a franchise team proves that new technology works in this company, develops some materials, and then exports the technology for teams to complete the implementation. In training, a similar type of franchise becomes a "train the trainer" model. In the larger technology framework, it also creates "champions" who enthusiastically support technology.

- In the frontal assault model, teams are told they must change; the technology transition manager and team go on site to provide them with tools and information.

- An infiltration model selects individuals who are brought into the technology transition manager's camp and given a period of training and hands-on experience. The trainee then returns to the team to do the work of the technology transition manager. This is slightly tongue-in-cheek; it should not be confused with the more legitimate model, where the technology transition manager has an on-site representative at each team. These representatives become the eyes, ears, and hands that fulfill the technology change.

- A variation of the preceding model has special teams created to use the new technology, with one team member being expert in the technology and its use. Upon successful completion of this project, some team members join other newly forming teams.

- In the "potted plant" model, which is my favorite, a project is carefully selected to allow new technology a fair chance for success. The project is "potted" in the sense that all nutrients are provided in balanced proportion, and all independent variables are controlled to the greatest extent possible. Every team member receives full training; there is also ongoing consulting. A full set of metrics is used to measure success and to allow a detailed examination in the event of failure. Every team member has all tools running in the correct environment. The programming project to be completed using the new technology requires some innovation, but it is demonstrably doable by another existing tool or technology.

Movers and shakers like to do potted plant projects. They have a higher probability of success than some of the other models, and success is well documented. The same formula can then be used to initiate other projects using the same technology.

A word of caution concerning my enthusiasm for the potted-plant approach. I have seen it work well in U.S.-based software laboratories. It may be that another approach will prove better suited to other cultures. The Japanese term KAIZEN takes the guiding principle of continuous improvement and applies it to all activities. KAIZEN includes work improvements, home improvements, personal improvements, and so on. Many Japanese quality and productivity gains are attributed to Kaizen.

The KAIZEN approach is process-focused; results will improve if process improvements are attained. This process approach is suited to long-term planning. KAIZEN focuses on change that is planned, methodical, and consistent. In contrast, many innovations are revolutionary in nature and are done with sudden shocks to the old process.

Perhaps most importantly, KAIZEN involves all, while potted plants involve a few. The potted-plant approach will allow selected projects to shine, but it will ultimately require a KAIZEN approach to get everyone using the new technology. KAIZEN involves the group; innovation involves individuals who are often willing to risk failure by attempting new techniques.

The potted-plant approach allows the best opportunity for a new technology to succeed. If the infrastructure then allows others to share in success by adopting new technology over time, the potted-plant/KAIZEN concatenation allows new technologies to prove themselves and then be adopted in an orderly transition.

The preceding approaches listed can also be influenced by the nature and origin of the software engineering platform or tools used in the experiment. If the tools are accepted practices and are purchased from a reputable vendor, then training, support, and ways to ensure success should be readily available. If the platform or tools are closer to a pioneering practice, then the vendor should be willing to provide additional support or incentives. The hardware options can be categorized as follows:

- Homegrown tools come in two categories: tools for internal use only and tools for internal use and then for sale. Internal tools generally receive poorer documentation and support, and the trend is to attempt to upgrade them to meet standards and then to sell them to customers.
- Purchased tools that are available as either components or turnkey systems. The trend is components, but many vendors promise all of the remaining components in the fabled next release.
- A whole new system or new components that must be integrated into an existing system.
- Distributed or centralized platforms.

The type of hardware, maturity of the platform and tools, and documentation, support, and training all affect model selection.

In all these approaches a successful wide-scale implementation must include promotion of the technology and its advantages, recognition for those who pioneer and succeed, and a continued promotion of ongoing change processes. Even potted plants die without attention.

The technology transition manager is a big job, but it can done by one individual who is "big" in spirit. If all activities and choices seem overwhelming, it is because you have not gotten started. As soon as technology transition managers or change teams get started, they begin to gain confidence. Successful teams usually have a good plan that is properly executed, but others have done it with intuition and cleverness.

There are other approaches to the technology transition manager role. It is possible to have a middle manager or an individual engineer be successful in this work. It is also possible for informal groups to achieve remarkable success. If you don't think you can do a full-blown plan, follow your best instincts. But get started. The Silicon Valley story is told of the engineer who complained to an executive that the company seemed to follow a policy of "ready, fire, aim." The executive responded that such a policy was superior to another policy of "ready, ready, ready." If you don't shoot, you cannot hit the target. There should be a policy to encourage technology transitions, and a system of rewards for recognizing success.

13

Software Engineering Transition Planning

THE BUSINESS OF SOFTWARE TECHNOLOGY TRANSITION

Planning is the Achilles' heel of technology transition processes. Only a few schools of engineering place emphasis on business or project planning, and of those who are skilled in planning, not all are intimately familiar with technology transitions. As most impetus for technology change comes from those who believe that they understand the technology to be changed, there is a tendency to minimize planning. There are bound to be some readers who at this point are wondering if it really is worth the effort to read on; the good parts have already been read. But the enormous changes that must occur in the transition to software engineering surely require planning. As an inducement to those who must have their technology "fix," there is a return to software technology futures later in the book. An M.B.A. degree is not required; a little common sense, combined with experience, will go a long way.

Technology transition planning includes both long-term and short-term elements. Even a one-time project should have some of the planning elements that are outlined in this chapter. There are many reasons for developing, reviewing, gaining approval, and sharing a plan. Let's look at the key reasons.

PLANNING VALIDATION

Technical validation of a plan is critical to its success. There will doubtless be lively debate if some reviewers are normal, healthy engineers and technical managers, but the review process does not mean adopting all proposed changes or fully answering objections to everyone's satisfaction. The technical review looks at the plan from the perspective of objectives, resources, schedules, and metrics. It is quite possible that a reviewer will spot a flaw in the plan that can be corrected prior to getting in trouble. The reason for emphasizing the technical review is that there is often a tendency to go for management approval and the money and then get on with it.

Validation can also be done by outside sources. This is especially helpful if outside reviewers are familiar with the process and can provide a valid critique of the proposed approach. Timing of outside validation varies according to the temper and climate of the group. Usually an inside review is held first to see if the plan is in the ballpark and to avoid wasting higher-priced reviewer time. However, if inside reviewers have the power of instant termination, then outside reviewers may go first. Outside reviewers are sometimes used to provide validation, which top management requires before giving approval. And they are occasionally used as an insurance policy by a wary technical manager. If the project should fail, the technical manager points to the outside reviewers and says, "Don't blame me; they said it would work."

One word of caution to those who decide to try outside reviewers for the first time: Most of the consultants and reviewers are some of the hardest-working, most dedicated professionals I know. However, there is the possibility that the reviewer sees this as a chance to get additional contract time. Watch for the item in the report stating that the project holds great promise but should have some ongoing consulting, which the reviewer just happens to be able to provide. What do you do if this happens? Get a second opinion before signing the additional contract. This is not to say that the consultant would never provide full service; you just may not need what is being offered.

GOAL ALIGNMENT

Validation allows the project to be aligned and verified to see that it meets company goals or, if there is an existing technology change program, that it also meets those goals. Validation can spot duplicate efforts or efforts of a similar nature that are heading in different directions. If validation uncovers the fact that another group has already started to do a similar project, but they have chosen another methodology and tool, what do you do? First, avoid possible confrontations and thoughts of winning the contest. You want to do the correct technical solution. Try to determine why their plan led them in another direction. Then see if there is any objective data to prove that either side has a significantly weaker position. If the technology is new or if there is no clearly superior selection, then agree on criteria and hold a "bakeoff." Both groups give their projects the best possible run, gather data, and then see how their results compare to criteria. Do not attempt to bias criteria; do make every effort to have criteria accurately reflect the company's needs.

There is also the possibility of planning conflicts at higher levels. If the company is large enough to have more than one division or multiple groups, then it is possible that the potential conflict could occur well above the individual tool level—perhaps at the group level. This highlights the need for a common strategy, a common set of goals, and some sort of technology transition manager or change coordinator. When we spoke of the potential of potted plants, the positive values of providing all nutrients and focusing the sunshine of technical training, consulting, and support were discussed. If a larger company is truly interested in accomplishing the transition to software engineering, then it needs much more than a series of potted plants; it needs a planned community with the software "parks" and "lakes" becoming an integral part of the living software environment. If such a software engineering community were planned in your industrial park, then there should be minimal planning conflicts. If not, things can quickly degenerate to a crafter's version of Star Wars. The elements that can help to prevent such an unfortunate waste of company resources merit some discussion.

NEEDS ASSESSMENT

In needs assessment the customer is the software team. Internal team needs are dictated by the ultimate needs of external customers, and internal needs must be met by the planning process. What is the problem to be solved? What is needed to get the job done? What resources already exist?

The danger is that answers may not be suitable for the planning process. If the team says they need faster compilers, editors, and debuggers, they may be focusing on the present process without thought about process improvement. If the team says all new tools, it may be influenced by a technology transition using applied development or pioneering practices. The call for better and faster tools may also be inspired by the "creeping elegance" syndrome. This elegance also manifests itself in design specifications that grow to meet the minds of the designers. Although it is very important to ask the staff what they need and to have some of them review the project or transition plan, it is also necessary to check for some of these biases.

One of the best checks is to go back and see exactly what needs must be met. This validation can be done by internal data gathered as part of the normal business process and used to make certain that it solves the problem. Validation can be done by other groups or outside experts who use their own techniques. This same principle applies to validating the solution. You could have identified the correct problem and then selected the wrong solution. Or, you could have selected an answer to a question no one is asking. The plan should clearly state the problem and the solution. The problem should accurately state needs; the plan should fully address those needs.

There are many productivity factors to take into account in assessing needs and preparing the plan:

- processes and possible improvements
- tools and the degree of congruence with the process
- skills and the degree of obsolescence
- objectives and a competitive perspective
- facilities
- equipment and support
- motivation, morale, and the need to enjoy work
- management and project support
- documentation, training, and consulting
- marketing and promotion
- recognition and rewards

Much of this information should be available in the information systems used to run the company. Some information might be in human resources (personnel), some in financial databases, and a lot in project databases. As part of the planning process for a multiyear plan, planners should consider if a productivity and/or quality database is required. If there is missing information, which is almost always the case, then the planner has to ask how long one can go without the information. If it is possible to used crafted techniques to get the information, that will get the project started, but it will not guide improvements and transitions during the next 5 years.

A fully operational information system allows planners to know how team time is being spent now. Many teams state that they spend less than 20% of their time actually programming, and teams often state that 25% or more of their time is spent in meetings. This should be known, not only to understand long-term needs for changes to time allocations but also to accurately scope needs and requirements for doing shorter-term projects using new tools and technologies. Twenty-five percent of the time spent in meetings may be good, bad, or not enough. Even if the percentage is correct now, it may have to be increased in the future. Unless data are available to tell us where we are, meetings will probably follow present trends and consume larger percentages of available time.

There are also needs posed by software obsolescence. How can you tell when your software is obsolete? There are two guidelines. The first is time. The federal government estimates that software is probably obsolete when it is 8 to 10 years old or older. This estimate is based on software of the 1970s and early 1980s and changes in technologies that we have examined in this book. There are exceptions, and this obsolescence parameter will change over time, but for today it serves as a good guideline. The second guideline is to see if systems used today will fully meet the projected needs and requirements stated in the 3- to 5-year plan. If they do not, there is a problem, and a technology transition should be part of the plan.

After determining that some software systems are obsolete, the overall software plan should address obsolescence with one of these four options:

1. total replacement
2. major redesign and modification
3. conversion or enhancement
4. phase-out in the next 12 to 18 months

Remember that obsolete systems may also have personnel who need upgrading of skills. (No human being ever becomes obsolete; they can be denied the chance to learn. The only circumstance that should allow for a human being to be phased out is their own personal choice to transfer to another activity.)

The transition to new technologies presents a mandate for management to understand new technologies, the present rate of change within the company, and the rate of change necessary to attain a leadership position. Management must know which systems are obsolete, the estimated number of systems that will become obsolete in the next 3 to 5 years, and how to plan for proper resource management of technology transitions. Top-management objectives and plans should focus on software resources to meet the goals of the company, not merely on hasty implementation of software engineering tools in an attempt to correct an obsolescence problem.

The final caveat is to be certain that the company's needs can justify a major transition to software engineering. It is sometimes easy to sell technology with high-power demonstrations and vague promises of technological leadership. Software engineering must have demonstrated capacity to meet a proven need, and it must have a high probability of success in meeting the need.

GOALS AND OBJECTIVES

Corporate goals and objectives should make a definitive statement about where the company must go. Goals and objectives should be clear, concise, achievable, measurable, and consistent. They should fully meet the needs of customers. The clear statement of goals and objectives should also state the return on investment that is required by the company. Goals and objectives should be flexible enough to allow for some adjustments to the tactics that will be used to achieve them.

Corporate goals should be high-level and broad-brush and should allow for group and division creativity in selecting strategies and specific goals for success. President Kennedy set a very good high-level goal when he stated that the United States should put human beings on the moon and bring them back to earth safely within 10 years. The goal was clear, the criteria were clear, and there was no ambiguity about whether or not the goal would be achieved. The president did not say how to accomplish the goal. Thus NASA could have dematerialized the people here on earth and rematerialized them on the moon, they could send them in a bus, or they could use a rocket. It was up to the engineers to find the best tactical way to solve the problem.

If the high-level corporate goal is to become a leader in software engineering in the next 10 years, then there are a variety of ways to meet this goal. The corporate strategy could be to develop proprietary software engineering tools, or to have tools custom-made, or to purchase ready-made tools. A variety of strategies are discussed in a page or two. Project-level goals are far more specific. A project goal might be to use C++ to successfully deliver a completed version control program in 6 months. Notice even at this level the goal leaves many options and strategies available. Proper goal setting allows maximum creativity in solving technical objectives.

Some leading computer manufacturers have stated their software goals in publications or in speeches by their chief executives. These stated goals include

- a 10-times improvement in software quality in 10 years;
- a 10-times improvement in software quality in 5 years;
- a 20% to 30% quality improvement in each software release;
- halving development cycle time (while improving quality) in 5 years.

Software quality is often measured in customer-reported defects. There are several problems if success in meeting these goals is measured only in terms of customer-reported defects. First, a significant reduction in customer-reported defects could be made by simply stopping enhancements and allowing the code to remain the same. Second, the 10-times improvement could be attained but at the result of a higher cost to the company. Third, a 30% improvement in each subsequent release could be attained much more easily if releases were 5 years apart, as compared to the present 1-year to 18-month intervals. Those who set goals should be commended for having had the courage to take action and to publicly state that action. But goals must serve as a rallying point for software teams; their completion must meet the company's business objectives.

Goals and objectives must be believable, especially by those who will accomplish them. Kennedy's goal to put someone on the moon and return him or her to Earth was not believed by all the population, but it was believed and internalized by those working on the project. They understood the risk, they believed technology could meet the challenge, and they knew it was the first step toward the dream of space travel. Software engineering goals can also allow us to dream and make believable plans to move toward that dream. A transition to software engineering without goals can quickly turn a vision into a bad dream.

STRATEGY

Now that we have identified the goals and objectives, how will we meet the customer's needs; how will we win? A winning strategy meets all goals and objectives. Too often a winning strategy has the ring of a speech given at a motivational sales rally. A winning strategy is not hype; it involves approach, positioning, and timing.

A winning software strategy examines needs, goals, and objectives, the present position of the company, and the direction and speed at which the company wishes to move. Strategists must look at goals and determine the best ways to attain them. Perhaps the optimum strategy would be to use small incremental steps over a 10-year time frame. Perhaps it would be to begin with small steps and take a larger step later. Or it might be best to take a large step to catch up and then switch to smaller steps.

Strategists must also decide whether to stick with accepted and proven practices or to venture into the world of pioneering and unproven practices. Strategists must have an understanding of risks involved. It is not sufficient to be willing to take risk. There are some gamblers who simply want a chance to throw the dice; they just know that they will win if they get their chance. They do not understand the odds or betting strategies. The strategist knows the risks and has criteria for deciding where and when to bet. The strategist also knows the software game, strengths and weaknesses of the company, and management's ability to play the software game. The strategist understands the starting software position and whether the company has a good hardware position or a good competitive position.

Strategy includes recognition of the present position. If a large-scale conversion to a new software process is required, then the upgrade and conversion elements are included in the strategy. Are all preparations to be done in advance and then the entire company converted at midnight? Or is it to be a phased conversion, with each division coming on-line separately? When one of the Scandinavian countries switched from driving on the left side of the road to driving on the right, it was recognized that the strategy must be a midnight conversion. After months of planning and preparation, the entire road system was shut down one midnight, and thousands of workers began changing road signs and signals and repainting marks on the pavement. At dawn the conversion was complete, and all drivers began driving on the right side of the road. The transition was handled with a minimum of disruption and confusion. Imagine the pandemonium if the strategy had been to do a gradual conversion, starting with the freeways, over a 6-month period. An appropriate strategy is absolutely essential to success.

TACTICAL PLANS AND BUDGETS

If planning is anathema to most engineers, then budgeting surely ranks even lower in popularity. Let's try to see it from top management's perspective. Most companies operate in a sort of "venture capital" mode. There are lots of things to invest in, always more than there are funds to invest, and there are many potentially profitable ventures in the total set of investment options. At higher levels, management watches dollar flow. Dollars are the universal common denominator. Even if the analysis of investments in software and investments in shop floor control seem to be an apples and oranges comparison, it becomes straightforward when converted to dollars and return on investment. Dollars are the great "rationing coupons"; they should be allocated according to need, but the need must be customers' needs. Therefore, proposed software projects must ultimately be translated into how well they will meet those needs. Those who learn how to translate projects and technology transitions to investment dollars and return on investment will ultimately succeed; those who fight the system will get dollars that "can be spared."

The secret to translating software projects successfully to investments is to be able to state these projects in terms of potential risk of not doing them and in terms of both short-term and long-term return to the company. It is not sufficient to say that our competition will crush us; the potential loss or gain in dollars must be shown in terms of return on investment. There are many good books and courses available on financial return on investment, and our treatment here focuses on the special nature of software. There are several ways to approach the return factor, and all of them involve showing cost, which can be done in several ways:

- The cost of poor quality. A report can show the cost of poor quality software processes, or a projected trend to higher costs caused by quality degradation.

- The cost of development. In this case quality might be acceptable, but productivity is poor and getting worse. Once again, productivity can be accurately measured and compared to competitors. The cost of development can also be reported in terms of timely releases of new products.
- The cost of maintenance. Software is released, and it has the highest costs in the industry to keep it running. Or, it costs more due to more frequent upgrades and earlier obsolescence.

Software managers have (or can get) much of this software quality and productivity data. Business plans and reports using these data permit successful communication in the boardroom. Executive understanding and approval provides support for a successful tactical plan and accompanying budget. However, the tactical plan must show planned technology transitions, why these transitions will satisfy the goals and objectives, and the budget figures indicating how much they will cost and what will be returned to the company. There should also be several high-level charts to show technology gain (including positions of the competition); these gains should be clearly stated milestones.

Obviously the project size affects size of the tactical plan. We are dealing here with a multiyear plan to make a major software transition in a large company. However, elements of the plan apply to projects of all sizes, and the elements should be included in every top-notch plan.

The shortcut here is to get to the biggest problems today. If long-term needs and plans are not clear or are difficult to sell to executives, then focus on the near term. The best way to sell the plan to executives is to follow the principles just listed, but have the project solve one or more of the biggest existing problems. These problems are usually already known and prioritized; in many cases they are supplied by user's surveys or user's correspondence. User needs are the key to gaining approval for technology transitions. When attempting to sell a major long-term transition to a new software methodology, first sell the need and urgency and then begin to sell the solution. In the case of immediate needs that are clearly recognized, sell the solution. Go for deliverables; go for the shortest solid solution to the software problem; set aggressive schedules that can be met. If management agrees with the stated need, half the approval is attained. Even if management does not agree with a specific plan, they will probably agree to an iteration of the plan.

Returning to large-scale transitions, do not hesitate to be honest if the longer-term, larger software process change will not show a return on investment for another year or two. In this situation it is simply a longer investment period. Show cumulative payback and compare it with the cost of not doing the project. Being rigorously honest about the first year's start up costs saves the beating that will surely occur when executives review progress at the end of the first year and discover there is still no positive return on investment.

Another approach, which is used when executives do not favor multiyear investments in software, is mentioned here only to record that it has been done successfully, but it has risks. And I certainly do not endorse the "refrigerator sales strategy." This approach involves selling them in and then selling them up. The salesperson gets the customer to agree that a refrigerator is needed and then begins to sell up to more expensive models. If at any point the customer balks, the salesperson can always back down to a lower-priced model. But the customer is vulnerable to this sales strategy as long as it is agreed that a refrigerator is needed. The salesman will continue to try to sell more expensive models. This same scam has been worked by getting the executives to agree that something must be done about software but not telling them what CASE or software engineering might cost. The danger to such a strategy is that executives stay sold on the idea that something must be done about software but decide to replace the person who should do something about it.

Planning and budgeting remain weak areas for software development groups. This is unfortunate but understandable in the world of crafted software. Times are changing, and it is essential that software managers be able to scope, plan, budget, schedule, and complete software projects as planned. Software development groups and software tools are viewed as a "logical building"; they are an investment and can be compared to other investments. As knowledge is the "material" of the future, our logical software buildings are very attractive investment opportunities. We must know how to present them in the business language of decision makers.

14

Software Technology Transition Steps

GETTING SOFTWARE TECHNOLOGY TRANSITIONS STARTED

A well-planned technology transition program is the key to a timely and efficient technology transfer. It is very good management practice to have a program for any size transition; it is essential for software team, group, or company transitions. It would be easy to write a seemingly endless chapter by covering numerous permutations and combinations, including long checklists and lists of questions and exhortations to action; lists and exhortations will not work on all software development groups. The following generic guidelines and assumptions will help to guide us in our quest for a well-planned and well-executed program:

- Assume a crossing of technology boundaries; this could be a minor crossing such as initiation of a practice new to this group or it could be a major shift to artificial intelligence. The assumption is that the technology is new to this group and that it has not been used successfully by the group at an earlier time.
- An extension of this assumption is that technology transition has not been used successfully at any other location that is closely connected

with the team or group to be transitioned. The idea here is to face the challenge of starting a transition that otherwise might take a long time to occur "naturally." When a new practice is successfully used by some of the team or a nearby team, it will probably spread throughout your team.

- Assume software development teams only. This may be a multisite or companywide transition, but our transition steps apply to software development activities. The reason for this restriction is that many of the transition concepts discussed in this book have a generic application to all technologies. If a newly formed transition team decides to make their first attempt with a software development transition that also changes manufacturing, marketing, and support, it places the whole venture at risk. Better to begin with the development function only and then expand the transition practice as experience and confidence dictate.

- Assume an orderly transition with a definite completion date. Unless this is the "Johnny Appleseed" activity previously described, it should be a transition that is doable, controllable, and predictable. Even if the transition is one of those giant catch-up leaps forward, it must be done with risks understood and controlled.

- Assume that there is no external formula, recipe, or "cookbook" that will solve this specific transition problem. None will be given here. Variances between companies, among companies, and across multinationals are just too great to allow formula solutions. Transition experts have to create the recipe and develop their own best practices. After having some successes and understanding the process, it might be possible to develop more exacting guidelines to be used throughout your company. Be very careful when using recipes based on successes in other environments. When a typist, clerk, or someone not familiar with computers or PCs asks how to do something at the terminal, that person will frequently write exactly what they are told on a little sheet and post it nearby. They will then faithfully type the exact sequence each time the same situation arises. When the day comes that an almost identical situation occurs, they type the sequence, only to find that it does not work in this case. They often attempt permutations and in some cases do data damage before help arrives. The same thing can happen here. We must understand the process, the user's needs, and what has happened in order to be able to carefully modify the recipe.

Step One: Assess Needs

Everyone has a customer, and it is essential that the customer's needs are fully met. Even if you think that you understand those needs, it should be demonstrated that the proposed technology transition will meet a valid, high-priority customer need. If I "just know" that my customer must have something for his or her own good, it is probably a subjective judgment call. There is also a risk that the customer will tell me what is wanted rather than what is needed. The faster compiler might be wanted, but the design tools and methodologies are needed. One of the best techniques for learning about needs is a properly designed and administered survey. There are a variety of surveys; let us look at the ones that offer the most promise.

Product surveys will provide the surest sign of ultimate need. Information can be gathered from customer surveys, product marketing professionals, user groups, and reports of product problems. There are also a variety of other surveys and measurements. Please beware of peddlers who pretend to be product-marketing professionals. A peddler goes from door to door and tries to sell whatever happens to be in the bag that day. The professional salesperson, backed by the professional product manager, understands what the customer needs and how best to match products to that need. The professional marketeer can give valuable information; the peddler will mislead by encouraging another approach. Also, the ultimate need of the external customer may require some translation to plan a software transition to meet needs of the development team (the internal customer). For example, a request for performance improvement may be solved by the team providing an intelligent configurator rather than spending days trying to optimize code in order to compensate for less than optimum configurations.

Software baseline metrics provide one of the best ways to determine where the software development teams are and to point out where the team is less than average when compared with other teams or organizations. These metrics will not tell exactly what to do, they will not select the correct methodology or tool, but they will guide thinking about the most likely sources of the problem. Some managers who have reviewed results of these surveys are surprised to see areas where they are ahead or behind. The results often allow them to chart a new course for technology transitions. Other managers will say that such a survey taught them nothing new. They already knew about the problems and relative position of their teams compared with others. These managers will often admit that the survey did get them and their teams thinking about the problem in an organized way. The baseline survey caused them to stop and focus on their problems. For an external technology transition manager and/or change team, a baseline survey can be a way to get buy-in. Even a Silicon Valley–based team must want to change before any transition will take; all other software development groups are similar.

The need for change can come from obsolescence pressure. This is one of the most painful pressures, and it causes increasing discomfort over time. Early detection is the best course of action. This can be accomplished by having a good knowledge of the literature, current tools available, and the competition. Obsolescence can also be detected by the reactions of visitors from other teams within the company, honest consultant reports, and smug looks on the faces of technical visitors. If technology is truly obsolete, the need for change is obvious.

The need for change can be accurately assessed by consultants. However, this is trickier than it looks. There are many consultants who specialize in various subdisciplines of software. The problem is there are not as many who specialize in the processes described in this book. One of the great dangers of specialization is the natural tendency of the specialist to see everything from one perspective. A surgeon might fall into the trap of suggesting surgery for almost everything, whereas a neurologist or internal medicine specialist might recommend another method of treatment. The artificial intelligence or structured design software specialists might also be tempted to tell you that what you need is something from their toolkit. Please note that this is not done with any conscious intent to mislead; it is the normal way that specialists think. The problem is that all teams could do with better design, and so any recommendation to upgrade design tools is probably worthwhile; but design may not be the highest-priority problem. It may not even be near the top of the list. It may not solve the problem that is causing top management to worry about software. And there may possibly be a few consultants who would not hesitate to recommend a hearty measure of their services. Although free enterprise is good for transitions, consultant enterprises are hardly free.

The best way to handle the consultant process is to follow the medical example. Do not hesitate to get second and third opinions. If all consultants agree that design is needed, then revisit the list of those who can help, and select one, if appropriate. Consultants are one of the best ways to get started; they are also invaluable for transition groups that are still learning the transition craft.

Another very effective way to assess internal need is to hold a combination seminar and workshop. Gather some of the best technical movers and shakers from among various teams and bring them together for a day or two. Begin the session with an introduction about the need for software evolution and the needs of the company. Present technical information relating to the proposed area of change—for example, software inspections or analysis and design. Do not give detailed tutorials; they can come later. Just get everyone calibrated so workshops will not stray from stated objectives. Then hold workshop sessions, preferably dividing the big problem into its major components. Have workshop groups take half an hour to prepare reports. Then hear reports, agree on needs and proposed steps, and formulate an action plan. Get agreement before the meeting ends, and the transition is launched. This type of seminar or workshop works best in a focused area. If the session is held simply to agree that a problem exists, with no idea of a solution, the result is a phenomenon sociologists describe as a mutual celebration of traditional values (in this instance, the problem). The seminar workshop technique is presented here because it does have tremendous need validation and buy-in power.

The seminar workshop is but one form of verification. Another form is verification by walking around. If the transition team spends some time talking to engineers whose environment will be changed, it not only promotes approval and support, it also provides verification. A word of caution regarding the walking-around process; there are many different types of engineers, and universal agreement that a technology transition is a good idea should make the proposed transition suspect. Not everyone will agree; the trick is to be certain that transition specialists understand why they do not agree. If the problem is that they simply do not understand the potential of the transition, that objection can be overcome by the formal training and promotion elements of the program. If they say that the transition solves the wrong problem, dig deeper and understand what they think the problem is. If 100% of those engineers say it is a bad idea, consider a drastic rework of the technology transition program. If 100% of the people sampled say you are doomed to failure, they are probably correct (even if the program is 100% correct), because the program will not have their support. One approach here might be to hold a seminar and give them some technical information as well as benefits and proven results. If this still does not change their minds, be very cautious.

Verification should be done by some orderly process with categories and metrics. Try to quantify the problem, proposed solution, and responses to surveys and interviews; record some actual quotes. Be certain that everyone understands the proposed solution.

Part of this data should be used to prioritize team needs and customer needs and to show some connectivity between technology transition and customer needs. This sounds obvious, but it is not automatic as there is constant temptation to go ahead and do something without objectively knowing it is the top priority. The reason for stressing this activity is that Pareto lives. It will be true that about 80% of the total customer needs are included in the top 20% of the items on a complete list of needs. Working on a lower-priority item (in the lower 80%) will at best meet only 20% of the total customer needs.

After validation at the problem and solution level, move to a higher level of validation. If everyone agrees that a specific design methodology, tool, training, and metrics package would be just what is needed, validate that the customer's need is connected and met. A major team shift might produce the excitement and interest that will get everyone happy and productive, but it also might be similar to the classic "Hawthorne effect," in which any internal change produces temporary improvements, but over time things slide back into the regular pattern. If transition solves an immediate customer problem, it should also have longer-term effects and benefits.

One final word about needs. Be certain that the customer's problem will be solved by the one thing that you have selected to do from the team's internal needs list. For example, suppose the team list of needs contains 30 entries, listed in the following priority:

1. version control
2. structured testing
3. structured analysis
4. structured design
5. refresher courses

   .
   .
   .

28. quieter environment

   .
   .
   .

You have chosen to implement 3 and 4. However, 5 and 28 must also be implemented to achieve your projected targets. Understanding that the need for a better working environment can actually negate most of the gain from application of the new methodology and tools will help to avoid failure. This same problem can occur in meeting customer's needs. If you prioritize and group a total customer's needs list, find 95 separate needs, and decide to meet the top 10 needs, you may still miss some of the customers, who need 75 and 85. You may even attend to the top 10 needs and subsequently find that not one customer is satisfied. In this situation it would be better to derive your list from needs of the top 10 customers. If you fully meet the needs of your top 10 customers, not only are you in pretty good shape, but you have probably also satisfied many other customers.

If knowing the truth shall make you free, then knowing the customer's needs shall free you to pursue the correct solution. Now that we know what is needed, let us see what we have on hand.

Step Two: Assessing Existing Resources

Three caveats help us know our resources:

1. Do not reinvent the wheel.
2. Do not drag something that appears to be round.
3. Do not start large-scale hobby projects.

These can be expanded with some specific examples. If you need to teach the C programming language to engineers, do not automatically decide to get into the university business if the C course is offered at an existing educational institution. If you must teach C on-site, consider using an instructor from a local college or community college; consider using a qualified insider if one is available to teach. Only if C is not available from any other source do you want to consider getting into the training business. C is an easy example because it is taught at many existing educational institutions. Software methodologies and tools training may not be available from local institutions.

Know who is in the training business in your company. In some situations the continuing education program has the needed course; perhaps it is offered via satellite television. In other situations the course is offered by another training group within the company. If another training group already exists but does not offer the course, the group may be willing to start the course if it meets one of their existing needs.

Know how much training comes with tools. Often software tool companies are very anxious to help get their tools installed and used successfully. They will provide courses, often at your site. These courses will usually prove to be less expensive when taught to 12 or more engineers at your site, compared to having 5 engineers fly to a distant city and spend nights in hotels. This can be deceptive because the cost of having an instructor on-site usually runs in the thousands of dollars, but do consider all costs. In many cases it is less expensive and more productive to hold on-site training. Also, some vendors will allow one of your engineers to teach subsequent offerings of the course at your site as long as you buy the books or written materials from the vendor.

Know if you can recruit teachers from your own teams; know if they can work on a semipermanent or part-time basis. There are other advantages to having qualified trainers in the teams that are going to make the technology transition. Larger companies have an advantage here. A prophet is without honor in the home team. If the trainer does most training for other teams, it usually enhances the stature and effectiveness of the trainer. Trainers enjoy getting a bit of travel, and they learn a great deal about the operation of other teams.

If there is a separate change team with a technology transition manager, consider the "train the trainer" approach instead of the "have an institute" approach. The institute is necessary only for really large training programs. Focusing on thorough training of those who will be trainers is very effective from both an educational and cost point of view. Transition teams can also market the benefits of having a resident trainer; offer an incentive to those teams that agree to have one or more persons who are trained to be trainers.

The final point in assessing internal resources is to know the true cost of those resources. Nothing is free simply because it is internal. The closest thing to free is something already paid for and not presently in use or someone already drawing salary and not currently busy. Persons who appear to be available may require a very large investment before they are equal to a local professor or outside instructor who already knows the material. The professional can get you started quickly; the internal instructors can perhaps be just as effective in the long run. Internal instructors must be dedicated to software engineering education; if they are not, quality of education suffers. Continuing use of internal instructors requires an additional measure of quality control, which is discussed later in this chapter.

Step Three: Methodology Selection

After knowing what we need, where we are, and what we have at hand, methodology selection should be made. This is probably the most important choice that we will make; it is one of the most important ingredients in technology transition, and yet it often is ranked as far less important than tool selection. Methodology selection should be based on the following criteria:

- Where is the methodology on the generic technology transition cycle? If it is not advanced at least as far as the pioneering practice level and if it does not have any proven return on investment, then it should be approached with greater caution.

- Where is the present position of the team or group in relation to the proposed technology? This is a multidimensional positioning. There is an axis showing the position of the proposed technology; an axis showing our present position from a baseline perspective; and an axis showing "adaptability to change" of our team or group. The greater the cumulative distance that we must move, the greater the risk.

- How many factors must change? If change requires new facilities, new hardware, new technology, new personnel, new measures and new policies, then of course the risk is higher. Another way of stating this factor is to estimate the breadth of change.

- Does change fit the present path? Does it fit the long-term plans? It is possible to have a good long-term plan and yet implement a change that answers a question no one is asking? It is possible to take a path that is attractive in the short-term, but fails to meet long-term objectives?

- Who has done a similar technology transition successfully? Do any known success stories resemble our teams or groups? Were they in similar starting positions?

- Is this a proven methodology? Is it a leader?

- Is the methodology on the rise? Beware of climbing on board a methodology meteor to find that it is in reality a fading star.

- Once again, what do team "customers" (those who will use the methodology in the team) think? Do they know the methodology and fully understand it? If they do not, the transition will definitely take greater effort. If they do know and have objections, be certain that you understand the nature and merit of those objections.

If the answers point to high risk, do not be discouraged. The answer is often to set up a pilot project and verify results before running a large test. Think of the chemical engineers who prove a process on a small scale before building a billion-dollar refinery. In these software situations it would be good to run pilot projects with several teams or sites to allow for unseen variables.

To revisit our earlier discussion about problems in finding a true and global software engineering methodology, be certain that the transition team understands the implications of the methodology. If it is not expandable or does not appear suited to the longer term, be wary. If the technology transition manager is in a leadership position, there is great responsibility that goes along with this position. If a corporate group or equivalent technology transition group selects and promotes a methodology, there are savings in time and expense for the whole company. We have already discussed the fact that each individual team will attempt technology transitions and probably arrive at different standards, if left to their own transitions. However, a technology transition manager who has selected the first methodology to come along or a favorite methodology assumes global risk for the company if that methodology is promoted. Teams will assume that the transition manager conducted some sort of evaluation and that the winning methodology was selected based on its ability to meet selection criteria. An effective transition team can get teams to buy into transition on a large scale; the wrong methodology not only can cause a direct loss to the company, but it can also reset the "change clock" and cause a time delay before those teams are again willing to attempt technology transition. Of course, there are stories of the transition manager who simply knew the correct course of action and did it, but this is simply a change crafter who worked with glass and got it on the first crack. Probability dictates that luck will not work over the long haul in technology transition.

The great majority of methodologies, having copyrighted names and four-color promotional literature, were developed for commercial applications. The scientific domain may have some, but I have not seen the brochures at this writing. The selection guidelines just listed should apply to the scientific domain. Simply substitute the needs and requirements of the scientific customer.

Step Four: Tool Selection

Sizzling tools are fun to watch—they generate excitement and everyone hears the music and knows there is a technology parade nearby. Peddlers love music, parades, and tool fairs. Smiles, claims, and data to support claims are readily at hand. It seems so easy; you buy this tool and it solves your problem. What about all the other tools that were described in the software engineering toolboxes and platform? Of course, they are in the legendary next release, and the salesperson promises great return on the one tool that is presently for sale.

The tongue-in-cheek treatment is necessary because the demonstration of the tools can be hypnotic. In many cases tools are very expensive, and training and support place software packages on the luxury level. Tools are essential; tools should return their investment in a timely manner; tools are only as good as their user's skills.

When structured analysis and structured design first arrived on the commercial tool scene, I received a demonstration of these new tools from some very accomplished engineers who had recently acquired them. Their demonstrations were most impressive; I heard the music and was moved. Then I had occasion to visit one of the foremost companies that supplied a leading structured analysis and design tool, and I met with three key inventors. They gave me a demonstration and answered my questions. Their demonstration was akin to hearing well-performed Chopin on the piano, whereas the earlier demonstration had been "Chopsticks" as performed by first-year students. There simply was no comparison. The speed, range, and skill of accomplished analysts and designers was much greater than my colleagues. The question is, How quickly could my colleagues learn to play Chopin? The answer in this case was 6 to 12 months using the tools on a part-time basis.

A technology transition is not successful until the team can use tools effectively. When we are enamored by the sizzle of a polished demonstration, we must understand the true cost of skillful mastery.

Risk has a lot to do with tool selection. To buy one copy and let a knowledgeable engineer experiment is better than betting the team on a pioneering practice. To have proof of performance is superior to promise of performance. In many pricing structures, the price of a single tool can be five to ten times greater than the unit price on a volume purchase. The higher unit price may be worth it if it prevents an incorrect decision to purchase 200 copies of the tool. Another way to test tools on a cost-effective basis is to purchase a copy or two and use them in a sort of lending library approach; if several engineers are sharing, they check out the copy, use it, and return it. This return could take a day or several weeks. If you use the lending library, be certain that it does not violate the usage agreement that is part of the purchase.

If a volume purchase of the tool is anticipated, do not hesitate to negotiate a deal that includes earlier copies. For example, if you must buy individual copies at x per copy and the tool would be $0.35x$ in quantity purchases, negotiate a rebate of the $0.65x$ difference when you move to a volume purchase. Or, negotiate for the first copies on a lower per-copy price with the understanding that you will make a volume purchase if the tool meets your needs and expectations. This is another example of unnecessary expenses that might happen if every team is buying a copy of a tool at full list price. If teams are purchasing several tools for comparison, the situation gets even more expensive. If they are not working together and make volume purchases of different tools, the ultimate convergence could be most expensive.

There is a danger that technology transition managers can wind up running a company store, and this is not part of the plan. Volume purchases are often shipped to one location and paid in full upon receipt. Individual tools must then be shipped to various sites. Do not hesitate to negotiate for shipments to multiple locations by the vendor. In some situations, the technology transition manager agrees to take orders and send addresses to the vendor. If a large purchase is made, the vendor should also agree not to sell any additional copies to your company at list price. The vendor should agree to monitor orders and direct the company orders to the technology transition manager.

Who supports tools? This can be a replay of preceding paragraphs if each site buys a separate support contract from the vendor at full retail price. If the company gets a major support contract with discounts, it is sometimes necessary to have an internal support person who takes the calls and forwards them to the vendor only if they cannot be solved locally. Suddenly the technology transition manager and team find they are running the "company store."

Support contracts often include upgrades. What happens if the vendor comes out with a new release? Who negotiates the upgrade price? Who arranges for a timely upgrade of all sites? One technique that is effective is to have the vendor participate in an "upgrade fair," complete with booth and information at the company. Users can bring their old discs and proofs-of-purchase and receive the software on the spot. Remote sites can mail in discs and receive the upgrade. If each team has purchased the tool separately, the upgrade can be a nightmare.

Upgrade implications should be understood before distribution of the upgrade. Will the upgrade work with existing configurations? Is additional memory needed? What about other tools that interface with this tool? All change must be managed.

There is also overall company direction. If the company is moving to UNIX, then investments in other operating systems should be carefully considered. If the company is moving to laptops, then investment in new PC tools should be weighed.

The technology transition manager can help the company to achieve standardization. Even if it should become necessary to select one toolset today and change to an entirely new toolset several years later, it is easier to change the entire company from one toolset than from a variety of different toolsets.

There is another complication for those companies who have developed all or part of their tools as internal tools that were never intended for external release. Internal tools can give the company a big lead in technology; they can be focused and tailored to the company's exact needs, and they can track company movements precisely. They can also be poorly documented, developed and released without proper processes, and supported on an ad hoc basis. Be very cautious about homegrown tools, unless they are developed and released in accordance with external product practices. Be very wary of custom-built platforms; be opposed to a complete homegrown software engineering solution. Today's trend is away from homegrown for internal-use-only tools.

There is one final tool source. There will be some tools developed on an unofficial basis, with no project number or funding, to meet a specific need within one team or division. These tools often are successful in meeting a specific need, and someone asks for a copy in another group. News spreads, and distribution follows. Soon there are many users asking for support, enhancements, and so on. Developers usually enjoy their newfound fame, and they willingly comply with early requests. Later they will not answer the phone and often complain to their manager about harassment from other groups. At this point the custom tool either dies or begins genetic transformations at the hands of other crafters. If the tool was successful in more than one team, consider replacing it with a tool from an approved source. The bottom-line caution here is that tools require ongoing support of the shop that sold or distributed them. Those who deal in tools ultimately become shopkeepers.

Step Five: Education

Technology transition managers who deal in education often become dean of students or chancellor of the university. Education is an absolutely essential element of any technology transition program. The trick is to be able to develop and deliver training and ongoing consulting without being consumed by course development and delivery processes.

We have already spoken about education, but it is an absolutely vital step in the technology transition process. Software professionals must be well educated, or they will fail to make the technology transition grade.

The best advice was given in assessing needs and resources. Use all existing resources, and leverage those resources to provide what is not currently available. Use educators to help you know what to do and how to do it. Do not develop courses if you have no prior experience. Such attempts usually result in reinventing proven educational practices. Human resources departments often have educators trained in these practices. Do be willing to use newer technologies. Do be willing to consider proven technologies.

One of the best ways to ensure that engineers stay up-to-date is to use continuing education. Many of these programs, especially master's degree programs, provide a solid foundation for software engineering and also help the engineer in existing assignments. There is a built-in recognition and reward structure, and students know they must study. There are many excellent books and constant promotion of continuing education by academic experts. This is simply one more endorsement and a reminder not to forget a standard educational practice in the new world of software technology transition. There are several caveats here.

- Watch the types of master's degree. There are engineers who have always wanted to study another field. The master's program should be approved in advance, and it should improve job skills and performance. In companies that have financial subsidies for graduate education, there usually is an approval process and committee.
- Watch for schools teaching accredited but older curricula. If your goal is to bring engineers up-to-date, be certain that the school is up-to-date.
- Beware the diploma mills. Some of these schools charge very large tuition and fees, and they provide very little education. They often grant massive amounts of credit for on-the-job experience, assuming fees are paid. There should be no trouble in identifying these schools; they may be allowed to grant degrees under state law, but they will not be approved by the legitimate accrediting associations.

For minor technology shifts you need some training; for major technology process changes, you need a curriculum. There is no way around this requirement. The curriculum may already be in place, or it may have to be invented for development or pioneering situations. The curriculum must include the following:

- All the baseline subjects. If the transition is to object-oriented practice and if C is the language, then everyone must know C and the object version of C. If artificial intelligence is the goal, then students must know a language such as LISP, fundamental concepts of logic, and so on.
- Methodology and any special extensions of the methodology.
- Tools and how to use them. These may include workstations, software tools, support tools, and the like. They may also include operating systems, networks, and databases.
- Metrics. Everyone should understand what is to be measured, why, and how to understand the process. This does not mean that everyone has to review metrics on a daily basis or analyze all metrics at once.
- Actual accomplishments to date; major work that has been done, references, sources. Part of the transition success depends on understanding and insights of participants.

The approach here is to figure out educational needs, resources available, and resources needed to meet the curriculum. There is a temptation to reverse the order by seeing what is available and then sort of molding the curriculum to fit what is available. This decreases the chances for success. Consider developing the full curriculum outline first, and then look at the baseline curriculum necessary to ensure success. There are very expert sources to assist you in curriculum development, and you do not have to start from scratch. Professional educators are always publishing suggested or proposed curricula in journals. Get some of these and use them as a reference in developing the transition curriculum.

When the transition team has the curriculum and some supporting information, they are in an excellent position to search for one or more contractors or teachers to deliver the curriculum. In some cases, they may contact a community college or university to find that they have been working on a similar curriculum and will agree to a joint project. In other cases, the transition team can piece the sources together to get a curriculum into a pilot phase. If contracting with some institutions of higher learning, be aware of the fact that they often place a premium on delivery of corporate courses. The university "markup" can be as high as an additional 50%. Individual contracts with professors can be significantly less expensive. Graduate students are another good source of high-quality, less-expensive teachers. Beware of all instructors who understand software engineering theory but not its practice.

Any new curriculum must be piloted, probably two or three times. Feedback and critique should come from within; if there is another educational department, they can often be of great assistance. Do not hesitate to have some of the upper-level team and group team managers attend the second pilot (think carefully about having them attend the first pilot). Their feedback is valuable, and their attendance works toward future support for your technology transition.

If the curriculum begins with the pioneering practice level, do not hesitate to use the "experimenter" model. In this curriculum do not teach any specific applications; rather, teach methodology and tools, show past successes, give some suggestions, and let students become experimenters who will find best ways to apply this new technology. If implementing this experimenter model, be certain to put the best and brightest mover-and-shaker engineers in the class. The results can be simply amazing.

Two advantages of having formal educational structures are (1) maintenance of quality through consistency of courses and curricula and (2) planning and control of educational transitions. Formal curricula require fully supported educational programs to ensure success. As the program—or even an individual course—is taught by more teachers at more locations, there is a normal tendency for the quality to decrease. This is especially true where a professor taught pilot versions and approved the final curriculum but inhouse part-time teachers were drafted to deliver the final product. Quality degradation can even occur when the course was videotaped by the professor and student proctors show tapes, do examples, and answer questions. Proctor quality determines the quality of the course, and proctors vary in their delivery. Some will start skipping parts of the tapes; others will only work one example. If you offer the curriculum at more than one site, there must be some method to ensure program quality. There are a variety of traditional education techniques that can be used here. The important point to remember is that technology transfer is a delicate learning process. Education must be of the highest quality to allow technology to flourish and transitions to succeed.

Step Six: Selecting Metrics

In an earlier chapter we discussed product, baseline, and process metrics. Technology transition must be supported by a good set of metrics for several very important reasons:

- to measure and verify success
- to begin a baseline for the new process
- to establish a baseline for similar technology transfer in other teams
- to allow for improvement of future technology transfers
- to be able to know what went right and what went wrong in the event of a less than desired or negative result

There are lots of metrics information sources, but they do not tell you exactly which metrics to use. Product metrics are too late and too little for technology leadership. Baseline metrics will give some indication of how well the project has gone, but baselines do not provide process information. Actual software process metrics can be difficult, depending on the uniqueness of the selected methodology and tools. There is less published information about technology transitions, but some metrics can be planned and implemented.

If technology transition is to use structured analysis and structured design, it can be guided by some baseline indication of how long crafted projects have spent in design (% of total project time), total time to design and code a project, number of defects found in testing prior to release, and defects reported in the first 60 or 90 days after release. The transition team can also get some indication of the level of satisfaction that engineers had using the new process, places where they had the greatest difficulty, and changes they observed. One word of caution: in an analysis/design implementation, data may reveal that the amount of time spent in the analysis/design phase is a significantly higher percentage of total time than was spent in the former process. In most cases, coding time is also a smaller percentage of the total project time, thanks to structured analysis and design. But real gains from the implementation of structured analysis and design tend to be in the ongoing support (number of defects, ease of maintenance, ease of enhancement).

Beware of incorrect interpretations, and beware of gathering the wrong metrics. Lines of code per programmer per day may not tell the entire story. If you are measuring training, the total number of student hours per month does not tell the whole story. In our example, it could be that structured analysis and structured design save no total development hours, but they reduce support time by 75% and enhancement time by 50%. Such gains would more than offset the cost of using these methodologies and tools.

There should be some regular measuring and reporting structure for metrics. There should be regular reports, and they should have several summation-type metrics and charts that allow project monitoring from several key metrics points. If more than one site participates in the transfer, summation charts should also be used to report the entire project.

This is a difficult area. Those who are not enamored with measurement will gladly skip over these words and get on with the action. Those who are devotees will heap abuse on my cursory treatment of this most important subject and proceed, in all likelihood, to excess measurement of technology transfer. Part of the difficulty is that many problems encountered in software development projects are human errors. In some cases, errors are based upon flaws in tools or methodologies; in other cases, they are simply errors.

Specific tool errors can be grouped into the following categories:

- human interface due to: incorrect data, misunderstanding, or failure of the module to protect itself
- functional faults within the module
- system or database interactions

Human errors can be grouped into the following categories:

- failure to understand the problem to be solved
- failure to design the proper solution
- failure to translate the design to code
- failure to understand the system

Actual source of the errors can include:

- user misunderstanding
- poor documentation or training
- operator problems
- system or environment problems
- incorrect analysis or design

Metrics should be sufficient to allow the problem area to be detected and few enough in number to be described in one page. Ideally, the total number of metrics could be counted upon the fingers of one hand. Part of the key to successful metrics use is to have metrics point the way. It should be possible to follow the metrics pointer into a specific area to determine the source of the problem.

Some traditional metrics are

- cumulative project months, with a breakdown by activity;
- analysis and design months, with note of redesign by area and time;
- coding time, size of code (source and object), first-time success rate at module, unit, and system levels (note that it may be necessary to do some normalization by language and also that the code may have to be normalized by type of machine);
- cost per line of code;
- costing models;
- function points and complexity;
- analysis of error types and causes;
- analysis of where and when defects are being found;
- time to correct defects and number of attempts to correct defects;
- adherence to planned schedules;
- engineering, productivity, and ease-of-use metrics;
- verification that metrics do not unduly disturb the processes that they are measuring.

There are many metrics experts who bemoan the fact that we still use lines of code in metrics. Although it is true that this leaves much to be desired, the fact is that all we have is desire; there does not seem to be a better proven subject to be measured. Remember that if we do not consider other factors, we can be deceived by lines of code. Suppose that we switch to another language. Lines of code per programmer workday can be decreasing, but product functionality per programmer workday is increasing. Remember, the goal is not to have maximum lines of code in the product. Also remember that the measure of lines of code is reliable as a metric only when the software process being measured is not undergoing transition. It is meaningless when used as an absolute productivity metric or when used to compare different types of software development teams.

Although these are suggested guidelines, there is another problem to confront. We need a standard set of proven software metrics, and we need a baseline set of data that is based upon these metrics. When measuring something for the first time, measurement has little meaning without a known baseline. It is true that organizations can establish their own metrics and conduct enough measurements to establish a baseline. Such a process would be slow and would also run the risk of having selected a poor set of metrics.

We need software metrics that are

- measuring something of value;
- clearly defining what they measure (no ambiguity);
- able to be validated;
- able to allow actions to be taken in time to be beneficial.

If you are going to derive your own metrics, consult the literature that is available regarding software reliability and testing. Most importantly, decide what you must know about your software project, and ask yourself if you can use the reports that will be generated. One way to check your metrics is to ask if they will tell you how to better spend your money on the next project. If they do not, ask yourself why you are taking the time to use these metrics.

If metrics help you to improve the process, then the metrics also help you to understand why the process worked well. A set of successful metrics can then be used with subsequent projects to increase the probability of success.

Step Seven: Selecting Other Supporting Activities

There is a whole collection of supporting activities that can aid success of technology transitions, and some of them are essential to success in specific companies. A complete program will have elements of all these activities.

Keeping management informed is essential. A one-time trial of one new tool probably does not require interim reports to top management. A full program of software engineering transition requires regular reports, periodic briefings, site visits, and show-and-tell sessions. The required frequency of contact decreases somewhat as we move up the corporate ladder, but importance increases with magnitude of the project. The greater the number of dollars being spent per year, the greater the importance of keeping management informed. Also, any breakthrough on the positive side deserves extra attention. If the technology transition manager comes from an engineering background, there might be a tendency to minimize this obligation. Management support is vital, and good news should be shared.

Promotion is also essential, especially when the object is to achieve a technology transfer across the company. A newsletter, even an electronic newsletter, can be most effective. Formal reports are good, both to management and to the engineering community. Some companies have an internal luncheon (brown bag) series of technical reports and discussions. Reports and papers at conferences, both internal and external, are good. Of course, it may not be possible to publish all good news in an external report. But employees can share many things, and management can be surprising in their willingness to grant permission to publish in respected journals.

Scheduled demonstrations or a booth at one of the internal conferences will help to spread the word. Videotapes can be made quite inexpensively and can be used both for promotion and for instruction. Computer video screens come out surprisingly well on video, and the audio portion can describe step-by-step ways to take advantage of tools and best practices. A very effective demonstration tape can be made showing video screens, with background voice narration describing activities taking place on the screen.

Internal information dissemination channels can take the form of conferences, briefings, seminars, workshops, proceedings, and informal channels. Conferences and proceedings are the best way to bring experts together to share information and the best way to retain information. However, only larger companies can afford to put on 3- or 4-day conferences for engineers. Smaller companies can resort to electronic mail systems and use special shared files, but it is not quite the same. Formal conferences usually have a system for selecting papers, and they enforce a certain standard for publication. Seminars and workshops can be put on by many companies, and they can be videotaped for future use. Briefings can be conducted for both managers and engineers, especially interim briefings. The informal channel is trickiest. It cannot be controlled by management, and attempts to do so usually result in a strengthening of negative information on the channel, which otherwise could be a tremendous source of support. The best way to handle informal channels is to be as open and truthful as possible and allow the informal channel to work positively to support the program.

Informal channels work through the entire infrastructure. This includes other groups, perhaps even some of those groups in "friendly competition." It is important to maintain positive relationships with all these groups and to attempt to work with them. This sounds a bit overwhelming, but their support is essential to the overall success of a major technology transition. They can also help you to stay informed, with an active feedback channel.

There should be a conscious and planned effort to maintain positive and active relationships with technology transfer groups in other companies and with professional societies and standards groups. This is done for three reasons. First, your company should be known and be an active participant in the global community. Second, there is a wealth of information and advice out there. Third, there must be a calibration with the outside world in order to know if you are gaining or losing ground. Larger companies have specialists who know standards, attend and participate in standards groups, and actually take a leadership role. Smaller companies also have such persons, but they usually do these duties on a part-time basis. The global community also works toward evolution and standardization of terminology and processes. Regular attendance reaches out and keeps you informed.

A paragraph about keeping informed seems necessary here. How many computer societies do you belong to? How often do you attend chapter meetings? How often do you attend national conferences? How many journals and technical magazines do you receive each month? How many do you regularly read? In general, in the United States the answers to these questions tend to be one or two, occasionally, and sometimes. We are very busy people. The answers from Japan, Korea, and other countries seem to be three to five, regularly, and read cover to cover. In the technology transition game, it is necessary to keep informed on a broadband basis.

An information system becomes necessary at some point. A companywide database for metrics regarding quality, productivity, baselines, and all other required information is essential for a companywide program. If some new transfer is underway, there may be other groups who want to link up. If regular reporting is necessary for scheduled reports and studies, it is much easier to gather electronically than by some crafted process. This is another one of those areas that tends to get ignored or overdone. You can begin simply and add things as required. It may not be necessary to create an entirely separate information system; it may be possible to work as part of an existing system. A working system will provide facts and data for analysis, a means of monitoring and control, a source of help (including where to go to get what).

Post mortems have been mentioned before, but they should not be dismissed as an option. You can learn a great deal from failure, especially if you have gathered data along the way. Failure is part of all our lives (every legal trial has a winner and a loser), and learning usually happens as a result of failure. Do not walk away from the crashes. Have a formal post mortem, and avoid all negative criticism or attempts to level blame. List both the things that went right and the things that went wrong. List possible actions to avoid errors in the future. If you do not know any such actions, note that fact and then see if there is someone who knows. This is another reason to collect and save the post mortems; it may prevent another team from reliving the same mistakes at a later date.

Potted plants have been discussed earlier; they allow for precise post mortems. A potted-plant technology transition attempts to control all independent variables, and this should enhance the likelihood of success. If results are very negative, it also allows an earlier decision to abandon that path of technology transfer and begin another route or select another tool. If variables have not been controlled and understood, there will be several additional attempts at the same experiment or one with only few modifications.

Aerospace developers used "skunkwork" projects with sometimes sensational success (high-flying spy planes and sophisticated satellites). The term has a special connotation of being left alone by the rest of the community. Skunkworks were set up in a special isolated hangar or location, the team was basically a potted-plant setup (everything they needed for success), and they were allowed to keep to themselves. Skunkwork projects could work well in advanced development or very early pioneering projects. In this situation project funding is probably covert, and upper management is told only that something worthwhile is going on. If one is trying to make a significant score by making a leading-edge technology breakthrough, skunkwork is a pretty good idea. By sealing the small team off, negative criticism does not reach them to say that the project cannot be done. Privacy allows a focused creative effort free of distractions. This would be ideal for proving the feasibility of a state-of-the-art technology. It could also provide the definitive data for making a larger investment when such data and confirmation could not be obtained by any other means. And it is just plain fun. Do not be afraid to buy one or two of those state-of-the-art workstations; do not be afraid to turn a couple of your best engineers loose; do not be afraid to let someone dream. Processes are for proven practices; skunkworks are for visions yet to be practices. A successful skunkworks project can allow you to make significant strides on the software engineering path.

Step Eight: Getting the Program Started

The following steps should come in order. The program should be treated as any formal program, project, or development effort.

- Needs assessment and validation should be in order.
- Plans should be in place; the budgeting and targeting should be part of the planning process.
- Orientation and sign-up of team members should follow accepted guidelines.
- The schedule should be explained and published. Significant objectives and corresponding milestones should be clearly understood.
- Initial training must occur.
- Environment setup (including hardware and support) should be in place and fully checked out at the start of the project.
- Metrics should be validated and operational at the start of the project.
- If the potted-plant model is used, all variables must be covered.
- If this is a larger or multistage project, check each phase or step for planning completeness and integration.
- Get started as soon as possible; do not overplan.
- Follow progress carefully; ensure that ongoing consulting and support is provided; field all problems as quickly as possible.

All these steps are obvious. They are listed here because they may be obvious, but they do not seem to be mandatory. The default seems to be to grab the tool and run with it. Every undone or missing element increases risk of failure. All these elements have some probability for total success associated with them; if you simply apply the rules of probability, technology transition becomes difficult even if all these elements had a probability of 0.9, and this is a high percentage for some of the variables.

Obvious steps can fail because the technology transition manager underestimated the intensity of resistance to change. Everyone gets comfortable with their familiar routine and their surroundings. There are many programmers and technical managers who will issue calls or even demands for change. But they presume that change will be in alignment with their present position, beliefs, values, and needs. If change is not, it may cause doubt, uncertainty, or fear, and it will be opposed. If change does not bring a better assignment, a promotion, the possibility of future gain, or a seat near the window, it will be opposed. If change advances a peer competitor, it will probably be denounced.

Although all change steps in this chapter appear to be based on logical principles, many technology transition managers fail to anticipate the level and duration of resistance to change. They do not analyze starting positions of engineers and managers. They cannot imagine how C or object-oriented languages could possibly be terrifying to some engineers.

Managers often assume that resistance to change is based on superstition and fear; this is true in only a small percentage of the cases. Even the most logical and best planned of changes can produce irrational responses. Some components of resistance are

- lack of knowledge of new technology;
- lack of understanding as to why change will benefit programmers, management, and the development team;
- for some individuals, a basic disdain for change;
- lack of understanding of outside pressures that mandate change.

There are techniques that technology transition managers can use to overcome this resistance to change. The key is to have everyone involved as a participant in the change process. Get everyone started; get them early information and education; let them see how the change helps them; and let them understand how they play an important role in the change and its success. Bring generic fears out into the open and deal with them.

If there are still some who oppose the change, it may require one-on-one negotiation. This is especially important in situations where the individual will not gain directly, but the team will gain.

There is also the possibility that change is being oversold, and the resistance is informed and justified. There are losers in the technology transition game. A successful transition to an oversold technology will come up short on results. A successful transition to an excellent technology may still require a lengthy learning curve before the technology returns its investment.

There are courses, books, and consultants available to help technology transition managers and change teams. The point is to acknowledge that not everyone will enthusiastically support the change, and they must be converted. It is helpful to remember that so much of the software process is in the human mind and that the goal of software engineering is to allow full expression of that mind. There are quite a few crafters who do not accept the premise that software engineering frees the engineer to create. When you have convinced them, they will be your strongest supporters.

BALANCED TECHNOLOGY TRANSITION PLANS

Larger programs involving numerous projects or entire groups or companies should have balanced technology transition plans that include detection or correction and prevention elements. This should not be an after-the-plan analysis that attempts to justify strategy and tactics based upon the already being implemented plan. Rather it should be based on 3- to 5-year goals and objectives.

The role of the technology transition manager was outlined in an earlier chapter. To get the program moving and keep it moving, a "change mover" is needed. In some situations the technology transition manager might also double as change mover, but it limits progress. The change mover spends all of his or her time implementing tactical plans. The change mover knows how to work within the bureaucracy and when—and how—to go around the system. The many elements of the program outlined earlier in this chapter do not automatically come together. A seemingly simple event such as a 1-day seminar by an outside expert takes about 2 full-time weeks of internal effort to plan and execute (2 weeks' effort is actually spread over 3 to 4 months). Orderly transition of a team or group is an order of magnitude greater. Large-scale technology transitions require technology transition managers who can also function as tactical change movers. Large transitions require vision and supporting strategy.

A technology transition program that teams a visionary who is also a strategist with one or more change movers has every chance of producing outstanding results. The combination of a clear vision and good tactics to implement the vision allow efficient technology transition.

The quicker path to success is a well-defined, near-term program. If resources to establish a permanent software technology transition team are not available, it is still possible to make significant gains in detection and correction phases. Key software problems facing a team can be known and described in one day simply by using verification. Some solutions involve simple process changes and can be done without training or support. One example would be to make certain that no new code is added to a "completed" release that is in testing. Another would be to ensure that any modules that are being corrected after a defect was detected during testing do not have additional last-minute code added.

The quicker path works well with proven or accepted practices. In many cases these are not presently being used, and they have the potential to make significant improvements. One of the best examples is software inspections. Many software engineers know about this technique, and they usually acknowledge that it has merit. But I have often heard the comment, "That was a technique for an earlier era; we want to use today's methods." As long as the development group is not using some form of software engineering that includes design and code validation, inspections are one of the best tools in the detection and correction arsenal. One of the quicker paths to success is to get formal inspections started and be certain to focus on those code modules that have the highest risk of defects. This will require some preparation and training, but experts and courses are already available. Baseline results are available. This technique is also well suited to a train-the-trainer approach. If I were getting started in an environment that was software-defect-plagued and under great pressure, inspections would be one of the first things that I would do.

Summing up the quicker-path approach, detection and correction works best with smaller, shorter programs that use known and proven practices. Although it will not bring leadership, it will bring everyone up to date. Benefits that will accrue just might be sufficient to convince top management that a complete technology transition program will bring leadership over 3 to 5 years. There have been instances where very dedicated movers have single-handedly caused all elements described in this chapter to occur and contracted (using both internal and external sources) technology transition programs. These dedicated movers have been able to do this in larger, dedicated complexes where the problem can be well described and where there are a sufficient number of engineers to justify the cost of doing the program.

COSTS OF TECHNOLOGY TRANSITIONS

All these programs cost money. They are an investment that should have a proven return equal to or better than other investments (skunkworks are understood to be a higher risk). There might be a temptation to look at the cost of a 1-week seminar or program and decide to skimp on the instructor, tools, or support. Consider the complete cost of having 20 of your best project managers or top engineers sitting in a room for 1 week. The fully loaded cost of each person (salary, benefits, facilities, computing support, and so on) can easily be in the $1000 to $2000 per person range for the week. If they have traveled to attend class and are staying in hotels, the cost can increase by $500 to $1000 per person per week. Now you have 20 people spending a week with you, and the direct costs are $25,000 to $40,000; that does not include the impact of having them "off-line" for a week. Using a lesser instructor or cutting corners to save several hundred dollars does not make sense in this situation.

These costs also highlight the need for technology transition managers and change movers. It costs money to change; it will cost more not to change. But the investment in change must be taken seriously. This is the reason that I referred to our logical "software buildings" and how these buildings must be sold to top management. Suppose we invested the $25,000 to teach software inspections to 20 key engineers, and suppose they initiated the technique on key projects. Software defects found by customers can cost the company $5000 to $40,000 per defect, depending upon the nature of the defect. If the use of inspections detects and corrects just ten such defects, it is a good return on investment.

These numbers are based on some averages in Silicon Valley, and of course they will vary according to circumstances. But what do you think the return will be in your company? Can you begin to do similar projections on the costs of software change, and the returns?

A serious long-term program of transition to software engineering will require big bucks. If early investments do not bring a return, top management will not only be hesitant to continue the programs, they will begin to "adjust" the organization to find someone who can produce return on investment. Top managers are usually not enamored by sizzle; they are enamored by solid results gotten quickly.

There is no one path or existing formula guaranteed to be a certain winner in a software organization just beginning to deal with the transition to software engineering. There are proven techniques that will help to guarantee early wins. There are multiple ways to get to any destination, and a program that closely matches the needs of the software organization has the best chance of success. The problem has been that very few professionals have the experience needed to develop these programs. Perhaps universities will begin to initiate programs or options to the software programs that will teach some of these techniques. I am working with universities now, and first results are encouraging.

15

Corporate Technology Transition Coordination

GAINING LEADERSHIP BY COORDINATING TECHNOLOGY TRANSITIONS

Various software teams, groups, entities, and special interests can be viewed as crafters traveling in wagons. Without an agreed direction and purpose, they will each drift off in their own direction searching for truth. The natural tendency to move in different directions is enhanced by company growth. As there are development teams in different locations, as there are manufacturing operations in different locations, and as companies move toward multinational status, the technology wagons will just keep drifting apart.

This natural tendency to drift is accelerated by new ventures. New groups are sort of venture-capital operations and usually move into areas of business previously unknown. Venture capital may leverage existing technology to provide new products and patents, and this leveraging process will almost always result in a new development team being established.

Acquisitions bring rapid growth, but they also bring a whole new culture that is most likely headed off in yet another technology direction. New partnerships or alliances bring additional pressures. The demands of the very largest customers or original equipment manufacturers (OEMs) bring another set of pressures.

IMPORTANCE OF TECHNOLOGY COORDINATION
TO CORPORATE SUCCESS

Everyone must do some coordination. If a company desires to have technology leadership, then there must be a clear direction, management must insist that all the wagons move in that direction, and technology coordination becomes a polite way of facilitating shifts in direction as everyone aligns the technology wagons. If a company desires to stay in business, there must be technology coordination to prevent redundancy and loss of time.

One of the most common strategies for coordination is to get all technology wagons going in the same direction in wagon-train formation; one wagon follows behind the other, with their wheels moving in the same tracks. This is done by some sort of corporate directives: Everyone will code in Ada; everyone will use this CASE set. It appears to be a form of dictatorship that is a very efficient form of government . . . assuming you have a wise and benevolent dictator. In the Ada example, corporate "dictators" may not have a choice; government agencies have made the decision for some companies. Technology wagon trains will work only if the wagon master knows the territory and how to avoid leading the wagons into unnecessary risk.

In any event, dictatorship will not work for high-technology companies who gain advantage by their state-of-the-art discoveries and products. But even these companies cannot afford the luxury of letting teams move in any direction they choose. High-technology companies do well by setting and clearly giving direction to the team management and team members and then letting the wagons travel in tandem, with some taking the high road and others taking the low road. Groups can maintain contact, share many things in common, and accelerate the overall company progress. Coordination is an almost perfect tool for this tactical advancement. There are built-in peer pressures to keep in step, and yet there is enough flexibility to allow teams to maximize their productivity. Coordination is conducive to the flowering of creativity.

COORDINATION SCOPE

The argument for coordinating activities should be strong enough to stand on its own merits in the software development environment. However, there is a much stronger argument to consider. As companies move toward one integrated product process, it will be necessary to have all the functional wagons not only moving in the same direction but closely coupled (it still does not have to be a wagon train). CASE and software engineering apply to far more than software development.

Many groups will be buying or building software. They will be using information systems within the company and connecting to information networks outside the company. When we discussed the concept of design for manufacturability and supportability, it assumed coordination and integration as required elements in the formula for success.

If software development teams are successful in their coordination efforts without considering all other groups, then we will have to begin all over in 5 or 10 years as we start to coordinate these various functions. If we wait for the master integrated proven practice to connect all these functions, our company will probably either strangle on its own information or be pulled apart by all those wagons going full-speed in all directions.

Figure 15.1 shows the traditional approach to discrete technology transitions. Each department set its own goals, objectives, and timetables. Although the traditional approach may keep a company in a competitive position, it will not place the company in a leadership position. Figure 15.2 shows a concurrent approach to integrated technology transitions. Properly planned and coordinated transitions at the company level can attain—and maintain—technology leadership. Companywide coordination requires a companywide transition manager.

Who is the companywide technology transition manager for the internal processes of the company? Who is the companywide doer? Are these change managers and doers the same people who make transitions in software research and development activities? These cannot be philosophers who strive to understand the problem. They must be visionaries who can select a strategy and get the first phase of the plan into place. A companywide technology transition manager must ensure that all functions are working to get their areas under control and moving together. There must be repeatable, predictable processes in any area before serious integration is attempted. Coordination can be started now, but it is more of an information and direction

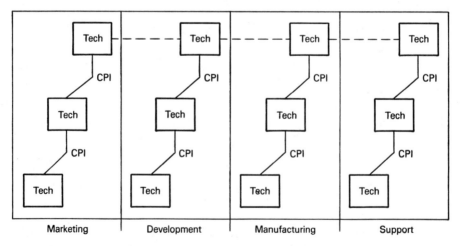

Figure 15.1 Traditional approach to departmental discrete technology transitions.

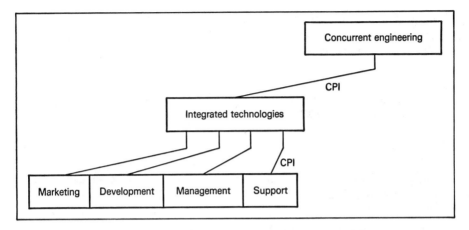

Figure 15.2 Concurrent approach to integrated technology transitions.

sharing at first. Communication now can be a very positive factor in getting the big team together later. Communication can also go a long way toward getting new initiatives moving in the right direction.

Of course, the size and diversity of a business affects the effort required to get this coordination in place. The extent to which products of one division are used as components of another division also affects the effort. In some cases, a large company has such diverse businesses that it is hard to see how the puppy chow operation can be linked to the medical pacemaker operation. But even these extremes have one thing in common . . . software.

Software is an integral part of business, and software is becoming the differentiating element in computing. Software is a common necessity and concern for all companies who do 90% of the gross national product in the United States. There may still be thousands of one-person shops, but they do a very small dollar volume. Software is even an integral part of all large, illegal business operations.

If you spent a summer Sunday afternoon sitting on the front porch of a typical Iowa farmhouse, you would be amazed at one topic of conversation (unless you are a regular invitee). Many of those farms are run by personal computers, and the farmers not only know they need computing support to run their farms, they are able to discuss pros and cons of software applications with the same ease that they discuss tractors. If a farmer has children who also have farms of their own, they are concerned about coordination and linking of software to permit volume purchases of equipment and supplies and volume sales of products.

While many businesses are users only of software applications, larger businesses are very much developers and integrators of all types of software. The important perspective to be gained is that all these groups have the need for coordination of their activities, and many of these supposedly "nonmembers" of the software fraternity are probably doing a better job of coordination than charter members of the software development community.

CONCURRENT TECHNOLOGY TRANSITIONS IN A RAPIDLY CHANGING MARKETPLACE

Technology coordination in large companies involves strategic, tactical development, purchasing or licensing, integration, and reporting. Coordination in smaller companies can involve simply purchasing or licensing, tracking, and reporting. This allows smaller companies to make faster moves and conversions; it allows larger companies to set directions and be aligned with advanced development and pioneering practices.

The traditional departmental approach is not well suited to a rapidly changing marketplace. Figure 15.3 shows the difficulties encountered in this approach. In this situation, marketing waited for more than half the time period before beginning a transition and then selected a technology transition that made only a small gain. Development did two rapid transitions and attained rapid gain but overspent their budget by 50%. Manufacturing attempted a transition that produced less gain than would have been achieved by staying with the original process. Support did not attempt a transition, but instead stayed with a process that showed no improvement.

This scenario is bad enough, but what happens if the market requirements shifted at the same time? In a team approach, supported by concurrent engineering, it is possible to make changes in direction in the shortest possible

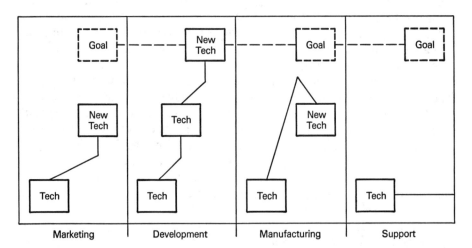

Figure 15.3 Traditional technology transitions in a rapidly changing marketplace.

time. If a company is operating in the mode shown in Figure 15.2, it will be able to react quickly. If the company is in the Figure 15.3 mode, it simply will not be able to react in time.

There are more and more industries today that must master the concept of concurrent engineering and concurrent technology transition. All companies that have significant investments in computers must attend to this need. But these examples are given to show the emergence of corporate technology transition discipline. It is possible to begin with coordination only, and this will provide immediate benefits today. It will not set the stage for the transition to concurrent engineering tomorrow.

TECHNOLOGY TRANSITION COORDINATION— THE FIRST STEP

If no technology transition manager and change mover are available, there is still much to be gained from providing technological coordination. Some techniques were described in the previous chapter: newsletters, reports, bulletins, reviews, workshops, and conferences. The point is that these techniques can be used in a coordinating role without worrying about the final direction. It is more important to have everyone moving in the same direction than to have them moving on exactly the right coordinates. Of course, there is greater value in a technology transition manager who assumes a leadership role and ensures that technology is completely in line with the company's business direction. But there is much conventional wisdom in management at all levels, and it is unlikely that technical managers will steer technology in the wrong direction. It is likely that they will move more slowly and perhaps encounter some dead-end paths along their route. Coordination can help them to spot the dead-end paths and help to move them along more quickly.

Coordination can occur within, and even across, major functional areas. If teams have not had an opportunity to share, bringing them together will be a positive experience. If Information Systems (IS) groups have not worked together, they will enjoy the experience. Even if only one, two, or a few representatives from each group come together, it can cause positive changes in direction when they return to their groups. In many cases they will be amazed to find that other groups have been working on the same problem, have already evaluated outside suppliers, or have a solution in hand.

The coordinator has the ability to function as a Swiss neutral. Teams that would not ordinarily come to easy agreement will do so more readily if there is a wise and independent party who is not in a win-or-lose position with respect to the outcome. The coordinator can serve in a sort of mediation role. If mediation becomes part of the job description, then coordination becomes a minor element. The idea is to have an ad hoc mediator as situations arise.

In this sense the coordinator functions at the subcrafter level. The crafts-person is directly responsible for the product. The coordinator can be very important but is not directly responsible for the product. Coordination can be viewed as a craft, but the raw material is lack of direction (perhaps chaos), and the product is a coordinated activity.

The Johnny Appleseed model can be combined with coordination ac-tivities to produce a very powerful technology transition technique. Spread seeds of change, and coordinate growth of the changed processes. This as-sumes the collective wisdom of technical management and engineers, but wisdom is there. As long as consensus is reached by collective participation and not by dictatorship, results can be impressive. This may not allow world-class leadership, but it has potential for maximum technology yield with minimum investment.

The quicker coordination path is to follow a minimum Johnny Appleseed model. Disseminate information with a minimum of preaching or direction setting. Just encourage technical managers and engineers to plant the seeds of transition. Bring planters together logically and, if possible, physically. Promote successes; warn everyone of failures and potential failures; keep everyone focused on their seedlings and maintain a friendly competition. Know what is going on outside, and share winning stories.

To some this will all seem obvious; to others it will seem strange; and to yet others it will seem unnecessary. Coordination of technology transitions is an essential component in the evolution of software engineering for the following reasons:

- It is essential to all types of engineering technologies, and software is joining the engineering community.
- It is essential to establishing a companywide process and is absolutely essential to getting an integrated concurrent product process.
- Omission of this activity inevitably results in mixed results or failure to meet established goals.
- This has been an essential element in all successful software transitions to date.

TECHNOLOGY TRANSITION COORDINATION—
A MULTIDISCIPLINARY APPROACH

Coordination includes much more than the engineering community. Coor-dination includes technology, methodology, social processes, and organiza-tions. There is a complex behavioral model of software development pro-cesses, which includes programmers, technical managers, programming team, division or group, company, and customers.

The behavioral components of software have been researched, discussed, and documented. Even physical environment has a major impact; software engineering technologies account for less than 50% of the software success factors.

Successful coordination must include all layers if we are to have consistent software engineering throughout the company. Coordination activities must take into account group dynamics and team motivation. At the programmer level there is very specific in-depth technical knowledge, which has to be coordinated with other team members and with other groups. As the large-scale integration and multisite projects must come together, there are higher levels of knowledge that must come into play. For example, a programmer may have in-depth knowledge of telephone-switching software, and the complete project is a new telephone-switching system. As the project moves to higher levels of technical management, coordination moves from specific technical concepts to system coordination.

Earlier chapters have examined the challenge of getting crafters to function in a team environment; the challenge becomes greater as we move up to company and customer levels. Coordination that results in everyone agreeing to use the same CASE tool is not enough. (In some situations, it may even be wrong.) Customers view the company as prime contractor for the total solution. They expect the company to deal successfully with changes to requirements, with conflicts between subcontractors, and with all other unforeseen problems that arise. They expect the company to have complete coordination at all levels, and they expect the company to be able to deal with all problems. Giving them a tour of software teams with the latest CASE tools and demonstrating those tools is impressive only if accompanied by results.

The final software platform must function as an integrated communication platform for engineering information flow. There must be a coordination and integration of methodologies, tools, metrics, and engineers. Information must be coordinated, controlled, integrated, and catalogued. The ultimate success of software projects depends upon successful technology transitions that are coordinated in a multidisciplinary manner.

16

Business Challenges to Technology Transitions

OPPORTUNITIES TO IMPROVE THE TRANSITION PROCESS

There are numerous internal and external pressures, both technical and non-technical, that affect software engineering and our ability to put it into action. These pressures present a challenge to technology transition managers and major obstacles to those who would attempt technology transitions on a part-time basis.

There is another element of frustration in the change process. Colleges and universities love to publish alumni newsletters, magazines, and bulletins to advance their cause. This is all well and good, but they never publish failures. We all fail in some portion of our endeavors. If we do not, then we are not working to our true potential. Every graduating class has some individuals who will excel in their work. The problem is that we read all these success stories and perhaps conclude that our own accomplishments are not sufficient. Or we decide that these successful people have some special power, some magic talent, that allows them to succeed. They do possess talent, but most of them will tell you it is determination, drive, and plenty of hard work that leads to success.

The same thing seems to be happening with CASE and software engineering. Most of the books tell you now is the time and you should be doing something. Many books and articles tell you the sky is falling, and even while you are reading you are getting further behind. Very few books and articles tell you about the problems encountered in making technology transitions. Even when some brave person steps forward and admits that something did not work as planned, many rush to make judgments and decide that there must be something wrong with that person and their work. Very few publications list successes and failures in any format that allows you to know the probability of success for any given transition at any point in time.

It must be noted that many CASE installations have been successful. There are well-controlled, well-measured, well-reported projects that have proven CASE to be a success and a proven return on investment. It should also be noted that CASE advocates and vendors want to put their best tools forward. There should be a positive, optimistic atmosphere. But major technology transitions are always accompanied by some setbacks. The problem is that many failures are not reported, not analyzed, and not understood. But they do happen.

In the foreword to this book I mentioned that the material was gathered from many sources, including sharing and discussions at many companies around the world. The bibliography lists many published works, which contain additional information or opposing points of view. Part of the material and reports in this chapter cannot be found in the bibliography; they have been gathered on an informal basis as part of the lunchtime and after-hours discussions and gatherings.

USER COMMENTS

It is often hard for professionals to admit that something did not work well or that they simply do not understand how they encountered these problems. Informal conversations outside of the normal work environment usually reveal a common thread of difficulty in implementing CASE/IPSE tools. There are numerous instances of failed technology transitions. The universal conclusion from all of these discussions is:

CASE AND SOFTWARE ENGINEERING TECHNOLOGY
TRANSITIONS
DO NOT ALWAYS WORK

The reasons for failure vary widely. Some of the more common reasons given for having severe difficulty or outright failure are technology, transition, and management.

Technology

- Structured analysis is used as a design tool. Structured analysis is poorly suited for design; some users find it difficult to deal with abstraction levels. Structured analysis often has no way to combine separate functions.
- A gap exists between structured analysis and structured design; a tool is needed to bridge that gap.
- Most of the tools are no good. (Remember, this is the conclusion reported in informal sessions. It may or may not be a fact that the tools were no good. But the fact that these persons are telling this version of the story to whomever will listen does have an effect.)
- CASE is a "front-end mask" attempting to cover a major software crisis.

Transition

- You cannot inject one dramatically advanced software development tool in the midst of older technology teams with tight schedules.
- Many developers will still do things by hand according to their traditional ways and then submit their work at the last possible moment. They either cannot see the advantages to using new tools or they cannot break with old skills.
- Miraculous success, especially with a very feeble attempt at change, is expected.
- The way something was done in another location is exactly duplicated, without regard to the differences between that team and this team.

Management

- The wrong problem is solved; a technical question is answered that no one is asking.
- Introduction of structured analysis and structured design cause imbalances in some projects through delay of the start of actual programming. Managers find it difficult to know what is going on. This initial reaction is abated in subsequent projects as managers learn how to know what is going on and how to coordinate this project with other projects.
- The project turned out to be bigger than thought.
- The presumption that whatever CASE tool is selected, whatever is decided to do, as long as it involves bubbles and arrows, it must be right.

The list goes on. But these most frequently heard problems and objections allow us to get the flavor of the objections. Many managers have been "burned" when they pushed for change, talked upper management into providing funding and support, and then failed to deliver. Although we should not dwell on the negative, we must understand the fact that technology transition is not an automatic process.

INTERNATIONAL BUSINESS TECHNOLOGY TRANSITION CHALLENGES

The Japanese SIGMA project was reported in an earlier chapter, and the overall impression is that the Japanese have another winner. Although SIGMA is having success, it seems to be only a partial success. Not all companies have subscribed, networking is still less than desired, and software tools need much work before there are complete toolboxes and platforms. Some critics are now saying that the project is in trouble; others note some success and urge SIGMA to press on. SIGMA's future will be determined by the recently formed SIGMA Operating Company.

One trait that has lead to Japan's success in technology is tenacity; the Japanese keep on trying until they succeed. MITI is actually on its fourth try with software engineering funding. The first project was begun in 1976 and met with limited success. The second project focused on developing tools for writing software; it met with limited success. The third program is the 5-year SIGMA program, which has already been discussed. The fourth program is funded and underway.

One trait that has allowed Silicon Valley to make significant gains is innovative spirit. In our enthusiasm to discover the path to software engineering, we sometimes tend to discard ideas or technologies because of reported difficulty or because of failure to meet all the goals. The tenacity of the Japanese allows them to learn from each attempt, to look for alternative paths, and to try new technologies within their proposed model. If we hear a report that software engineering projects, software factories, or CASE tools have failed, we should understand the degree of failure, the nature of the project that failed, and the lessons that can be learned for the next attempt.

Japan appears to be trailing the United States in formal computer science programs. Although some universities have outstanding programs, only a limited number of universities offer computer science; however, the number is increasing each year. Many of the most recent college graduates have degrees in fields other than computer science, and when these graduates are hired in programming positions, they must be taught computer fundamentals and programming. The largest Japanese computer companies run large training institutes and programs.

Starting salaries of Ph.D.s who work in Japan are less than in the United States; in many situations the young Ph.D. receives little or no more pay than a person with a B.A. or B.S. Part of the justification is that the Ph.D. holder should have additional knowledge and skills, which will allow for rapid advancement.

Although many Japanese managers believe that software engineering tools and techniques are the right answer, they do not believe that the right tools and techniques are available. They continue to search for the right ones. A number of Japanese firms still have programmers sharing terminals, and there are fewer workstations in comparison with some U.S. companies, where every engineer has a workstation or personal computer. Some U.S. programmers have two or three. It should be noted that some advanced Japanese teams have the very latest in workstations, fiber optics, networking, and the like. In general, Japanese management is frustrated at the lack of an integrated technology to implement an ideal practical programming and support environment.

Japanese software companies are seen to be less prestigious than hardware companies. As a result, some software companies have very elegant offices and decor in an attempt to impress their customers and to be able to recruit the best college graduates. Software companies work very hard to build a successful image.

There have been multicompany attempts to develop software engineering platforms independent of the SIGMA project. These efforts have not had much success, primarily due to coordination problems. They will offer informal comments that technical management is weak, proper goals are not set, and projects are not sold to top management properly. (Sounds familiar, doesn't it?)

Software is not always seen as a scientific discipline in Japan. It is a sort of "soft science discipline." Many attempts to do structured analysis and structured design have met with mixed results. An informal compilation of the reasons for experiencing difficulty in attaining software excellence in Japan include the following:

- Lack of genuine top-management support. Executives all want quality and productivity, but they often attempt to direct it to be done rather than taking an active role in the management process. There seems to be a lack of technology transition managers.
- Lack of clear plans and directions. The announcement of top-level directives often causes a wide range of activities to follow, but lack of a technology transition manager means that activities are done without clear policy, goals, objectives, and coordinated tactical plans.
- Lack of a dedicated program team to implement the program.
- Overall lack of a companywide team or team spirit.

We give a special note of caution when thinking about these factors. The reasons for difficulty are the same in Japan as in the United States. Do not come to the conclusion that Japan is not hard at work on these problems. They are working harder than most U.S. and European companies. They have enjoyed major successes. They intend to master software engineering and produce software products of the highest quality. We should study their work and their successes; all companies and all countries should continue to work together and to share in the development of the software engineering profession. There will be ample benefits and rewards for all.

Europeans will likewise complain, but they have much wider process variation. In one country they will tell you that structured analysis and structured design is the key to the solution. Another country will say structured testing is vital. Part of the reason for the variation is that computer science programs vary widely from country to country and region to region. The United Kingdom has some very advanced groups that consider all present techniques to be passé. They advocate formal methods, artificial intelligence, and neural networks as the answer.

Europeans are also developing a wide variety of software tools, and some of these tools have had success in the United States. Europeans have standards groups, which were described earlier. Informal feedback sessions will offer numerous reasons for failures. Critics say that it will take years to have full software engineering because it will take years to develop standards. They also point out that there are major cultural differences throughout Europe, and even with standards and platforms, there will still be a wide range of preferences for tools, metrics, and training. When you consider the possibility of one particular tool gaining universal acceptance across Europe, remember that other high-technology products offer few examples of prior universal acceptance. It could happen; it is unlikely.

The Soviet Union has a surprisingly well-informed computer science community. Even if they do not have all the western equipment, they read journals and attend conferences. In Moscow, Kiev, and Leningrad I had very stimulating conversations about software engineering. University professors and students were delightful. In several conversations they made reference to some of the latest mainframes and minicomputers manufactured by the United States. Wondering how it was possible that they should have had "hands-on" experience with these machines, I asked them. They smiled in a very knowing sort of way and replied that it was difficult to get spare parts. The recent changes in international relations may bring the Soviet Union closer to the international software engineering movement.

The point is that they have experience on the newest equipment, and they do manufacture their own computers. They have arrived at the software breaking point, and they understand very well the importance of software engineering. They have fewer software engineering or CASE tools and therefore have had fewer failures in this area. The Soviets still approach the CASE concept with a much higher level of hope than is found in Silicon Valley. They do understand the enormous scope of the conversion to software engineering and are prepared to make the investment. As you might expect, most of their software work is scientific in nature; they have less of a management information system and very little factory automation. Retail computing and on-line transaction processing is almost nonexistent.

China has an understanding and appreciation of software engineering, and they do some contract programming for western countries. They understand the need for software engineering. The political situation may make it more difficult for them to get information on a worldwide scale.

Taiwan has a similar appreciation and is at least a decade ahead of mainland China. The principal software houses in Taiwan can do large-scale systems or application programming, and they are concerned about CASE. Their experiments to date indicate less than a 50% success rate with specific CASE tools.

Korea has very large and very prestigious software companies. The executives in these companies have the finest business offices that I have ever seen (compared with those of other software executives). All software executives are chauffeured to work. This seems to be a part of their culture more than a specific attempt at image building. It also means that software projects must be successful and return significant profits. Koreans are very knowledgeable in matters of CASE and software engineering. They have tasted both success and failure with early software tools. They understand the importance of software reuse, and they understand the emerging economic significance of software. As software engineering moves into the proven practice domain, Koreans will be major players.

India has some of the largest software companies in the world. The largest companies have more than 8000 college-trained programmers on staff. They are ready to do contract programming on a worldwide basis. They were some of the first to get into large-scale contract programming and do tens of millions of dollars in contract programming in Silicon Valley each year. These companies are very knowledgeable in software engineering and CASE tools, and they have developed their own modular tools, platforms, and processes.

Bangladesh offers contract software services, including software development in a variety of languages. They have training institutes and support and will do the work there or at your site. They too are well into software engineering.

The list could go on for many pages. All these countries will tell of the same problems with software engineering; many of the present-day tools have been oversold. Start-up times and learning curves have taken 12 to 18 months. Although these countries agree on the start-up problems, they understand the importance of the transition to software engineering. They expect to be among the very first to make the transition to software engineering. Many developing nations understand the difficulty in attracting major foreign capital investments to their country. They also understand that software development can be done with less capital and that there is still time to be one of the pioneers. While developing countries have not had major successes in their first attempts at software engineering, they all know that they have a good chance of future success. They all understand the great promise of reward to those who are first to cross the finish line.

One of the reasons for lengthy explanations of technology transition problems, which are universal, is to help you understand that many of these failures happened because well-intentioned professionals simply got caught in the transition trap. They did not understand where they were or how far they were attempting to move forward; they did not plan well; and they did not consider the potted-plant approach.

INTERFERENCE PHENOMENA IN TECHNOLOGY TRANSITION

Even after we take away all the leapt-before-looking excuses (didn't prepare properly, didn't really care, it wasn't really my job, and so on), there are still some very legitimate interference phenomena that can hinder technology transitions. All failures cannot be blamed on improper planning or improper dedication. Technology transition is hard work. It requires skilled technology transition managers to plan and guide the transition process. Even while writing this book, I have gone on lecture tours and have met with many customers. Informal comments and feedback sessions have not changed. The fact is that the percentage of failures is significant, and it is not diminishing.

This seems strange in light of all that is written, all that is claimed to be known, and all that is promised. There are many good books on CASE and software engineering. Some are up-to-date; some are dated; and some seem timeless. Many of these books have lists. Many experts have lists. Many experienced managers have lists of doubts. Many of those who have tried and failed now have self-doubts.

How did we come to this state of affairs? Part of the problem is the idea that if you try and fail, then you personally have failed. But what is one failure along the way? Who could possibly conceive of doing technology transitions on the scale described in this book without allowing for some failures along the way?

To answer these serious questions, we must return to the rational world of planned transitions. You can successfully plan for and make the transition to software engineering. Part of the answer to the questions and objections that we have posed is that we did not fully understand the problem, and we did not understand the level of effort and commitment that it would take to solve the problem.

Many books that contain lists have perfectly good cookbooks, charts, metrics, feedback loops, partial methodologies, sample contracts, and schedules. The problem is that they do not consider all the variables described in this chapter and in several preceding chapters. These books deal in a much simpler, tidier world where the customer is rarely mentioned, change is rarely mentioned, and we are solving a static problem. Some of the best books are directed to information system departments or other internal departments that have focused internal objectives. These internal customer needs are often much easier to characterize and meet than the more varied and demanding needs of external customers.

The static occurs when we realize that we are plowing new ground and that our customer's expectations are changing even as you read this book. We should consider looking at the big picture, which includes much more than the software development environment. There is much more to the software engineering problem than one or two of the toolboxes described in earlier chapters. The software engineering solution must include installation and building and support toolboxes. Software engineering methodology must ultimately integrate these toolboxes, or the methodology will not satisfy customer's needs.

THE ENTIRE SOFTWARE SOLUTION

To see the entire picture we must remember the following:

- Software is designed and built by software development teams.
- Software is often installed and customized in the field.
- Software "lives"; software undergoes permutation.
- Almost all maintenance (except perhaps some documentation) is done by the labs that designed and developed the software or at least involves those labs.
- Technology transition can fail because theories advanced by entrepreneurs or academics were not proven in the business environment. Technology transition must improve productivity and quality of software products.
- Software engineering must of necessity be involved in and able to deal with all these phases and activities.

Considering these factors makes it easier to understand some of the failures. There is another problem with changing the existing process. Software has a built-in slowness factor; it takes more and more time to bring out subsequent releases. Touch the process and you slow the process. Even if process improvements will ultimately result in efficiency and savings, in the short term any perturbation of the process slows the process.

"SOFTWARE FACTORY" CHALLENGES

In an earlier reference to the term software factory, I stated that the concept was no longer in fashion. The original idea behind the term was that software development should be divided into two main activities. The first activity would involve need, analysis, and design. The second activity would involve the factory where the design was "produced" as completed software. The idea had great appeal because it would allow strict control of "manufacturing" activity, and design would be completed and verified prior to any development. Those who worked in the factory would never be allowed to make any design modifications, and they would produce code exactly to the original specification.

There have been some software factories, and a significant number of them have reported success. Some Japanese software companies have used this term in their published papers. There have been some efforts in the United States, most notably in the petroleum and chemical industries. One of the major benefits to this approach is that it is supposed to control process slippages and the "touch it and you slow it" problem. The approach is also supposed to lend itself to software reuse because factory development engineers determine when and where to reuse modules to meet design specifications. These engineers even maintain catalogs of reusable modules and can make the decision to have a new module developed for reuse based upon actual need.

Reports of success generally come from those applications where needs are relatively stable, and there is every opportunity to allow reuse. This coincides with reported successes in using large software houses to do major software projects. Some U.S. companies have contracted for major software developments projects using companies in India, Korea, Taiwan, China, and other nations. Major successes have been reported, with significant dollar savings when compared with projects completed in the United States. There have been significant improvements in documentation and support tools and publications. In all these cases and in software factory cases, applications have been well known and well understood. If you attempt to have one of these groups design or develop a state-of-the-art tool or application, many advantages vanish.

The following are the major objections to the software factory approach:

- It attempts to solve the software engineering problem by copying an existing hardware solution.
- It is a great leap backward.
- It delays investigation and development of the new software paradigm.
- It does not solve future problems.

- It will not fit into integrated product processes.

The term software factory seems to be out of fashion due to semantic problems and emotional posturing. The semantic problem is associated with the old-style understanding of the word factory. Engineers and engineering managers do not want to be put into factories. The original meaning of factory implied rigidity, monotony, and strict tradition, whereas modern factories allow flexibility and timely change. A comparison of crafters, traditional manufacturing, and flexible manufacturing is given in Table 16.1.

This comparison is true for hardware and also appears to be true for software. The three basic software options are as follows:

1. Software crafters build a customized software product.
2. Software vendors provide a semicustomized software product.
3. Software vendors sell a standard software product.

The semantics problem is making an issue where there should be no issue. Just as flexible manufacturing is the current manufacturing technique of choice, so it will be with software engineering.

Emotional reactions produced when the term software factory is used range from the sublime to the ridiculous. On one of those rare occasions when an informal software conversation with managers is slowing to a crawl, I will ask if they think we will have a software factory in the near future. The outburst is something to behold. Some heads instantly nod in agreement; some begin to ponder; and others become absolutely vehement in their objection to the term software factory.

There are valid reasons for taking any one of these three positions. The strong objections seem to be centered on the theme that you cannot mass-produce masterpieces. While there are some "original art painting" assembly lines where each painter quickly does one part of the painting, real works of art are usually produced by one artist. If software were used only to create very low priced masterpieces, then the artistic argument might have merit.

The problem with this position is that it would deny the vast majority of citizens the benefits of software technology. The software factory is not intended to produce one-of-a-kind masterpieces or to reproduce masterpieces

TABLE 16.1   Impact of Technology Change on Product Cost

	Ability to Change	Product Cost
Crafters	Rapid	Higher
Traditional manufacturing	Slow	Lowest
Flexible manufacturing	Timely	Lower

in large numbers. Existing software factories are one way of attempting to produce well-engineered software that fully meets the customer's needs. There should be flexibility in the software engineering system, but software must be designed and built to specifications and standards. The best course of action for future discussion of software factories is to use the term with caution in the United States and with objectivity in Europe and to be prepared to discuss the pros and cons in Japan.

REVERSE ENGINEERING

There are a number of tools—and, to some extent, methodologies—to support reverse engineering of software and databases. The concept involves taking the final software product and working backward toward the source, either language or design. There are a number of good reasons for reverse engineering:

- To allow source to source code translation. This would allow older programs to be recompiled in fourth generation languages.
- To recreate (or perhaps generate for the the first time) the module designs. This allows CASE tools to be used on software that was developed before the tools existed.
- To allow analysis of the code for test coverage and to allow analysis of databases for functionality enhancement and performance improvement.
- To create cross references.

Although there is value in this rapidly emerging discipline, there are inherent dangers and limitations. The idea of returning to design seems to be a panacea for software ills. If we could have designs expressed in modern-day format, then we could reengineer the weak spots in design. We could also add additional modules and functions with apparent ease.

Informal research reports indicate that this simply is not happening. Much older code was conceived in the mind of the creator, and in attempts at reverse engineering, first formal examinations of designs often appear confusing and illogical. Part of the reason that old code causes problems is variation in the minds of crafters.

Even when old code was well done, there is the philosophical problem of the automated reconstruction of design context and levels of complexity. Each human mind bases its understanding of the external world on perceived relationships and values, which are not always communicated in the end software product. Well-engineered software would be designed according to agreed-upon principles and standards. Crafted software is the product of human genius; engineered software is the product of science applied to software.

Thus it is not always possible to reverse engineer code and arrive at an understanding of the design. However, there is important work in design recovery; the fruit of this work will be better software maintenance; object-oriented techniques will allow some software reuse within these older programs. The formal reverse engineering techniques can be combined with interpersonal data gathering and interviews to make it possible to understand much of the original program logic.

Early uses of these types of automated techniques have very mixed reactions. Reverse engineering is beginning to address data and part of the functionality. Reverse engineering will continue to be developed, but it is not certain that it will ever be able to handle context fully. There will be much additional progress in this area because reverse engineering is vital to maintain a balance between old and new software. We cannot simply discard old software because it was crafted. We cannot simply put a fence around old software with a sign that states Do Not Enter. There must be constant improvements in all software as long as it remains in use.

A BALANCED SOFTWARE PROGRAM

Another reason for informally reported failures is lack of appreciation for a balanced program that involves elements of detection and correction and process improvement. We have discussed these in an earlier chapter, but here we consider the possibility that an improvement is suggested as a near-term fix for a very pressing and immediate detection and correction problem. In one sense, every problem that is detected could be solved by a major process improvement; in some cases the solution would be only one of the minor benefits to accrue from the major transition. However, most detection and correction items are very pressing, and customers simply cannot wait for the new factory to be built or the new software process to be implemented. If well-intentioned but misguided technology transition managers sell longer-term transitions on the basis of near-term results, there will be a perceived failure even if the long-term program is valid. Converting to C may indeed solve many problems with today's code (written in Neanderthal III), but it will not provide immediate relief to critical defects, and it may not provide a solid release for another year or two.

In many situations the best engineers are busy with existing code, and they cannot participate in conversion to C. These engineers are needed on-line simply to maintain the status quo. If a company has more than 50% of its total software development resources involved in current releases and maintaining status quo, then the realities of the desperate situation in which business finds itself prevent any long-term solutions from being implemented. All companies suffer this interference phenomenon to some extent.

Regarding this interference effect, managers know; engineers know; field support engineers know. Many of them will simply say, "That's the way it is, and that is most likely the way it will stay. Little or nothing can be done to change it." Team managers also know that proposed solutions often do not work. They share information; they attend conferences; they have friends in other companies. These managers want a business solution with an 85% to 90% chance of success. Then they will agree to actively participate in the change process.

Just about everyone knows and just about everyone agrees that something must be done; many are willing to try a change. But who shall lead them? In an earlier chapter we discussed the concept of technology transition manager. The need and concept are valid, but it is a new concept and does not fit into business planning. Does the technology transition manager have the experience and skill to understand detection and correction versus improvement balance? Should the technology transition manager be able to dictate the overall schedule for technology transition across the company? If we are going to switch and have all engineers driving on the other side of the technology road, can team and general managers have the right to block the switch in their territory?

SOFTWARE TECHNOLOGY RESPONSIBILITY AND AUTHORITY

Many technology transition managers are doomed to failure at the time they are given their charter. Many technology transition managers, under whatever department and title they operate, are given responsibility for making change happen but not the authority to make the change. There are some who can find a way to function under these adverse conditions. One technique is to bluff and claim you have the authority. If everyone believes you, then you do have it, by definition. Another approach is to use political skills to get all the line managers working together and supporting change. But the fact remains that traditional business organizations do not allow for technology transition managers who must function rapidly over a long time span.

In business, schedules dominate. It is a race, and the prize definitely goes to the swift. This will continue for at least another decade or two, and this hard cold fact must be combined with the reality that software lives and permutes. Thus the technology transition manager must operate in business environments that did not envision this problem, that must live with the software they have produced, and that, in many cases, are being strangled by the level of software support required.

This is one of the reasons that top management generally likes the portion of a presentation that speaks of software chips and an orderly end to crafted software. This solution appeals to their sense of logic, and it begins to make software sound more like the hardware world that they have been able to control successfully. Software chips seem to promise clean new designs, they allow high levels of reuse, and they can be measured with an understanding of the return on investment.

The paradox is that prior failures of software tools and techniques simply whet the appetites of top management for the software chips solution. If the technology transition managers do not soon change their expectations, they will expect this sort of result in the near term.

In this real-world chapter we are saying again that the transition to software engineering is difficult to fit into standard business plans, partly because software is "soft" and partly because those who have an understanding of the technical needs and transitions are usually not the same persons who have an understanding of the business of change.

MANAGING SOFTWARE SUCCESS

From a business perspective, the advice is the same. Find your worst problems today. This includes a realistic appraisal of the demands upon development time. If you do not have an understandable and repeatable process, *manage* your way into such a process. This is the *only way* to attain short-term gains:

> MANAGE YOUR WAY OUT OF CHAOS

The reason that the original crafted life cycle was subject to some ridicule was the fact that it was not used on a day-to-day basis. Managers did not set milestones or conduct reviews based upon a life cycle. If such a situation exists today, then manage your way out of it. If the designs are to be completed by a certain date, conduct a full review of all the designs at that time. If 50% of the code is due by a certain date, then inspect code and demand testing reports. In other words, manage the crafters to work in a more structured world.

If this seems difficult, consider that there must be some sort of process already going on. Things cannot be completed in a completely chaotic situation. Oh, there is indeed a process; the crafters simply do not want management to be a part of that process. In many cases the process that is going on simply does not match the manager's idea of a process.

Therefore, some sort of process must exist. And it must be possible to manage that process into something that fits the traditional idea of a software life cycle. Please remember that this should be done only to establish a platform for technology transitions. By managing the existing process and making it into something that is repeatable and understandable, there is the temptation to stop there and enjoy a few years of success. If you stop to enjoy, success will be temporary.

If a life cycle is considered to be a laughing matter by programmers today, it will not be so humorous when deliverables are requested. It will be serious if such elements as designs, code, and test results all have to be delivered on schedule and evaluated.

Not knowing what the crafters are doing is only one dimension of the management dilemma. As you manage your way into controlling the situation, it will become evident that there are many outside influences and demands that are causing some of the schedule problems. This is also part of the process that we said must exist but was not fully understood. These outside sources can include requests for assistance from other teams, skunkwork projects with no hope of success, organized playtime that uses valuable company resources, and so on.

MANAGING YOUR WAY TO A SOFTWARE PROCESS

As you gain management control, attempt small changes. If you see that something is radically wrong, try to find ways to correct it such that it produces minimum upset to the existing process. Bet on sure things; praise all good results. Limit new tools to pilot projects, new projects, or those situations where there is no other way. Managing your way into a process that you understand does not mean managing your way into a pioneering process at the same time.

All changes to the mainstream process should be made to solve specific customer problems; they should have a very high probability of success. The business perspective is that if you manage your way into a process such that productivity dips dramatically, you will find top management asking you to manage to get right back to where you began. A few caveats are listed here:

- Do not hand the managers cookbooks and ask them to get cooking.
- Do not get cooking with a stale recipe.
- Do not get cooking in a kitchen in which you do not know where things are located or how many meals you must serve.
- If you cannot say precisely what you are planning, why it must be served, and what it will do, reconsider the menu.

After you have considered all these things, existing software cookbooks that feature numerous lists will begin to make sense. If you have never before been a cook, then recipes and lists will not guarantee success.

SOFTWARE PROGRAMMERS AND COMPUTER SCIENTISTS

Management is required for success; the personnel who design, develop, release, and support software are absolutely essential to success. Many programmers who have so faithfully worked long hours and kept systems up and running by sheer force of determination and copious amounts of perspiration may not be ready for software engineering.

On the other hand, many current computer science graduates are not ready to become contributing team members in the software community. New computer scientists have much of the latest theory and methodology, which experienced programmers may lack, but they do not know how to work under many of the conditions described in this book. They have a basic understanding of schedules and deadlines but little or no knowledge of costs, customers, and commitments. Many medical doctors who know how to practice medicine take an additional medical research degree at the master's or Ph.D. level before attempting medical research. Computer scientists are placed in the opposite starting position. They might be better suited to research or theory than to the "practice" of software engineering in industry.

There have been programs developed to turn dedicated electrical, mechanical, or industrial engineers into software engineers. It seems easier to add software knowledge to someone who already understands good engineering principles and practice than it is to teach software engineering to many present-day programmers.

Pressures for change in the educational process are mounting. Whether academia will produce bachelor's-level graduates who will be ready to practice software engineering or whether they will modify their existing curricula to support the practice is not clear. It is clear that they will have to make changes in undergraduate curricula or risk increasing irrelevancy. But graduating software engineers is just the beginning; engineers are the starting point for successful implementation of software engineering.

SOFTWARE ENGINEERS AND SUCCESS

Managers must remember that software engineers will determine their success. As part of the overall plan, consider the potential of trust between engineers and management; you really must. Understand where they are; understand their concerns; understand what the distribution of their attitudes is. Remember that the difference between the oldest and best crafters and the newest and brightest college graduates is greater than the difference between college freshmen and graduate students. Remember that some will look at your plan and say, "of course," whereas others will say, "what a mountain" or "impossible." Do not expect universal acceptance of a plan.

Just as it must be sold to top management, it must be even more successfully sold to engineers. If engineers do not buy the software technology transition plan, they cannot make it happen.

Understand that engineers are your customers in this activity. They must believe in the change. Be aware of the psychology of persons undergoing change. Be aware of the stress under which they are already working. Be aware of their desire for and, at the same time, fear of change.

The importance of a well-motivated team cannot be overemphasized. In many technology transition attempts that meet with mediocre or no success, there is a lack of teamwork. Change requires team support. Change from a crafted to a team environment requires team building.

The team must have a common understanding of and agreement to meet goals and objectives of the technology transition. Where there was fear, there must be team bonding and self-confidence. Where there were varying opinions regarding the direction, there must be alignment. Where no team existed, there must be a team created. Where informal teams or older teams exist, they must be upgraded.

One of the main reasons for failure of technology transition is lack of teamwork. There is the story of the famous football coach who could take his team and beat your team; he could then swap teams with you, and one week later he would win again. Any team, even an average team, can beat a collection of individuals, even if they are the most talented individuals in the business.

This same team element is essential when recruiting a new project team that must use a new technology. Truly creative software innovators are necessary for success: Creativity must be supported by the team. Individuals may be gifted, but they must want to win as a team. They must believe that it is more important for the team to win than it is for them to be individually recognized. They must want individual recognition only as part of the team recognition.

Clearly stated goals and objectives are necessary for a winning team. When explaining these goals and objectives, watch for the individual who stares at the floor or looks away. Watch for those who say that it cannot be done or that it must be done their way. Encourage individual thought and discussion, but watch for anyone who will not sign up for the final decision.

There must be clearly stated team rules regarding the project, new technology, and ongoing behavior of the team and individuals. Some key items are

- Rules of conduct for meetings.
- Rules for resolving conflicts.
- Methods for keeping the flower of creativity alive. When attempting a new approach or when trying to diagnose a problem, there must be no negative criticism that will stop the creative flow. Everyone should be

allowed to share their thoughts, which will be evaluated and categorized later. This behavior is absolutely essential if the project has encountered a seemingly insurmountable obstacle. Creativity and inspiration are the only hope; they must be given a chance to work.

- The process issues of: criteria and priorities (how to set them and when to change them); a list of the problems being addressed (do not solve problems that do not require solution), and measurements.
- Rewards and recognition.

Lack of teamwork is usually manifested in the content and substance of other remarks. In the majority of the projects with problems, managers fail to recognize lack of teamwork as a cause; they see it as a symptom. Managers' comments often indicate that the tool is to blame for destroying team spirit, when in fact no spirit ever took root. Decomposition of the team is blamed upon lack of proper tools and platforms, when in fact it was the team platform that failed. In some of these projects the tool was never given a chance to fail.

It is essential that technology transition have every chance for success. The team should be stronger at the end of the project, no matter what the outcome of the project. If the project was not successful, the team should be eager for another opportunity. Pure basic research projects can have all sorts of outcomes, and failure is accepted as part of research. Skunkworks without teamwork can fail. The most expensive technology transitions without team-work can fail. Team psychology, winning spirit, enthusiasm, confidence, and a positive mental image are vital to technology transition success.

All these elements are included in those informal conversations that were outlined at the beginning of this chapter. Whenever someone tells me that something did not work, I attempt to find out what they did, what they thought, what they believed, and what they thought they were going to achieve. The caveats and guiding principles presented here are some of the main reasons why failures occurred. Many of those who failed were some of the most dedicated and technical and, at the same time, the most naive business professionals that I have met. When some principles discussed in this chapter were mentioned, they would display pure contempt for having to consider such notions. In many cases, blame would be placed on others; in many cases, they believed that it was simply a case of the wrong tool or language.

A SUMMARY OF SOFTWARE MANAGEMENT ADVICE

I am in no way attempting to place blame or judgment on these dedicated, hard-working technical pros. Rather, I am simply pointing out that in a lot of these cases they did not have a chance. If I could sum up advice to them, it would be as follows:

- You need predictability before attempting change. It is highly unlikely that you can use technology transitions to bring predictability to an environment that had never had it.
- You need schedules. A good technical manager can manage his or her way into predictability and schedules.
- You need cost control, which should be a lot easier if you have the first two steps under control.
- Ad hoc attacks will not win the battle; they may not even win the day.
- Getting lots of things done does not equal progress; trying endless variations of the same theme in the hope of a winning outcome the next time is not a viable alternative.
- Do not reward activity; reward results. If you continually reward activity, you will be rewarded with even more activity and, probably, fewer results. Do not confuse motion with progress.
- If you believe that you are gaining on the situation, does present status show progress? Do others believe that you are making progress? Do you have measures to show progress?
- Do you know what your critical processes are? Do you know how much the inefficient administration of these processes is costing the company? Does your analysis include all the activities in the software process?
- Do you know your key customer issues? Can you recite the top ten issues without using notes? Are your plans addressing these key customer issues?
- Will the transition to software engineering cause an impact on your team and your schedules? (If the answer is no, justification is needed.) Can you handle the impact of these changes? Do you have backout plans in the event these changes fail to meet targets?

The bottom line to this very sobering and very pragmatic chapter is that if managers who have failed or managers who are about to try technology transitions do not agree that these are important parameters, then they have a high probability of future failure. Technology transitions are moving us toward software engineering. The idea of an engineering professional implies someone who can fully meet the customer's expectations. This requires engineering professionals with a broader perspective. This requires engineering professionals who not only can understand how to meet customer's needs but also can be willing participants in the production process changes that integrate marketing, manufacturing, and support. The ultimate challenge is not to get it working; the ultimate challenge is not to make it defect-free; the ultimate challenge is the customer.

17

Customers:
The Ultimate Engineering
Challenge

Our last chapter discussed the reality of software engineering in the existing business situation. This chapter brings us to the top of the engineering mountain. Customers are the reason we are here; they are recipients of engineered products and they call the shots.

If this book had been written for customers who buy our products, I would have organized it in an entirely different manner. Customers should come first; they should drive the software engineering process. But the book is organized and written in its present form because you, the reader, are my customer. Some of you do have external customers, some of you have internal customers, and some of you are primarily your own customer. We did determine that the needs and requirements of the customer, no matter who that customer is, come first.

You are my customer, and you will make software engineering happen; you will be a major player in the ultimate software technology transition. However, the entire process is still being driven, motivated, and controlled by the end-user customer. Internal customers are very important, but they pay with the transfer of internal funds. When the customer is oneself, the customer is still very important, but once again self is not usually the ultimate source of revenue.

THE RELATION OF CUSTOMERS TO SOFTWARE ENGINEERING

The external customer, the one who purchases all these computer systems, personal computers, and accessories, is the one who is now demanding fundamental changes in the software development process. These customers are the ones who simply are not going to take excuses or second-best software any longer. These customers are becoming very sophisticated, and they cannot be distracted by jargon or promises of future success. They want us to stop delivering defective software products. They want the highest-quality computer systems at the lowest possible cost of ownership.

In order to understand these customers who are so often at a great distance from our software teams, we must go back to the very early days of computers. The very earliest users were scientists in research laboratories who were willing to write their own programs and work with the most rudimentary sort of programs, reports, and interfaces. Those who hooked computers to real-time experiments were some of the bravest, and they were willing to learn programming and work around all sorts of difficulties. Others waited hours or days for a few minutes on the early vacuum-tube machines; they also had to do programming under less-than-ideal conditions.

The advent of the punched card, with its origins in the census bureau, allowed the earliest forms of commercial computing. There was great respect for this miraculous card, and the prize went to those who could design machines to move cards, sort cards, print cards, and store cards. Some businesses actually expected to be able to mail the card to the user with a copy of the invoice, have the card returned with payment, punch the payment amount onto the card, and once again run it through 2000-card-per-minute equipment. Sometimes it worked; often the card crumbled.

Thus the very earliest uses of computers in large businesses involved financial transactions, inventory and equipment tracking, and report generation. These activities proved to be successful, and soon computers were moving into factories, railroads, and hospitals. As they gained wider acceptance, there was a movement to expand beyond using equipment to generate reports to using equipment to run the business.

In the meantime, hardware was evolving. Several major customer steps ultimately affected the programmers.

- Early vacuum tube machines and plug-in programming boards on early punched-card equipment required customers either to be very math- and science-oriented or to be specialists who knew how to place the wires to get equipment to generate the correct reports and sort cards correctly.
- Early solid-state machines allowed a greater degree of reliability and a greater degree of dependence on the reports. Large-information-system

customers began their batch-processing reports, and their modern descendents can be seen in any large corporation today.

- The largest institutions, including railroads, purchased vacuum-tube computers; some of them were still using those machines into the early 1960s.

- Along the way the largest corporations began to hire and train large programming teams. The early orientation was that customers developed all their own proprietary applications.

- Meanwhile, technology moved from tubes to solid-state to integrated-state and from mainframes to minicomputers to personal computers. Programmers followed the flow, reinventing the same programs on each new class of machine. Each supposedly new medium did adopt the content of the last, nearest medium. Each new hardware family also began in kit or near-kit form. Early programming on each new family tended to begin at the machine or assembler level. Customers often grumbled, but they always ordered the new machines.

- All other software, including file systems, database systems, networking, windowing, applications, and support, followed the same path. Some programmers enjoyed enormous success by leaving mainframe companies and simply creating the same types of software on personal computers. Customers could then purchase packaged programming solutions that met their needs.

- Today, computers have arrived just about everywhere. They are operated by very young children and very old adults. They are programmed by millions; they are feared by many of the older generation and mastered by most of the younger generation. Worldwide customers now number in the hundreds of millions.

Customers and Programs

The programming craze seems to have passed. Many first purchasers of each level of machine were very concerned about programming that machine. Today most personal computer owners do not want to take the time or effort to create their own programs. They want a wide selection of programs with options that meet their needs. They want to be able to accomplish more than ever with their computers; they do not want to be able to program more than ever.

This brings us to a central point of thinking that may not have been obvious in earlier chapters. Customers are not concerned about software engineering; they are concerned about the benefits that accrue when software engineering is used to develop software which they purchase. At the same time the customer base for software engineering is still expanding, for several reasons:

- Existing industries that use computer systems are still growing.
- Emergence of the world markets is still underway.
- The number of computer users, especially of personal computers and laptops, is growing.
- Applications and uses of computers and microchips are still growing.

The software engineering market is growing, but it is much smaller than the ultimate end-user market. What if the software engineering market follows a path that is similar to the original progression of the computer industry? There are signs that this is happening, leading us to the following conclusions:

- The earliest software engineering markets are developing in the scientific world of aerospace and defense. Scientists need workstations connected together in a software engineering environment in order to complete successfully the very large engineering projects which are planned.
- Software engineering has had early successes in the information system (IS) community, and this trend will continue. IS is well defined, needs are well understood, and there is an appreciation for controlled software development processes.
- Software engineering has already attracted the attention and dollars of the largest commercial corporations, including transportation, banking, insurance, manufacturing, fast foods, and service. The earliest expectations are for better reporting and information-gathering systems; later these large corporations will want intelligent systems.
- Software engineering is already on minicomputers and personal computers.
- CASE and software engineering are natural for workstations. There is already an ongoing and significant competition between workstations and personal computers. As personal computers grow in size and performance, it is sometimes difficult to tell the difference. No matter how the final user stations evolve, software engineering will be part of the development platform.

Customers and Software Engineering Benefits

The story takes a different path at this point. If software applications for personal computers can be sold for very low prices and if there can be large profits because sales can be in millions of units, then defect-free software becomes essential. As we explained earlier, personal computer owners do not want software engineering directly, they want the benefits. But at the same time, some crafters who moved from mainframes to personal computers and enjoyed success because personal computer programs were small enough in size and simple enough in function to craft will soon find that they need software engineering tools because newer programs are becoming much bigger in size and complexity. Other personal computer programmers are newcomers to the field, and they are entering as crafters.

What does all of this mean to us? The trends are as follows:

- Software engineering products are for everyone; customers are everywhere.
- Personal computer and workstation applications, software chips, and software boards are multibillion-dollar businesses; they will continue to grow.
- Although there is no doubt that the largest companies will have tightly integrated software engineering platforms, it may be less obvious that the personal computer, workstation software engineering tools, and platforms will also have to be tightly integrated for the same reasons. Closed systems are passe; standards are in. Applications on the smaller machines will have to be engineered to standards.
- There will be a much greater dollar volume in sales of end-user applications than there will be in software engineering tools and services. This is analogous to the dollar volumes for makers of printing equipment versus dollar volumes of magazine, newspaper, and book sales.
- Don't bet the farm on end-user software engineering tools that will appeal to the general public buying small computers.
- Do bet on software engineering specialists, software chip specialists, and software board specialists. Do bet on all sorts of education, consulting, and support services for those who will purchase and learn to use these tools.
- Do expect standards at the tools, code, chip, boards, applications, databases, and networking levels.

There is another major area of specialization whose tools and methodologies will be used by engineers and managers. Visualization, using image-processing techniques and computer graphics, is a rapidly emerging science, which is needed to transform data into visual images that can be understood and manipulated. Visualization techniques can be applied to every form of scientific endeavor: Medical images can be generated directly from scanning systems; geoscience models can show storms, earthquakes, and other planetary changes; astrophysics, mathematics, and finite element analysis can benefit from modeling. Visualization techniques can also benefit managers who need to understand business trends, financial positions, and product plans.

Scientific customers need a full set of tools to support visualization. In addition to megaflops and teraflops of computing power, they also need software tools to handle lines, surfaces, images, color, rotation, three dimensions, and volume. Networking support is needed to provide image transfer, compression, decomposition, security, and cataloging. Software engineering tool developers would do well to stay in close contact with visualization developers. Our software engineering medium may have adopted the flowcharts of the last, nearest software medium, but visualization pioneers have processes to allow us to see our software engineering future.

The difficulty of developing user interfaces at all levels will cause another spin-off of software engineering technology to produce a generic tool for computer users. There is a need for rapid interface prototyping, interface tools, human factors analysis, and testing of interfaces. This includes hypertext and natural language interfaces, which allow logical connections to both programs and data. These interfaces will be combined with visualization methodologies.

Interface standardization is necessary but is still a future hope. User interfaces must have some sort of consistent framework that provides a uniform view and interaction as well as data portability and transformability. This will require still-to-be-developed protocols and frameworks (platforms). These includes graphics, windows, commands, help, and support. Once again there is the possibility that software engineering developers may be able to share research and leverage development successes as they work with interface specialists. These joint projects include future work in natural languages, graphics, speech, gesture, and pattern recognition. They also include artificial intelligence contributions that will allow dynamic interface customization based on user preferences.

SOFTWARE ENGINEERING SPECIALITIES

Software engineering is already with us. Software engineering specialization will arrive first in the networked workstation environment. The first application specialists are working in large commercial and government projects. The first successful software engineering methodologies and tools are serving these large customers. As these customers are served, software engineering is branching into other areas. The first areas are aerospace and government. The second area is big business. If you are betting on the near term, focus on these customers. If you are betting on the personal computers, take a cautious approach because the market is in the embryonic stage.

Although there will be millions of dollars invested in personal computer software, there will be billions of dollars invested in workstation software. This is analogous to very large building and civil engineering projects. Although there are more than one million family homes built in the United States each year, billions of dollars can be spent on a single commercial or government project. It will always take larger and more sophisticated software engineering tools and platforms to provide engineering support to these giant projects than it will take to develop applications for the personal computer.

Crafters have already moved toward the personal computer; they will undoubtedly continue to flourish there. The most sophisticated crafters have retreated to the best research teams; they will emerge in the world of neural networks, large parallel processors, and biochemical computing.

Finally, there will be a smaller band of amateur crafters, assemblers, tinkerers, and experimenters who will have need of lower-priced CASE products. These are the folks who still make some of there own printed circuit boards. They basically want to hook up and experiment; they usually are not interested in large-scale new designs. Somewhere in this small group of customers there will be a few legitimate designers and program developers. They will plan and execute their own technology transitions.

The largest systems and software engineering systems have a clearly defined customer base. They are the professionals who are going to do the largest-scale projects. Workstations and personal computers can be used both by some of the larger customers, who will network them together, and by smaller companies and individuals.

The following list serves as a summary:

- Software engineering will specialize by business and engineering functional areas to better meet customer's needs.
- Software engineering is starting with the biggest customers and will work its way down to the smaller customers.
- Of course software engineering tools start as high-priced items; costs come down over time.
- Software engineering must meet the customer's needs at each level; this may seem obvious, but there will be a number of tool suppliers who will fail because they attempt to force customers to adapt to their products.
- As areas of specialization in software engineering emerge, there will be more than one set of toolkits in response to customers needs.
- Do not be panicked into making major investments in software engineering today (unless you serve very large commercial or government customers). The generic software engineering tools of today will not be able to compete with the specialized tools of tomorrow.

GLOBAL CUSTOMER COMPUTER NEEDS

We have examined the needs of customers who will buy and use software engineering tools. However, there is a more global set of needs that includes all customers who will buy and use computers. These are mainstream users; they are the ones who want software that meets their needs and has quality throughout.

There are computer megatrends at work here. These trends will influence software engineering by dictating what the software products must do to be successful. The first trend is that customers are angry; they are not going to take it any more. Customers know that they have had to change the way they do business, have had to work around hardware and software problems, and have had to protect themselves from some of the system features. Customers now understand that things can be different, and they are demanding change.

The second trend is to open architectures. This trend is universal and will become pervasive across all levels of software development. Customers want peripherals to work on all systems. They want databases and information to be accessible from all systems. They want published interfaces and graphics. They want applications to be able to be run across systems. The trend to open architectures is so powerful and universal that it is surprising that the computer industry has been able to resist it for so long.

The third trend is to standards. This means standards for everything and at all levels—systems, databases, peripherals, data communications, local area networks, and so on. How can you link dependencies if you cannot link systems? How can you expect human teamwork if the computers don't work as a team? There are thousands of examples showing the benefit of standards for both customers and manufacturers. One is the rapid success of cellular telephones. Dozens of manufacturers can provide a wide variety of telephones ranging from under-the-dashboard units to small, hand-held units weighing only a few ounces. Another example is facsimile machines, which have become a totally separate medium of communication. Today there are even some advertising companies that send ads to fax receivers. The progression here seems to be from language-independent to machine-independent, to data-independent, to company-independent.

The fourth trend is to have data available in seconds rather than days. Information is the fuel of future process and product flow. Large customers have voracious appetites for terabytes; even smaller customers now want gigabytes. As retail products become very similar, one of the best ways to differentiate is to provide high-quality systems and service. Some examples of the competitive advantages of on-line information are

- knowing where the order or shipment is at all times;
- being able to bank anywhere, at any ATM, and at many banks;
- being able to refill prescriptions at any pharmacy in the network and having medical information on line to detect any possible problems with prescriptions (such as a side effect because of another medication);
- being able to check nearby stores when out of stock;
- being able to have automobile repairs estimated automatically when visiting a claim center;

- being able to take state and federal rules and regulations into account when processing transactions.

The fifth trend is a logical product of the fourth trend, providing gigabytes in seconds. The deluge of information coming from computers, satellites, cables, telephones, and the printed media is changing the way in which we allocate our time. There is much information-scanning; in-depth study and analysis is rare. Cable television news is available every half-hour of the day, but we may watch it only daily or perhaps weekly.

In the world of on-line computer information, we are becoming much more selective about kinds of reports and frequency of reports. We are learning to pass over normal information flow and watch for exceptions or variations. We focus on change in information. Managers are learning to consult outside information sources on a regular basis. They want information filtered, preprocessed, and put into concise report form. They are learning to ask for information that meets their specific interest.

The sixth trend is that major corporations are still increasing their investments in high technology, but computer mainframes are no longer the principal investment. Corporations are investing in networks, workstations, personal computers, and servers. They are moving from large monolithic computer systems to local- and wide-area networks. This allows the creation of global information systems. It also allows the creation of distributed processing networks, which are very cost-efficient and productive in handling large volumes of transactions. Networks span companies and continents. There is still a need for network control, and there will be one controlling point for network analysis and control systems. Optimization will be automatic. Customers want networks that

- are operated from one central control point;
- are automated at all other points and automated to the greatest extent possible at the central control point;
- require a minimum of specialized training for operators and can be operated by anyone familiar with the system.

COMPUTER COMMODITIES

All these examples illustrate not only the benefit of providing superior service in areas that are difficult to differentiate, but also the proven return on investment in terms of more efficient operations. We have more than enough computer-processing cycles necessary to store, retrieve, and manipulate the information. Speed and accuracy of information access become the most important factors.

Computer companies are also finding that their products are tending to become more and more like commodities. If customers can no longer differentiate at basic computing levels, then they must differentiate at higher levels, such as applications, utilities, interfaces, support, or the ultimate differentiater, quality. As the move toward standards brings customers closer together, there will be even greater emphasis on quality, service, and reliability. This will place great pressure on upgrading programs written in esoteric languages and programs that use nonstandard services. There will be pressure to produce these new programs using standard development tools and practices.

If customers' needs and requirements are being met in a standard way, it becomes simpler for them. If products interface in a standard way, it becomes simpler to buy and connect them. If integrated applications, platforms, and networks are standard, it becomes simple to connect worldwide networks. These almost obvious observations are also the driving force behind the obsolescence of any software that is more than 8 to 10 years old. There is very little chance that this software meets today's standards. The old software can be compared to buildings that are not up to earthquake code; it presents clear and present danger to the customers.

Software companies are under great pressure to upgrade and change to software engineering. The progression is as follows:

> Companies must upgrade to software engineering to allow systems that are simpler to use and meet standards that allows customers to connect systems and do things more automatically, which provides better services. This broadens the customer's base as computer systems become an integral part of life in our society.

Any company that is internally focused and not looking at this global perspective is probably in for a very difficult time. Any company that is centered on simple defect detection and correction will likewise have difficulty. Internal focus allows your processes to be made obsolete by the competition as technology transitions continue. Internal focus robs a company of the possibility of benefiting from a software vision. Internal focus prevents a company from sensing when a specific technology race is about to end and a winning standard is about to be declared. Internal focus prevents a company from knowing when principles of good practice are emerging.

World-class companies must understand software engineering in a world of customer-oriented software products. Experimentation and development must, of course, come first, but customer needs are now understood, and standards that support those needs are underway. Welcome to a whole new ball game. The move to standards will be fueled by customers who need computing power and services. Those customers have not always had the best treatment or the best service from earlier systems. Those customers have overcome their awe and fear of computers, and they know what they want. Those customers expect their needs to be met by computer professionals. The only way that software can live up to its promised potential is to be well engineered by professionals. Let us take a look at our almost certain destiny.

18

Software Engineering—
The Profession

There are multidimensional activities that must come together to allow software to gain full admission to the professional engineering community. Although these activities are moving in their own dimensions at their own paces, the relentless march of business and technology today is moving software downstream through a series of technology transition rapids.

All these elements and dimensions must be understood and harnessed to bring the full promise of software engineering to those who are now "shooting the rapids." If those on the journey could stop by the shore and rest, could make a proper plan, or could know what lies ahead, then the journey would have less risk. It would also probably be dull. The journey is exciting; we are going where no humans have gone before and we are truly pioneering this new discipline.

This final chapter is intended to be a summary of the transition to software engineering and a recruiting pitch. The computer industry is still in its earliest stages. Successful transition to software engineering requires the very best professionals; it requires you.

THE SOFTWARE ENGINEERING SET

We began this book by reviewing the software journey to date, enjoying some of the early stories, remembering how it was easier to understand it all in those days. We have looked at the promise and complexity of large toolboxes, integrated sets, and complex platforms. We have also looked at the other dimensions that can make or break our journey. And we have indulged in some extrapolations, which give us a "sneak preview" of the very exciting software engineering world which awaits us just a few years ahead. The set of things that must come together to produce software engineering includes

- the software creators and builders who advance through apprenticed crafter, journeyperson, specialist, professional, and "board certified professional";
- the software tools that have been advanced through manual phase with few tools, tooled phase supported with standalone tools, engineered phase, which loosely links tools in all phases, automated engineering phase with integrated toolsets, automated intelligent engineering with artificial intelligence, and other advanced techniques;
- the methodologies finding their origins in established practices, supporting separate functions and tools, emerging as processes link tools and platforms, and integrating all engineering processes;
- metrics having origins in products measurements used by quality departments, began to focus on software development through baselines, moved into software process as repeatable, predictable processes evolved, followed the transition into quality control and continuous process improvement, and will continue to evolve as the integrated engineering environment comes into use;
- education, training, and consulting, which found their origins in apprenticeship learning, moved to journeyperson learning as the universities began to develop the computer science curricula, are moving into specialization as the body of knowledge increases, will develop into professional education as the profession emerges, and will develop into an area of specialization within the overall integrated engineering profession;
- software engineering platforms, which began as stand-alone computer systems, embraced the best of time sharing and networking, began again in the almost stand-alone world of workstations and personal computers, embraced the best of local area networks and early forms of engineering networking, are moving to the truly distributed software platform, and will ultimately become the integrated engineering platform;
- the overall software engineering evolution, which had its origins in the

crafters who are true adventurers, visionaries, and dreamers, moved crafters into the tooled phase as they needed more support to cope with increasing software size and complexity, causes tools and methodologies to become linked as they begin to be engineering practices, brings pressure to link and integrate the tools as automated engineering emerges, and will finally bring us out of the rapids and into the world of automated intelligent engineering;

- the technology transitions, which always move through basic research, empirical research, empirical development, pioneering practice, proven practice, and accepted practice to finally become a standard.

- the integration with hardware engineering, which acknowledges that software design has many similarities to hardware chip design, recognizes that software must be designed and developed as an integral part of the system, requires that software engineering principles and good practices must emerge, and allows "engineering" to begin a closer integration into the emerging product process.

The multidimensional model can be awesome indeed. But those engineers who saw the early moves toward integrated circuits and visionaries who could dream of large-scale integrated circuits must surely have felt a similar awe as they worked with vacuum tubes and transistors. The goal is exhilarating, attainable, and understandable. Other disciplines have come through similar evolutions. As we move toward logical software buildings, let us remember that the journey consists of many steps, and each one of those steps is achievable by all of us.

PARADIGMS AND COSMIC GLUE

All these dimensions can be threaded together in a simple logical progression:

- Programmers began by specifying how the computer would get the answer.

- Modern relational databases and programming tools allow the programmers of today to specify what they want without having to specify how to get it.

- Future system users will specify what they need, and the system will deal with "want" and "how to."

What is needed is some "cosmic glue" that will bring all these concepts together and fashion a new paradigm to permit software engineering to take its rightful place in the engineering community. The paradigm will include new life cycles, new tools, new platforms, and new metrics. It will require education, training, and consulting—and then probably require them again. Cosmic glue is tricky stuff. If you use it to paste together things that were never really meant to be put together, they will soon unravel. In this sense cosmic glue resembles the weak force of gravity, which is wonderful because it allows us to move about and try things. If gravity were as strong as some of the other forces in the universe, we could never make a move. Cosmic glue has the property of holding together those things that should be held together and then allowing for orderly transitions, which are part of continuous process improvement. The only problem is that we do not have the new set of software engineering things that belongs together. We are still attempting to paste things together with older life cycles and tools that have adopted the content of the last nearest medium. The important thing to understand is that you cannot yet purchase paradigm glue, things to be glued, or the instruction manual. But you can prepare your "worktable," "toolboxes," and "platforms" to be ready when the "big kit" is available. Here are things that can be done today to prepare for the advanced engineering of tomorrow.

Gain a proper perspective of where you are, where software is going, where your competitors are (industrial, academic, or other), and, most importantly, where you want to be and how soon you want to be there. This book should help. If you require additional information, especially detailed and specific information regarding management techniques, tools, metrics, methodologies, and so on, consult some of the books listed in the bibliography. Become a member of professional organizations and attend local meetings. Attend some national conferences. Read journals, or at least scan them for those articles of specific interest. These are not things that can be attended to on a one-time basis.

Knowing where you are must include understanding the reality of your software world, your customers, and what needs to be done today. The quality of existing software is paramount to future success. If there are severe problems existing today, then the bulk of a program must be focused on defect detection and correction. Failure to do so will only delay timely technology transitions or cause a false indication that those programs are not successful when in fact they never had a chance.

The same is true of massive upgrade programs designed to catapult software teams into the future. They can bring all kinds of trouble, disappointment, and failure, which results in a "technology transition winter" that prevents progress for some time to come. This does not mean that massive upgrades and rollovers cannot succeed; it simply means that the greater the technology jump, the greater the risk. Larger jumps require better expertise, planning, and execution.

Massive upgrades are attempted because of rational planning and foresight, lunatic bravado, or black despair. Rational planning is based upon the western philosophy of people as rational animals. There is the premise that inspiration and creativity, combined with accurate information, allow management to make the best choices and follow through in the development and execution of rational plans. One of the commonly assumed causes of failure is the lack of timely or accurate information.

If rationality drives the engineering process, then the optimal tools are those that exactly suit user's needs and perform in a manner that is perfectly predictable by the user. Tools become an extension of the user. The rational engineer is in complete control at all times, and all decisions are based upon full disclosures, complete information, and complete understanding of information and data.

This is a very active and involved role. It assumes that the user is in charge; it will not work if the user is poorly informed, confused, or bewildered. It assumes that different individuals, if confronted with the same information and data, would arrive at approximately the same logical engineering conclusion. The problem with this utopian world is that, in reality, the software engineer is the recipient of software tools just as the end user is the recipient of applications and computer systems. Most software engineers are not creators of the tools that they use, and yet those tools are supposed to be faithful extensions of themselves.

This is the reason that crafters have success. They are fearless in searching through toolsets, in adapting tools, or even in developing their own tools. They refuse to be put in a strange environment. They refuse to use tools that do not make sense in their jobs. This adaption and selection, which makes them successful, also moves them away from engineering.

The other side of the philosophical coin, which many companies have been following, has tools as the right answer. Software builders are supposed to adapt to the tools. Management demands a role in selection of tools and mandates their use throughout the team, group, or company. Young, enthusiastic engineers with a new toolset are like young riders who have just taken the saddle of a wild mustang. They thirst for success; the boss demands victory; the riders wind up simply trying to survive the ride.

There are several ways to approach the rationality and control issue. The pragmatic way of resolving this issue is to return to the idea of fully meeting customer's needs. If this is done for software engineering, then software engineers can use tools in a rational manner. Software engineers do not have time to craft their own tools. Other types of manufacturers are able to meet my needs for clothing, food, shelter, and transportation in a rational way and sometimes at a rational price. But massive upgrades to bring us into software engineering are extremely difficult because today's programmers do not fully know what types of tools they need, and software tool inventors do not fully understand the software engineering environment or their customer's needs. Massive upgrades are therefore very risky; caution and a tempered approach are the best course of action.

As we discussed in the chapter on automated software engineering, tools of the future and their products for end users may turn us into the ultimate rational crafters. It all began with adjustable car seats and adjustable rearview mirrors. It continues with option selection on computer interfaces, and it will ultimately be reflected in software engineering products and tools that continue to learn about their owners long after they are in use. These tools and systems will continue to recognize their user's patterns and adjust themselves accordingly. After some period of time, my software engineering tools will be the right tools for me. They will be a logical extension of myself and yet function within agreed-upon rules for software engineering. Today it may not be the right tool for me—or perhaps for anyone. But I cannot wait for tools of the future; I must continue to prosper in order to get to the future. Thus today's tools should be selected based on rational needs and criteria as established by my organization.

THINGS THAT CAN BE DONE TODAY

Recognize the real pace that is best for you. Understand that these transitions require time, and that it is not wise to risk all that one has for promise of the unbelievable growth of a super technology beanstalk. Do not panic; be happy. Identify technology transition managers and change movers, and know how to get everyone involved as change managers (even individual contributors should manage their own change). Know some of these things that can be done today:

- inspections (of just about all phases of software and perhaps even other dependent processes)
- structured analysis and structured design
- structured testing
- defect tracking and analysis
- configuration management
- project management tools and practices.

Know some of the benefits that can be attained today:

- Selected divisions in some companies report software reuse in the 60% to 80% category, with impressive gains in software quality. Reuse is here and it should be implemented in almost all areas (with the possible exception of the very advanced development activities, and even those groups can reuse math libraries, utilities, and the like).
- Gains of 30% to 50% in code production using structured analysis and structured design, accompanied by a reduction in customer-reported product defects of two to four times, can be achieved.
- Significant gains through proper use of software inspections are possible.

In a recent seminar a distinguished speaker referred to inspections as a viable technique of the 1970s that had been replaced by formal methods for program proving. The old inspections horse isn't dead yet, and program proving remains to be proven as a generic tool for widespread use.

- Software reengineering is coming into its own. There are now some consultants who specialize in the area, and there are reports of significant gains. If you are going to continue to use your existing systems, learn about this discipline.
- There are selected groups within some companies who are now measuring software defects per million lines of code. This is done to keep interest in quality high. A defect rate of 0.01 per thousand lines of code does not arouse the same sense of urgency as a rate of 10 defects per million lines of code. Set your goals high, and be sure to keep raising the bar.

THE SOFTWARE JOURNEY HAS JUST BEGUN

We are really just beginning the software adventure. This may come as a bit of a shock to those of us who have labored for many years in the software vineyard, but the emergence of other disciplines has taken 100 to 200 years, or longer. Software had its origins as some sort of add-on that had to be loaded into the real computer. As long as it remained some sort of addition that did not have full membership in the engineering community, software could not become an integral part of the systems needed to take us into the next millennium. We have looked at some ways software development might benefit from integration, tight coupling, and knowledge processing. Let's take a look from the customers' point of view, and understand that in these needs is an even-higher calling for software.

There is a pressing need for fully automated factories. This no longer means a giant building filled with robots moving about in the dark (those fully robotized factories today are eerie; robots need no light and no heat, and you can hear them moving about in the dark, cold building). It does mean a fully integrated factory in which the managers and workers can use robots where they should be used, have information to know where they are and where they are going, and see how to improve and change processes as needed. The "light of knowledge" shines brightly throughout the factory of the future.

The fully automated factory will be part of the fully integrated business environment. The capabilities and optimum potential of the factories are known to other business units who plan for future directions of the business. Change is no longer a major problem; concentration is on strategies that tell when and how to change. Information becomes the new material; timely information becomes fusion power.

Medical miracles will be achieved. The laser is a most promising medical tool. Perhaps the surgeon of the future is today's young person who can score highest on contemporary arcade games. The surgeons of earlier centuries were massive men who could hack off a limb in 30 seconds before shock killed the patient, who had only alcoholic stupor to ward off pain. Many of today's best surgeons learned techniques of the scalpel and how to control bleeding. The laser takes us full circle to a new breed who "shoot" diseases as they pass by. How will these surgeons use computers? What knowledge will they require? What role will software play in the medical and surgical processes?

In a more traditional medical mode there are medical records, automated testing, and all sorts of patient monitoring, including monitoring at home and while moving about. The possibilities for software connections, artificial intelligence, expert systems, and high-definition displays are sufficient to keep an entire generation of software experts busy. As we come to engineer software, tomorrow's software experts will find this a fertile valley.

The permanent space station orbiting above earth becomes a necessity for many reasons, the most humane of which is to have a base for launching missions to explore other planets and beyond. The space station requires software so large in scope and so well integrated and tested that it is almost beyond our present ability to comprehend, let alone deliver. There are also biosphere experiments to allow closed systems, or communities, of people to live and function on the moon and on other planets and moons. These prototypes require massive amounts of new software and systems and constant monitoring of the environment within the biosphere. The space and biosphere experiments have system requirements that cannot be met by shopping in software catalogs or stores and seeing what is available to be "loaded" onto a computer.

There will also be an ongoing series of probes into our solar system and far into outer space. The wonderful results to date, the beautiful pictures returned to us, have only whetted our appetites to know more. The mystery of black holes and the question of how the universe started will compel us to build and launch bigger and much more sophisticated probes and space telescopes. Gathering and analysis of these data will require very sophisticated software.

Computers for the most part are silicon-based. This has caused some Silicon Valley thinkers to wonder if silicon is not smarter than we think. It has us carefully molding it into chips, taking it into our homes and businesses and feeding it power, protecting it from all harm, carrying it with us in laptop form, protecting it from harmful viruses, and singing its praises to all who will listen. While this is a bit tongue-in-cheek, consider the development of bioelectrical computers, which can be grown and mutated, can self-repair, and can adapt as required. What types of software will best suit these potential neural network systems? What will be the relationship of these systems to today's best silicon efforts? Once again, the reason for mentioning these things here is to give the perspective that all our efforts to date have been round 1 in a much larger contest.

The main event may be the integration of hardware and software microengineering. There should be large integrated engineering systems, which produce systems that cannot be seen by the naked eye. Exciting and embryonic nanotechnology discipline uses motors, gears, sensors, and other tools smaller than the width of a human hair and shrinking with each new iteration.

Once again it was the Japanese who first began to miniaturize transistor radios and other electronic devices. Today all leading electronics and appliance companies are working to make things smaller and simpler.

The excitement becomes greatest when considering miniature robots. It will be possible to have small robots enter the human body and repair damaged human parts. It will be possible to have smaller and much more efficient factories. It will be possible to have sensors monitoring every part of our homes, automobiles, and factories to allow continuous process monitoring and improvement.

The far-reaching goal of nanotechnology is to be able to assemble molecules and to "grow" machines, robots, medicines, and so on. The combination of microelectronics, nanotechnology, and software engineering could well produce tiny systems that will support the knowledge-driven world of the future. We are just beginning to understand the possibilities of very small systems, which can continue to learn how to serve as they become a logical extension of their users.

The purpose of this delightful sort of speculation, based on actual scientific achievements of today, is to confirm the fact that the engineering journey is only in the beginning stages. There are no technical limitations close at hand as we make this journey into the future. We can continue to work toward software engineering today; we can be assured that we will still be making exciting breakthroughs when we retire. This is one of many benefits to being a pioneer in software engineering.

There are personal benefits to be gained from the use of software in heretofore unexplored areas of existing technology. The final frontier may include satisfying the author's wish that software could help to create an appliance and electronic device that "learns" how to meet the user's preferences.

Thus far computers have done a great deal to allow us to communicate and calculate more efficiently. It is my fondest hope that they will also be a major contributor in raisi·g the standard of living for all and in making our world a wonderful place for all to reach their full potential. We have considered some major challenges for software engineering in the future. There are many other challenges, as well as some that have not yet been recognized.

Perhaps software will be able to make additional, original contributions in other areas that need help today, such as the environment, substance abuse, and poverty.

Somewhere along the way, you, the true professionals, will raise software to a true profession. You will then manage that profession as it attains its rightful place in the hierarchy of engineering professions. I hope we will all take the time to enjoy the journey fully, to remember what we have done, and simply to make software serve our customers.

Bibliography

There are many very good books related to software engineering and technology transitions. This bibliography includes the ones that I have found useful in understanding software engineering. Although other books have been reviewed and deliberately been omitted from this list, I am certain that there are still others not on the list due to my lack of awareness, or oversight. However, many of the books listed here do point the way to other books and sources of information. The computer societies are also very helpful in connecting engineers and information.

There are also a few references to articles that deal with software engineering as a profession. These articles also point the way to additional work in the field.

GENERAL INTEREST

ABERNATHY, W. *Industrial Renaissance* (New York: Basil Books, 1983).
ACM/SIGGRAPH Conference Proceedings, *Computer Graphics* (Reading, Mass.: Addison-Wesley, 1989).
BENTLEY, J., *More Programming Pearls: Confessions of a Coder* (Reading, Mass.: Addison-Wesley, 1988).

BROOKS, F., *The Mythical Man Month* (Reading, Mass.: Addison-Wesley, 1982).

CHANDLER, A., *Strategy and Structure: Chapters in the History of American Industrial Enterprise* (Cambridge, Mass.: MIT Press, 1962).

CUSUMANO, M., *The Japanese Automobile Industry: Technology and Management at Nissan and Toyota* (Cambridge, Mass.: Harvard University Press, 1985).

DRUCKER, P., *Innovation and Entrepreneurship: Practice and Principles* (New York: Harper & Row, 1985).

GALE, A. *Psychophysiology and the Electronic Workplace* (New York: John Wiley, 1987).

GLEICK, J. *Chaos: Making a New Science* (New York: Penguin Books, 1987).

GOLDSTEIN, H., *The Computer from Pascal to Von Neumann* (Princeton, N.J.: Princeton University Press, 1972).

HOUSE, R., *The Human Side of Project Management* (Reading, Mass.: Addison-Wesley, 1988).

IMAI, M., *Kaizen* (New York: Random House, 1986).

KANTER, R., *The Change Master* (New York: Simon and Schuster, 1983).

KIDDER, T., *The Soul of a New Machine* (Boston, Mass.: Little, Brown, 1981).

McLUHAN, M., *Understanding Media: The Extensions of Man* (New York: McGraw-Hill, 1964).

MORITA, A., *Made in Japan* (New York: E. P. Dutton, 1989).

PLUNKETT, L., *The Proactive Manager* (New York: John Wiley, 1982).

SHINGO, S., *The Sayings of Shigeo Shingo*, English trans. (Cambridge, Mass.: Productivity Press, 1987).

SPECHLER, J., *When America Does It Right* (Norcross, Ga.: Industrial Engineering and Management Press, 1988).

TOFFLER, A., *Future Shock* (New York: Random House, 1970).

SOFTWARE AND SOFTWARE ENGINEERING

BEIZER, B., *Software System Testing and Quality Assurance* (New York: Van Nostrand Reinhold, 1984).

BIGGERSTAFF, T., *Software Reusability*, Vols. I and II (Reading, Mass.: Addison-Wesley, 1989).

BOEHM, B., "Software Engineering," *IEEE Transactions Computers* (December 1976), pp. 1226–1241.

BOOCH, G., *Software Engineering with ADA*, 2d ed. (Reading, Mass.: Addison-Wesley, 1987).

BROOKS, F., "No Silver Bullet: Essence and Accidents of Software Engineering," *Information Processing* 86, pp. 1069–1076.

COX, B., *Object Oriented Programming, An Evolutionary Approach* (Reading, Mass.: Addison-Wesley, 1986).

DEMARCO, T., *Controlling Software Projects* (New York: Yourdon Press, 1982).

DIJKSTRA, E. "On the Cruelty of Really Teaching Computer Science," *Communications of the ACM* (December 1989), pp. 1398–1404.

FAIRLEY, R., *Software Engineering Concepts* (New York: McGraw-Hill, 1985).

FREEMAN, P., *Software Perspectives* (Reading, Mass.: Addison-Wesley, 1987).

GILB, T., *Principles of Software Engineering Management* (Reading, Mass.: Addison-Wesley, 1989).

HATLEY, D., *Strategies for Real-Time System Specification* (New York: Dorset House Publishing, 1987).

HETZEL, W., *The Complete Guide to Software Testing* (Ann Arbor, Mich.: Q.E.D. Press, 1984).

HUMPHREY, W., *Managing the Software Process* (Reading, Mass.: Addison-Wesley, 1989).

JONES, T., *Programming Productivity* (New York: McGraw-Hill, 1986).

MACRO, A., and J. BUXTON, *The Craft of Software Engineering* (Reading, Mass.: Addison-Wesley, 1987).

MATSUMOTO, Y., and Y. OHNO, *Japanese Perspectives in Software Engineering* (Reading, Mass.: Addison-Wesley, 1989).

McCABE, T., *Structured Testing* (IEEE Computer Society, 1982).

MURPHY, E., "Software R&D: from an art to a science," *IEEE SPECTRUM* (October 1990), pp. 44–46.

MUSA, J., *Software Reliability* (New York: McGraw-Hill, 1987).

PAGE-JONES, M., *Practical Project Management* (New York: Dorset House Publishing, 1985).

PARIKH, G., *Handbook of Software Maintenance* (New York: John Wiley, 1986).

PRESSMAN, R., *Software Engineering: A Practitioner's Approach*, 2d ed. (New York: McGraw-Hill, 1987).

PRESSMAN, R., *Making Software Engineering Happen* (Englewood Cliffs, N.J.: Prentice Hall, 1988).

SHAW, M., "Prospects for an Engineering Discipline of Software," *IEEE Software* (November 1990), pp. 15–24.

QUALITY, PRODUCTIVITY, AND STANDARDS

COMER, D., *Internetworking with TCP/IP: Principles, Protocols, and Architecture* (Englewood Cliffs, N.J.: Prentice Hall, 1988).

CROSBY, P., *Quality is Free* (New York: McGraw-Hill, 1979).

DEMING, W., *Out of the Crisis* (Cambridge, Mass.: Massachusetts Institute of Technology, Center for Advanced Study, 1986).

FEIGENBAUM, A., *Total Quality Control*, 3d ed. (New York: McGraw-Hill, 1983).

HARRINGTON, H., *The Improvement Process* (New York: McGraw-Hill, 1987).

ISHIKAWA, K., *What is Total Quality Control?: The Japanese Way* (Englewood Cliffs, N.J.: Prentice Hall, 1985).

JURAN, J., *Quality Control Handbook* (New York: McGraw-Hill, 4th ed., 1979).

JURAN, J., *Juran on Leadership for Quality* (New York: The Free Press, Macmillan, 1989).

JURAN, J., *Juran on Planning for Quality* (New York, The Free Press, 1988).

SHETTY, Y., *Competing Through Productivity and Quality* (Cambridge, Mass.: Productivity Press, 1988).

TAGUCHI, G., *Introduction to Quality Engineering: Designing Quality into Products and Processes* (White Plains: Unipub, 1986).

ADVANCED TECHNOLOGIES

CHARNIAK, E., *Introduction to Artificial Intelligence* (Reading, Mass.: Addison-Wesley, 1985).

HILLIS, W., *The Connection Machine* (Cambridge, Mass.: MIT Press, 1985).

OTHER SOURCES

American Society for Quality Control

Association for Computing Machinery

Institute of Electrical and Electronic Engineers

ADA Joint Program Office, Military Standard Common APSE Interface Set. Washington, D.C.

Index

Index

K

L

M

N

O